Unfolding Social Constructionism

HISTORY AND PHILOSOPHY OF PSYCHOLOGY

Series Editor: **Man Cheung Chung**, *University of Plymouth, Plymouth, United Kingdom*

DESTINED FOR DISTINGUISHED OBLIVION
The Scientific Vision of William Charles Wells (1757–1817)
Nicholas J. Wade

REDISCOVERING THE HISTORY OF PSYCHOLOGY
Essays Inspired by the Work of Kurt Danziger
Edited by Adrian Brock, Johann Louw, and Willem van Hoorn

UNFOLDING SOCIAL CONSTRUCTIONISM
Fiona J. Hibberd

A Continuation Order Plan is available for this series. A continuation order will bring delivery of each new volume immediately upon publication. Volumes are billed only upon actual shipment. For further information please contact the publisher.

Unfolding Social Constructionism

By

Fiona J. Hibberd

University of Sydney
Sydney, Australia

 Springer

KH

Library of Congress Cataloging-in-Publication Data

A C.I.P. Catalogue record for this book is available from the Library of Congress.

ISBN 0-387-22974-4   e-ISBN 0-387-22975-2   Printed on acid-free paper.

Printed in the United States of America

9 8 7 6 5 4 3 2 1

springeronline.com

9/19/06

PREFACE

For more than half of the 20th century, psychologists sought to locate the causes of behaviour in individuals and tended to neglect the possibility of locating the psychological in the social. In the late 1960s, a reaction to that neglect brought about a "crisis" in social psychology. This "crisis" did not affect all social psychologists; some remained seemingly oblivious to its presence; others dismissed its significance and continued much as before. But, in certain quarters, the psychological was re-conceptualised as the social, and the social was taken to be *sui generis*. Moreover, the possibility of developing general laws and theories to describe and explain social interaction was rejected on the grounds that, as social beings, our actions vary from occasion to occasion, and are, for many reasons, unrepeatable. There is, so it was thought, an inherent instability in the phenomena of interest. The nomothetic ideal was said to rest on individualistic cause-effect positivism of the kind which (arguably) characterised the natural sciences, but social psychology (so it was said) is an historical inquiry, and its conclusions are necessarily historically relative (Gergen, 1973).

Events outside psychology converged to give impetus to the "crisis" within. Notable among these were: (i) the failure of logical positivism as a philosophy of science; (ii) the impact of treatises such as Kuhn's *The Structure of Scientific Revolutions* (1962; 1970), Wittgenstein's *Philosophical Investigations* (1953), Feyerabend's *Against Method* (1975), Austin's *How to Do Things with Words* (1962) and Berger & Luckmann's *The Social Construction of Reality* (1966); (iii) an increase in the perceived relevance of both Continental and linguistic philosophy, and (iv) contributions from philosophers such as Rorty and Derrida. These reinforced the judgement that the previously unquestioned aim of social psychology—to establish general laws and theories through controlled observation—rested on an "old-fashioned" and mistaken epistemology.[1]

One consequence of these movements has been the development of social constructionism as a *metatheory* of psychology. Unsurprisingly, this development has corresponded to similar changes within other branches of the humanities and social sciences as they also have re-examined their supposed positivist foundations.

What is social constructionism? Of course, readers must read the constructionist literature if they are to gain a thorough understanding of this school of thought.[2] But in general, social constructionism emphasises the historicity, the context-dependence, and the socio-linguistically constituted character of all matters involving human activity. The psychological processes of human beings are, it is said, essentially social, and are acquired through the public practice of conversation. Some versions of constructionism extend this emphasis to the conceptual and methodological practices of psychologists, and to the epistemological and semantic assumptions which ground these practices; to the "meta-issues" of the discipline. In this case, the position is that all (psycho-)social facts are "constructed", in that they are constituted by human actions (usually by socio-linguistic activities such as negotiation and rhetoric). These social processes are said to *produce* the facts of the social sciences, and these facts are (it is alleged) sometimes revealed to be facts *about* social processes and the social milieu.

It is the "meta-issues" which this book examines, that is, social constructionism as an epistemology and, in particular, social constructionism as an alternative to positivist and realist philosophies of science—Hacking's (1999) "constructionalism".[3] I do not dispute the view that certain features of human psycho-social life have localised causes of a cultural kind. This is not a "meta-issue". For the same reason, I do not consider the sometimes valuable information about social groups (especially scientists) which social constructionists have unearthed in their empirical research. Nor do I consider research concerned with the nature of persons, conversational, discourse and rhetorical analysis, unless it is claimed that such findings have implications for social constructionism *as an epistemology*. I am not concerned with theories, methodologies or practices. For these reasons, I say little about the contributions from, for instance, Kurt Danziger or Rom Harré, significant though they may be. My intention is that of Locke's under-labourer, ". . . clearing the ground a little, and removing some of the rubbish that lies in the way to knowledge" (Locke, 1706/1924, p. 7).

To make clear the distinction between social constructionism as an epistemology and the socially constructed as a feature of some (or of all) psycho-social situations, an architectural analogy may be helpful. Imagine social constructionism to be two-tiered. The upper tier is the theoretical level and consists of social constructionist accounts of a wide range of psycho-social phenomena—social meaning, linguistics, morality, feminism, power relations, the educational process, emotions, the self, cognition, motivation, clinical diagnosis, narrative in the therapeutic encounter, management in organizations, social movements, and so on and so on. The lower tier is the metatheoretical level. This consists of a network of philosophical assumptions, largely about semantics, upon which the social constructionist theories of the upper level may depend. Sometimes social constructionism (the metatheory) underlies social constructionist theory, but the latter can also be consistent with some other metatheory, such as realism.

This lower tier is logically (but not necessarily temporally) prior to the upper tier. It is not less fallible than the upper tier, but its assumptions, claims, proposals, etc. are of a more general kind. Having certain views about what is open to observation and putting forward particular theoretical propositions and not others is, in part, a logical consequence of the adoption of a certain philosophical or metatheoretical position, whether or not this occurs consciously. If the (tacit) metatheoretical assumptions had been different, certain theoretical claims would still have been made, but others would not. For this reason the architectural analogy is imperfect. There is no *sharp* distinction between the two tiers. But because the assumptions, claims, and proposals of a metatheory are of a more general kind, it cannot comment on the particular features of situations. Social constructionist metatheory cannot, for example, specify the particular conditions under which certain psycho-social events might occur. The metatheory contains no analysis of psycho-social phenomena, although this does not preclude the possibility that controversies concerning psycho-social phenomena may alert us to metatheoretical problems.

As noted, social constructionism as a theory in psychology need not be inconsistent with realism as a philosophy. But some contributors to social constructionist theory have, *in varying degrees*, either expanded their accounts into a constructionist metatheory or have drawn epistemological conclusions from their research. In the present book, it is this expansion which is the focus of consideration, viz. the metatheoretical aspects of social constructionism. Their resolution is vitally important to a conceptually rigorous psycho-social science. Regrettably, and ironically, I doubt that these "expansionists" will engage at all with the metatheoretical issues raised in this book. They are of the view that these issues are misconceived, functioning only to conceal the context or background or "embeddedness" from which I construct these chapters; that I am not offering, on the basis of logical argument, an objective description of certain situations; that my writings are sufficiently rhetorical as to render them literary; that I am instead trying to persuade the reader to enter with me into an imaginary world. They, and others, may argue that my focus on metatheory is grounded in a mistaken adherence to "traditional epistemology"; that Quine and others long ago demonstrated the implausibility of such an approach; that there is really nothing to debate at this "level of abstraction" and that, in focussing on such issues, I ignore the recent research (of cultural historians, anthropologists, feminists, etc.) into post-constructionist science. I, however, am not persuaded that the case against traditional epistemology, and philosophy generally, is sound. Some of the arguments involve a

mischaracterization of these so-called "traditional" areas; others trade on ambiguity, a perverse form of pragmatism, and recent academic fads (see DePierris,
2003; Haack, 1993; Siegel, 1984; Smith, 1988). There is also Aristotle's (nd/1966)
point that if the genuine critic attempts to subordinate arguments to literary criticism and rhetoric, she or he can only do so *through* philosophical argument.
I do not, then, endorse the view that the metaphysical and epistemological claims
sometimes made by constructionists *should not be read as such*. In particular,
I do not believe that the import of these constructionist claims is only ever local
and performative, never global and descriptive. Even when an author writes as
carelessly as constructionists sometimes do, it is not the reader's job to disregard
what that author says, and either to guess at or to presume an alternative "real"
meaning. What constructionists say should be taken literally.

Contributions to social constructionist metatheory are disparate in several
respects. Some are less radical than others, some are complex and wide ranging,
some involve a denial that their exposition is metatheoretical, and some consist
of little more than an assumption or two. The present book does not ignore the
varieties of social constructionist metatheory—where relevant they, and the work
of Jonathan Potter (and his colleagues) and John Shotter in particular, will receive attention. However, in psychology, one particular theorist has dominated
social constructionism—K. J. Gergen. In 1985, Gergen published what is now referred to as a "landmark" paper in twentieth century psychology (Rychlak, 1992).
Entitled *The Social Constructionist Movement in Modern Psychology*, the paper
introduced mainstream psychology to social constructionism and advocated that
social constructionism replace positivism as a metatheory of psychological knowledge. Since then, Gergen has developed social constructionist metatheory to the
extent that it now exemplifies a post-modernist research program (see Rosenau,
1992). In particular, he has repeatedly pronounced on the status of psychology's
theoretical and observational statements, and on the ontological status of psycho-
social phenomena. His position involves arguments which go to the heart of social
constructionism's lower tier.

This emphasis on Gergen's metatheory may not please those who deem it
unworthy of discussion. However, it is not at all obvious that those constructionists critical of Gergen's metatheory do, in fact, repudiate the ideas which
he defends and which, I maintain, are problematical. Whereas some do not endorse Gergen's metatheory (Harré and Stam are cases), other accounts of social
constructionism often echo it. In fact, general descriptions of the constructionist
"paradigm" typically rely on the main features of Gergen's metatheory, though its
more radical elements and its exclusive focus on discourse are sometimes rejected
(e.g., Burr, 1995; Cromby & Nightingale, 1999; Potter, 1996a; 1996b). Moreover,
Gergen is far more explicit than others about his metatheoretical commitments,
and about why he thinks social constructionism (and not realism) is a viable alternative to positivism. To some extent, he explains and gives reasons for his

commitments, whereas others sometimes simply state them, and still others (e.g., Potter *et al.*) deny having them. Much to the chagrin of his constructionist colleagues, Gergen does not, to the same degree as other constructionists, pretend that his is not a theoretical position, nor does he always pretend that such a position involves no commitments of this kind. Thus he makes the metatheory more accessible, giving the critic ample material with which to work. An evaluation of Gergen's metatheory, despite (or because of) its radical nature, turns out to be particularly instructive for social constructionism and for the philosophy of psychology generally.

In the examination of social constructionism, three matters are addressed. Firstly, most critics of social constructionism maintain that it is relativistic and, therefore, incoherent. Secondly, critics and proponents alike judge it to be antithetical to a positivist philosophy of science. Thirdly, its proponents maintain that realism is not a contender for the metatheoretical "space" which has become vacant since the decline of 20th century empiricism, because realism is too similar to positivism. These notions are pervasive not only in psychology, but in the social sciences generally. I show that each of the three claims is false. Most theoretical and social psychologists, despite recognising some of the many defects of 20th century psychology, have not perceived important similarities between "old-fashioned" positivism and contemporary versions of social constructionism, and have, in consequence, unwittingly perpetuated some of the failings of the very metatheoretical system which they believe themselves so staunchly to oppose.

The philosophical system which underpins my analysis is realism. This requires comment because there is a sharp contrast between it and a widely held view of realist philosophy—that in seeking universal laws, realism ignores the particular and, therefore, ignores context. On the contrary, realism does *not* involve "the epistemological fiction of [an] ahistorical, decontextualized, emotionless subject" (Apfelbaum, 2000, p. 1010). The system of philosophy which permeates this work was developed and introduced into Australia in 1927 by the Scottish philosopher John Anderson. It is known as "direct realism", but might more accurately be referred to as "situational realism". Its most distinctive thesis is: whatever there is, is an occurrence or situation in space and time. Moreover, the located situation is surrounded (*Fr. environner*), and the environment in which the situation occurs will act upon that situation. Thus, *every* situation is contextualised. There is nothing above the situation; there is no God's eye view. Individuals cannot stand outside or above society; they do become caught up in social processes, of which they are sometimes unaware.

It may be tempting to dismiss this philosophy as anachronistic—as something which belongs to the 1920s or 1930s—of historical interest, but of no relevance to the current intellectual climate. That would be a mistake. Anderson's realist philosophical system has certain striking commonalities with social constructionism, i.e., social constructionism *as a metatheory*. For example, both:

- accept the Heraclitean doctrine that all things are constantly changing;
- recognise the reality of relations and interactions;
- reject the thesis of essentialism;
- hold the view that there are no such things as *pure* abstract universals;
- reject any epistemology which involves representationism;
- reject any theory of language which has statements or propositions as *linguistic entities* that are true if they correspond to reality;
- reject any theory of meaning which makes meaning a constituent of the mind;
- recognize the importance of context for social life;
- hold the view that there is no such thing as an individual unaffected by social processes;
- reject the view that scientific inquiry can be free from the motives of social interests.

There are, of course, substantial points of disagreement between social constructionism and situational realism. The latter, for example, does *not* reject the possibility of objective knowledge (of finding out what is the case), nor the possibility of objective description, though it recognises the many obstacles to achieving either. It also defends a pluralistic determinism, it locates the general *in the particular*, and it frequently draws our attention to the error of mistaking a *relation* between things, for a *quality* of one of those things. Nevertheless, there are, as I say, a number of points where these two seemingly disparate systems agree. This, I think, important. It affords some grounds for assimilation.

In Chapter 1, I outline the views of Jonathan Potter, John Shotter and Kenneth Gergen, and uncover Gergen's rationale for his relational account of meaning through an exegesis of his various writings. One negative thesis and three positive theses are extracted from his work. Critics of social constructionism maintain that the metatheory embodies epistemological relativism and is, therefore, self-refuting. These charges are considered in Chapter 2 and there I examine why these charges have had little impact. I argue that the differences between the various kinds of relativism are not always well understood, and that the charges have missed their target; the critics have attributed to social constructionists ideas which constructionists reject. In Chapter 3, I consider Gergen's reliance on Austin's concept of performative utterances—a concept crucial to his defence of constructionist metatheory. That defence does not succeed. Gergen fails to demonstrate that performatives are not, in part, reflexive statements about their speakers, and that truths and falsehoods are not conveyed by such statements. Nor is he able to exclude the possibility that *all* speech-acts have fact-stating components and communicate information, albeit in some disguised manner.

In psychology, and in the social sciences generally, the received view is that social constructionism is antithetical to logical positivism. The material of

Chapter 3 provides reason to question this. Chapter 4 unfolds the perceptions concerning positivism's failure as a metatheory for psychology and the judgement that the differences between logical positivism and social constructionism are substantial. Chapters 5, 6 and 7 suggest something to the contrary.

In Chapter 5, I demonstrate that the *a priori* elements of Gergen's relational account of meaning exemplify a conventionalism which evolved throughout the 20th century, and was clearly evident in logical positivist philosophy. Also, though neither Potter nor Shotter endorses certain features of Gergen's metatheory, connections between them and logical positivism are also apparent. I argue that conventionalism is an untenable thesis and, in doing so, I have much to say about a pervasive misuse of language among social constructionists, their neglect of logic (in particular, the logic of relations) and, not unrelatedly, their (mis)understanding of the subject–object distinction.

Chapter 6 examines the *a posteriori* elements of the conventionalism in Gergen's metatheory and in logical positivist philosophy. In the latter it pertains to the development of verificationism. In the former, it involves the thesis that language acquires meaning through its use in socio-linguistic practices. Both result from the influence of Wittgenstein's post-*Tractatus* dictum that the meaning of a word is its use. The connections between constructionism and operationism are also examined. I contend that use is not a sufficient condition for word meaning, that Wittgenstein's notion of family resemblance does not avoid the Socratic theory of definition, and that a realist philosophy does not entail a commitment to essentialism.

In Chapter 7, I argue that the similarities between logical positivism and social constructionism are not restricted to matters semantic. Both share the conviction that we can never know reality as unmodified things-in-themselves and both retain a link to Kantian philosophy. I also show that the constructionists' denial of unmediated knowledge relies on the winner of a worst-argument-in-the-world competition.

Chapter 8 contains a summary of my conclusions and I end on a somewhat speculative and provocative note. I suggest that the conventionalism and epistemic scepticism of constructionist metatheory is a futile strategy of survival deployed to defend against being mistaken, and so to defend against disappointment.

No doubt there are ideas about which more needs to be said, ideas which I overlook, gaps in my arguments, and hazy formulations. But my aim is to focus attention on certain lines of thought which, in various areas of psychology, still have not been put to rest. The spirit of this book is in keeping with Freud's (1909) observation that "... a thing which has not been understood inevitably reappears; like an unlaid ghost, it cannot rest until the mystery has been solved and the spell broken" (p. 122).

A little of the material from chapter 2 first appeared in *Relativism versus realism—all but a specious dichotomy*, and was published in *History of the Human*

Sciences, 14(3), 102-107. Abridged versions of chapters 5, 6 and 7 appeared in *Gergen's social constructionism, logical positivism and the continuity of error, Part 1: Conventionalism,* and in *Gergen's social constructionism, logical positivism and the continuity of error, Part 2: Meaning-as-use.* They were published in *Theory & Psychology, 11*(3), 297-321 and 323-346. The material from these three papers is reprinted here by permission of Sage Publications Ltd.

I was initially persuaded by Jim Good to undertake this book and I thank him for his interest and encouragement. Since then I have benefited from the support of many people. I am grateful to them all, but make special mention of David Hibberd for always providing, with characteristic Englishness, large amounts of humour and perspective. Perhaps the way the ideas in this book have been brought together is original, but the ideas *per se* are not. My intellectual debts are, therefore, substantial. Many are to those no longer alive but, of those still breathing, I single out Joel Michell and George Oliphant. Each has been teacher, supervisor, and colleague. I have benefited enormously from Joel's friendship, his integrity and, in particular, his understanding of philosophical matters and their implications for psychology. And George has given so generously of his time in order to comment on my work, that my debt to him is beyond measure.

NOTES

[1] Here, in limiting this list of influences to the intellectual, I am not suggesting that the wider socio-political context was of no relevance (see, for example, Parker, 1989).

[2] See Neimeyer *et al.* (1994) and Danziger (1997) for selective lists of references.

[3] In this book, I make no sharp distinction between epistemology and philosophy of science. Both are concerned with the conditions under which knowing occurs, the methods which may assist us in coming to know, the nature of evidence, and theories of justification.

CONTENTS

CHAPTER 1

SOCIAL CONSTRUCTIONISM AS A METATHEORY OF PSYCHOLOGICAL SCIENCE

1.1. A POST-MODERNIST PROGRAM

The central aim of social constructionist metatheory has been to provide a viable alternative to the positivist-empiricist philosophy of science which had long been supposed to ground the pursuit of psychological knowledge. This aim is in keeping with those in philosophy who have rejected "First Philosophy" or traditional epistemology (e.g., Fuller, 1989; Giere, 1988; Rorty, 1979). Here, a traditional understanding of epistemology and the philosophy of science as *a priori* disciplines has been abandoned in favour of naturalized epistemology, that is, in favour of epistemology as just another scientific discipline.

Yet social constructionists have also advanced a more radical agenda. Positivist-empiricist philosophy is condemned by them as embodying a "pretension towards invariance" and an "illusion of objectivity". Their opinion is exemplified in Margolis' (1991) suggestion that it is crucial that we discard:

> ... one by one, every last trace of the (grand, pretended) invariances—the perennial truths—of ultimate reality, knowledge, thought, rationality, virtue and value, logic, science, intelligibility, and the rest that have falsely reassured us all the while we disorder the planet (p. ix).

Social constructionism embraces the spirit of Margolis' position. Gergen (1994c), for example, forecasts that to many his view of psychological knowledge will prove deeply troubling because it challenges longstanding commitments to "... objectivity, truth, rational foundations, and individualism" (p. 64). These challenges in fact comprise much of the content of social constructionist metatheory, and in this respect the metatheory is post-modernist.[1] It is subversive, and what it intends to subvert is the positivist-empiricist philosophy of science.

Post-modernist in spirit, social constructionism is also post-modernist in method. The approach of social constructionists tends towards synthesis rather than analysis. Although some are an exception to this, Gergen's method, for example, is clearly that of a grand systematist. He has constructed a metatheory of psychology which relies heavily on his findings from a range of disciplines, notably contemporary non-realist philosophy of science, the philosophy of language, the sociology of knowledge, literary analysis, hermeneutics, social phenomenology, anthropology, feminist studies and social psychology.

Secondly, social constructionists of this kind often display the general post-modernist tendency not to consider the consequences of their own assumptions. For example, they will cite empirical evidence to support general conclusions, and then employ those conclusions as evidence against positivist-empiricist and realist positions and confirmatory of social constructionism. They will insist that their work not be read as a theoretical account to be judged by its truth or falsity. Yet throughout their accounts they have, of course, made assertions about what is the case. This lack of "self-examination" occurs despite their recommendation that constructionist scholars engage in "... self-reflexive deconstruction of their own theses..." (Gergen, 1994c, p. 48).[2]

But addressing such anomalies is not their concern. Their concern is to present to psychologists a number of ideas, ideas which are receiving increasing acceptance from philosophical systems as seemingly diverse as those of Continental and linguistic philosophy. When diverse philosophical systems arrive at the same destination, despite having begun at different starting-points and having taken quite different routes, they are obviously (so they believe) saying something of great import. It is this that they wish to attend to.

1.2. SOCIAL CONSTRUCTIONISM

The phrase "social constructionism" was introduced into recent academic debate through Berger & Luckmann's *The Social Construction of Reality* (1966). In some usages, the phrase appears to denote nothing more than "of social origin" (Sismondo, 1993). In others, its meaning is less vague, alluding to (i) the assembling or arranging of parts, in discrete stages, into larger structures for a certain purpose, and (ii) that such arranging is social in origin. Concepts, theories, scientific practices, and bodies of knowledge are all items which may, in this latter sense, be socially constructed.

For many, social constructionism enables an unconstrained and unlimited outlook (e.g., Burr, 1998). Their thinking is this: if some thing, event or process is social in origin, it is not given or established by nature. So, there is nothing fixed or inevitable about it. Social groups can, then, choose to replace old conventions, theories, ideologies, practices and bodies of knowledge with new ones. For example, the standard forms of academic writing can be discarded (Potter, 1998; Shotter & Lannamann, 2002). Of course, this thinking is contrary to the thesis of determinism, and much more besides, but determinism is a thesis which social constructionists dismiss.

The result of conjoining these two lines of thought, constructionism and "liberalism", is well captured in the following passage from Hacking's *The Social Construction of What?* Hacking (1999) notes that social constructionists tend to advance the following theses:

1. *X* need not have existed, or need not be at all as it is. *X*, or *X* as it is at present, is not determined by the nature of things; it is not inevitable.

Very often they go further, and urge that:

2. *X* is quite as bad as it is.
3. We would be much better off if *X* were done away with, or at least radically transformed (p. 6).

Now, if Hacking's generic *X* is replaced by the terms *theories* and *knowledge*, the following position materializes: theories and knowledge are not determined by the things they purport to be about. They are not given or established by the phenomena of interest. Our theories and knowledge have been assembled or constructed (brought into existence) by communities of scientists. These communities "carry" or embody social and linguistic conventions, histories, social forces, particular interests, etc. These factors could all have been different; there is no inevitability about them. Therefore, the theories and knowledge we have today could be different and, more radically, there is no reason why our current *conceptions* of theory and knowledge cannot be transformed.

This is the position of some social constructionists with respect to the discipline of psychology. Jonathan Potter, John Shotter and Kenneth J. Gergen have each contributed to social constructionism as a metatheory of psychology. Their contributions are disparate in many respects, but the general idea is as above. Theories, knowledge and facts in psychology are socially constructed and, this being so, they are constituted, via the discourse of psychologists, by social processes, conventions and milieux. This general idea is underpinned by two theses about which most social constructionists agree: (i) that the traditional categories of cognition (including perception and memory), motivation, emotion, learning, social behaviour, etc., are not properties in each individual's head, but are grounded in discourse, and (ii) that discourse is central to the constitution of at least *social* reality (e.g., Gergen, 1994c; Harré, 1993; Neimeyer et al., 1994; Potter, 1996a; Shotter, 1993b).[3] The practice of psychology (be it professional or academic) is just one aspect of social reality, and psychology's theories, facts and bodies of knowledge are its cultural artefacts. They too are discursively constituted. They too can be replaced, in order to transform social life (e.g., Gergen, 1999, p. 49).

In the remainder of this chapter, I shall outline the views of Potter, Shotter and Gergen, allowing them, for the most part, to speak for themselves. Some of their ideas will not be addressed at all in this chapter, and serious critical consideration of their accounts will begin only in later chapters. Potter and Shotter have less to say about metatheoretical issues than Gergen, and this will be reflected in the structure and content of the following sections. With regard to Gergen, my aim is to reconstruct aspects of his metatheory, making the reconstruction as faithful to the original as possible.

1.3. POTTER'S DISCOURSE ANALYSIS

Unlike Gergen's published work, much of Potter's (Shotter's too, for that matter) is explicitly ontological. Potter's principal research interest is discourse analysis and its application in psychology (discursive psychology). With Edwards (2001), he defines discourse as "... talk and texts, studied as social practices", and they regard it as "... the prime currency of interaction ..." (p. 104). Discourse analysis "... is concerned with the way people collectively construct versions of the world in the course of their practical interactions, and the way these versions are established as solid, real, and independent of the speaker" (Potter & Wetherell, 1998, p. 143). It involves explicating the uses of social representations (constructed discursive objects) in action, and describing the techniques used in "fact construction", especially those marshalled to make accounts of reality appear credible and difficult to reject.[4] As Potter (2003a) comments, discourse research asks questions of the "How is it done?" kind. These practical, relational questions are thought to replace causal questions, such as "Does X affect Y?" and "Why did she do that?". In the opinion of Potter and his cohorts, discursive constructions do not represent the speaker's cognitive states. Making sense of the nature of these constructions is best achieved by noting the social actions which the constructions accomplish (Edwards & Potter, 1992, pp. 2–3).

Importantly for the purposes of this book, Potter maintains that his research into discourse has epistemological implications, implications which Berger & Luckmann (1966) ignored. In exploring how factual accounts are generated, how events are described, and how cognitive states are attributed, Potter claims to be "... concerned with the nature of knowledge, cognition and reality ..." (Edwards & Potter, 1992, p. 2). Cognition and other cognate categories are re-conceptualised as "... participants' *ways of talking*" (Potter & Edwards, 2001, p. 105). Moreover, he believes his research to be validatory of Rorty's (1991) contention that philosophical discourse is rhetoric (Potter, 1996b). Like Rorty, Potter is dismissive of metatheory and traditional philosophy. He sees them as literary constructions, narratives which reify their terms and which become abstract and universal. Entering into metatheoretical debate should, he thinks, be resisted though not necessarily avoided (Potter, 1998)—resisted because taking part begins that process of reification, not avoided because of the opportunity to comment on the discursive processes at work. Indeed, when he engages in such debates, this is Potter's intention. He aims to reveal the "discursive moves" employed by his "opponent" for the account to appear coherent, factual and disinterested (see, for example, Potter, 1992).

This was the *raison d'être* for what has come to be known as "the Death and Furniture paper". In this paper, Potter and his colleagues argue that when the realist hits the table, in an attempt to refute relativism, this is a meaningful action, a rhetorical device. The realist is, at that moment, involved in a representational act and this undermines her position (Edwards et al., 1995). Realist philosophy, then, is patently mistaken. The world is not distinct from the processes involved in representing and interpreting it. Instances of brute reality are social accomplishments. Objective truth and validity are to be replaced by social process and practical reasoning. The concept of objectivity Potter thinks an abstraction, as is logic, and notions of truth and falsity are simply rhetorical elements of realist discourse (Potter, 1992). Potter's alleged relativism is a counter to his many strange beliefs about realism. For example, disputation, inquiry and argument all characterise relativism because, unlike realism, nothing ever has to be taken as indisputably true (Edwards et al., 1995). He does, however, prefer to conceptualise relativism as a "non-position" rather than "... a positive statement opposed to realism ... [because] ... positive statements orientate to the otherwise possible nature of things" (Edwards et al., 1995, pp. 41–42).

1.4. SHOTTER'S CONVERSATIONAL ANALYSIS

The philosophers Bakhtin, Harré, Vico, Vygotsky and Wittgenstein share an interest in the relational, social and cultural dimensions of knowing and language-use, and Shotter makes plain their influence upon him. His expressed aim is to understand "... our everyday, practical, social activities ..."; to grasp "... our continuously changing sense of living relatedness ..."; to discern "... relations-in-motion ..." (Shotter, 1996, p. 293). In his opinion, these (social) relations are linguistically constituted (Shotter, 1993b). This means that conversational activities are foundational to the construction of social reality; they provide the living basis of everything we do (Shotter, 1997, p. 10). Specifically, Shotter's (1996) focus is on the "... moment by moment changing circumstances surrounding our talk ..." (p. 293).

This he dubs the "dialogical, rhetorical-responsive, embodied, version of social constructionism". Like other versions, it rejects the representational paradigm in cognitive psychology (e.g., Shotter, 1993b). Memories, motives, perceptions, etc., are not psychological entities, but are constructed in conversation. Moreover, they are differentially constructed depending on circumstance and purpose, and this, Shotter claims, makes dialogical, responsive talk practical in nature.[5]

Given these views, it is not surprising that Shotter is highly critical of academic psychology, which, he says, is obsessed not only with representations but also with "... static, objective, systems of knowledge and factual information ..." (Shotter, 1996, p. 293). Academic psychology assumes that knowledge is the correct representation of an independent reality; that an outer reality can be "depicted" or "pictured". This he refers to as "the epistemology project". Shotter's (2002) judgement is that taking knowledge to be a correct representation of an independent reality assumes that we (as "knowers") are in a subject-object relation to our surroundings (2002, p. 590); that we can remove ourselves from the flux of social life and objectively examine that which we wish to learn more about. A consequence of this obsession is, Shotter thinks, that academics engage in a pointless "ritual", that of theory-criticism-and-debate. The discipline then continues to lack the conceptual resources to account for the features of "relations-in-motion".

To pursue this further: Shotter does not mean that psychology needs new and better theories. Theories are the problem. They are, he thinks, unsituated, abstractions. Theorists are entrapped within a closed disciplinary system, a system which disconnects itself from its social and historical roots (Shotter, 1993b). They use words "... in a wholly, lifeless, nomological, decontextualised manner and seek only a passive, representational kind of understanding ..." (Shotter, 1996, p. 303). This prevents our attending to "... the changing character of the moment by moment struggles between (and within) people as they 'orchestrate' their practices" (Shotter, 1996, n. 2, p. 308). The very act of theorising is said to distance the theorist from the flux of social life. A theoretical system "... creates the illusion of it being about "a world of things" existing independently of it and external to it" (Shotter, 1993b, p. 28).

For these reasons, Shotter would have no time for the material in this book (see Shotter & Lannamann, 2002). He would regard it as an epistemological project involving the unproductive "Ritual" of theory-criticism-and-debate. As such, he thinks it accepts implicitly a set of Cartesian assumptions which allows talk of processes, objects, events and causal relations between events, subjectively understood, i.e. understood by an individual knower (Shotter & Lannamann, 2002, p. 578), and it neglects the fact that inquiry is grounded "... within that realm of reciprocally interwoven, living, embodied activity, spontaneously and continuously occurring out in the world *between* people ..." (Shotter & Lannamann, 2002, p. 578).

Gergen's engagement in such debates is, Shotter believes, a mistake, as it undermines his (Gergen's) own professed position. Even though Gergen (2001a) has said that he "...no longer finds the tradition of argumentation a viable one" (2001a, p. 431), Shotter believes that he too (like the realist) has failed to realise his entrapment in Descartes' philosophy; he too is "...in the thrall of... 'the way of theory'..." (Shotter, 1995, p. 50); Gergen's version of social constructionism is a meta-critique or "grand narrative", instead of remaining a challenge to grand narratives in general.

Shotter's wish, then, is for psychologists to change their disciplinary practices—not to develop theories, but to provide local instructive accounts of activities of the formative, creative kind and to explore "...the scope and limits of a *practical procedure*..." (Shotter, 1993b, p. 33, italics in the original). More radically, he maintains that making knowledge is more important than discovery, for it can no longer be assumed that our knowledge of the world is independent of us; the character of anything beyond, or external to, our constructionist activities is unknowable to us. This, of course, is contrary to any realist philosophy, and Shotter (1995) takes it to be a feature of all versions of social constructionism. It is, then, not surprising that he judges the criterion of truth as "accuracy of representation" to be redundant. When assessing our accounts of activities and practices, "truth" must, he thinks, be replaced with notions of fruitfulness, adequacy, viability, and coherence.

1.5. GERGEN'S METATHEORY OF PSYCHOLOGICAL SCIENCE

In Gergen's opinion, a number of different philosophical systems maintain a thesis which psychologists find intellectually threatening. This thesis is that the nature of the relationship between language and the world has been misunderstood. Propositions about the world are not driven or required by particular characteristics of the world (e.g., Gergen, 2001b). Specifically:

A. Reality cannot be represented by language. There is no fixed relation between words and the world.

Neither claim follows from the other, but they frequently coexist in much of Gergen's work. Referring to theories as essentially discursive, Gergen (1994c) claims that:

...because disquisitions on the nature of things are framed in language, there is no grounding of science or any knowledge-generating enterprise in other than communities of interlocutors (p. ix).

Because 'whatever is' makes no necessary demands on our language (descriptions, explanations), ...our language serves to construct what we take to be the world.

And, because meaningful language is inherently a product of social coordination, the strong emphasis is on the socially constructed character of the real and the good (1998b, pp. 45–46).

To speak, then, of the material world and causal relations is not to describe accurately what there is, but to participate in a textual genre . . . (2001b, p. 805).

Similarly, Potter (1996a) claims that things cannot be described objectively (p. 125), while Shotter (e.g., 1992a, 1993 #811; 1992b; 1993b; 1996) maintains that language does have a representational function, but this function is derived from its primary function which is "rhetorical-responsive". The suggestion is that the "responsive forms of talk" are not, even in part, representational.

Gergen particularises thesis A in terms of the relationship between psychological theories and the states of affairs that such theories purport to be about.[6] This version of thesis A is expressed in three interrelated claims (henceforth, propositions A1, A2 and A3):

A1. Psychology's theories are not derived from observation.[7]

A2. Psychology's theories do not depict, map, mirror, contain, convey, picture, reflect, store or represent reality in any direct or decontextualised manner.[8]

A3. Psychological phenomena do not exist independently of the discourse that supposedly reflects such phenomena.[9]

Each of these propositions requires some elaboration before an account can be given of Gergen's rationale for them.

1.6. UNFOLDING THE RELATIONSHIP BETWEEN LANGUAGE AND REALITY

1.6.1. PSYCHOLOGY'S THEORIES ARE NOT DERIVED FROM OBSERVATION (A1)

In Gergen's opinion, there is little reason ". . . to suppose that conceptions of the psychological world are in any way derived from observation—either directly or by inference" (1987b, p. 11). His position on this issue is a composite one. When distilled, it is that theoretical categories are necessary in order to make observations, therefore such categories cannot be derived from observation.[10]

There are, however, a number of intermediate steps between his premise and conclusion. Firstly, Gergen rejects the view of Hanson (1958), Kuhn (1970) and others, that the *process* of observation is affected by the observer's theory. In his opinion, "[t]he argument that language determines the way events are registered on the senses is badly flawed" (Gergen, 1986a, p. 150). Secondly, in place of the process view, Gergen (1986a) suggests that:

It seems more promising to argue that the forestructure of the descriptive language will have a strong determining effect on the account to be rendered of the world (1986a, p. 150).

So, Gergen's belief is that the *process* of perceiving is not influenced by linguistic "forestructures", theoretical affiliations, or whatever, but that these variables influence the *descriptions* of what has been perceived. Thus, the nature of this "influence" is judged to be linguistic. It is, Gergen (1991a) suggests, psychology's theoretical language that "saturates" its descriptions (p. 15).

Typically, it is believed that proposition A1 sharply distinguishes between social constructionist metatheory and positivist-empiricist philosophy of science. The latter is said to accord observation a foundational role in the production of theory—foundational in the sense that direct knowledge of sense-data supposedly "trickles up" and informs our theories. Such knowledge is taken to be infallible, and is said to provide a neutral or objective observational base. Social constructionism, by contrast, maintains that the describers' experience of the (supposed) phenomena described play no part in what those descriptions mean. The meanings are said to "trickle down" from the theory, and observation is accorded a role that is, at best, marginal. The psychologist, Gergen assumes, will always be in the business of making observations, but there is no reason to believe that theoretical discourse is in any way derived from observation. Contrary to the positivist-empiricist view, then, observation is not the criterion for theory *evaluation*. In Gergen's opinion, the "forestructure of the descriptive language" is constituted by socio-linguistic practices, our "forms of life", and it is these which determine theoretical content. The social processes of rhetoric, conflict, communication and negotiation amongst scholars about the meanings of various theoretical terms, reveal the contexts in which each term may be used and these meanings trickle down to the descriptions of what has been perceived.[11] "In effect, the world does not determine the form of our utterances or our phonemes; we employ language together to determine what the world is for us"(Gergen, 1998a, p. 102).

Drawing on the work of Vygotsky, Shotter (1993c) makes general reference to "... language ... working to influence people's perception" (p. 464) and again emphasises that such higher mental abilities have their origins in relations between individuals. The term "perception" is here used loosely to mean "thinking conceptually" and for Shotter such thinking is a special social practice (p. 465). How far Shotter wishes to take this thesis (that language determines perception) is unclear, although the following question is perhaps rhetorical:

even the seeing of objects involves an active psychological process of construction involving socially derived knowledge—doesn't it? ... a way of speaking is what prevents us from seeing the facts (that is, our practices and procedures of usage) without prejudice (Shotter, 1992a, p. 61, p. 64).

The world is perceived through speech, and psychology as a discipline is situated within this everyday conversational background (Shotter, 1993a, p. 35).

Potter (1996b) similarly regards empiricism (which he incorrectly says is the doctrine that facts are a product of observation) as thoroughly compromised by the realisation that in seeing we are interpreting, i.e., we see x as *something* and this, he maintains, involves the imposition of language.[12] His argument is that in seeing x as *something*, theoretical assumptions are presupposed, and even if we try to determine the observational basis of these assumptions, this too is theory dependent.

Observations, then, provide no foundation for knowledge. The world is perceived through language (specifically through linguistic forestructures). Gergen reasons (albeit invalidly) that if the role of observation is properly deflated, the resultant body of psychological knowledge cannot be about psychological situations (e.g., 1999, p. 14). Thus, proposition A2 is judged to be a consequence of proposition A1.

1.6.2. PSYCHOLOGY'S THEORIES DO NOT DEPICT, MAP, MIRROR, CONTAIN, CONVEY, PICTURE, REFLECT, STORE, OR REPRESENT REALITY (A2)

Proposition A2 is said to exemplify the abandonment of the modernist commitment to representationalism (Gergen, 1994b; 1999). The point of a theory, according to Gergen (1988b), is not to copy reality, for:

> ... as post-modernist thought has made increasingly clear ..., the metaphor of theory as a 'map' or 'picture' of reality is deeply problematic (p. 286).

This excerpt suggests that Gergen might accept thesis A, but claim that the relation between words and the world (henceforth referred to as "external reference" or, in adjectival form, "referential") involves a non-correspondence notion.[13] This is not so. Although Gergen consistently identifies external reference with a correspondence theory (1.7.1), his position is more accurately represented as: not all notions of external reference are correspondence notions, but all notions of external reference must be rejected.[14] This is because he speaks generally of language bearing "... no determinate relationship to events external to language itself..." (Gergen, 1994c, p. 31). He claims, for example, that mental predicates are "semantically free-floating", in that there are no (general) links between these predicates and psychological phenomena (Gergen, 1987c, p. 118–119; 2001a, p. 421). Most of the time, however, Gergen takes external reference to imply correspondence, so that the notion of external reference collapses if a correspondence theory cannot be sustained. He does not distinguish between these two concepts—external reference and correspondence—and he offers no reason for thinking that his metatheory accepts the former whilst rejecting the latter.

From this Gergen (1999) reasons that theoretical statements containing mental predicates, and statements that are predicated upon the existence of a link between the mental predicate and reality, can be neither true nor false (p. 20). Even the non-psychological claim that the world is spherical and not flat is, he believes, "... neither true nor false in terms of pictorial value, i.e., correspondence with the objective world" (Gergen, 1987a, p. 6). The value of a psychological theory cannot, therefore, be assessed by employing the criterion of "correspondence with empirical fact" (Gergen, 1987a, p. 1; 1987b, p. 10; 1987c, p. 116; 1990b, pp. 212–213; 1999, p. 20). Furthermore, Gergen (1985a, p. 272) maintains, social constructionism cannot support the possibility of any alternative truth criteria. Here he is nihilistic about truth.

On this issue of truth, Shotter (1993a) is also dismissive. He insists that his work be judged not as a theory of either true or false statements, but as a toolbox replete with verbal resources which can be assessed as to whether they're instructive or not. In a similarly pragmatic vein, Harré (1990) insists that theories not be taken as sets of true or false statements but as "... guides to possible scientific acts" (p. 304). Potter (1996b) does not deny that a "story" may be true, but he prefers the obscure criterion of whether the story "works". Equally cryptic is his claim that "... truth and falsity can be studied as moves in a rhetorical game" (Potter, 1996b, p. 40). Elsewhere he maintains that objective truth and validity are to be replaced by social process and practical reasoning, and that facts are inseparable from judgements (Potter, Edwards, & Ashmore, 1999). In each case, interest lies with what is done with the statement or description in a context of social interaction, not with whether it is true.

Gergen's rationale for his truth nihilism is not obvious. It appears that he believes that any theory of truth requires external reference. Yet non-realist theories of truth require no such thing (Kirkham, 1992), and Gergen is surely aware of them. His suggestion that social constructionism cannot support *any* truth criteria, is perhaps motivated by thoughts of a Foucault-type analysis, in which power in social relations is considered to be a crucial ingredient of any conceptualisation of truth. He suggests, for instance, that the use of the term "truth" might function to justify one's own position and discredit one's opponent's (Gergen, 1985, p. 268). Presumably, then, he believes that neither a realist nor a non-realist theory of truth will reveal how the word "true" functions in social relations.

On other occasions, Gergen says that his position involves "... truth within traditions" (2001a, p. 422; 2001b, p. 806). This, he thinks, does not involve epistemological relativism. What it means is that whether an assertion "... can be considered true depends altogether on local agreements linking words with what we take to be wordly configurations" (2001a, p. 422). Still, Gergen remains concerned with what he judges to be the destructive aspects of the "truth game". "Local truths" are in no sense universal truths, nor must they become so, for this, he thinks, would involve the marginalisation of other perspectives. Clearly, though,

Gergen does not doubt that the negation of proposition A2 implies context-free correspondence between words and the world, and that such correspondence is a myth (Gergen, 1986a, pp. 138–139; 1987a, pp. 2–3; 1987b, p. 4; 2001a, p. 429). In his judgement, a text or utterance conveys different meanings across various subcultures and across history. In particular, what we understand about psychological phenomena is a function of culture and epoch (Gergen, 1997, p. 730) and, because of this, "... the specter of cultural and historical relativism remains robust" (Gergen, 1987b, p. 9).

Some of the time Shotter (1993c, p. 461) appears more moderate than Gergen in the eschewal of word-world, context-free representation. Shotter's position is that words are used primarily in non-representational ways, ways that maintain, reproduce, transform and create various modes of social relationships, and that the representation of facts to each other is a "refinement" of this primary discursive form (1996, p. 304). However, we must, he says, stop "... thinking of our sentences as *pictures*, in which we can *see* [in] the structure of the sentence the "things" they represent..." (Shotter, 1992a, p. 64). On other occasions though, Shotter omits any qualifications and appears to endorse a more radical position. Descriptions do not accurately represent reality (Shotter, 1993a, p. 183) and, elsewhere, he maintains that:

> ... a system of thought and expression can work to disconnect itself from its own social and historical origins, and also (seemingly) from its rooting or grounding in the social practices which maintain its appearance of autonomy, and creates the illusion of being about 'a world of things' existing independently of it and external to it (1992a, p. 65).

Potter (1996b) also rejects what he mistakenly takes to be a realist idea, that discourse mirrors reality. He does so, he says, for two reasons, neither of which, he says, have anything to do with truth or falsity. First, if we are to evaluate whether a description "mirrors" reality, the description must be compared to reality. But any reference to reality would involve another description and this assumes the very point which is at issue—whether this new description is descriptive (p. 98). Second, he maintains that the metaphor of "mirroring reality" precludes an investigation into how descriptions are constructed, what materials are used, and what they produce. Here, his reasoning appears to be "if not mirroring, then constructing"; he evidently thinks, like Gergen, that rejection of the "mirror" metaphor forces an adoption of "descriptions as constructed".

To return to Gergen. Having claimed that the meanings of theoretical and observational terms are not invariant but depend on culture and epoch, Gergen articulates the post-modernist rejection of the Western conception of knowledge as objective, individualistic and ahistorical. Knowledge is said to consist of linguistic renderings of the kind represented in linguistic propositions, stored on computer disks and found in journals and textbooks (Gergen, 1985a, p. 270). When in the form of general laws or conclusions, these renderings are merely rhetorical devices (used to promote one's own theory and demote the opposition's). They do not describe or report anything, and there is, he believes, a general failure amongst Western intellectuals, to recognise this fact—that scientific propositions are not truth-bearers (Gergen, 1990b, p. 213).

Given that psychological propositions are not truth-bearers, the question must be asked, "What do they reflect?" Gergen's answer involves a reiteration of the point made in the previous section: he thinks that a psychological theory reflects the various social negotiation processes and conventions of discourse that are shared by the community of psychologists responsible for the construction of that particular theory. An analysis of our theoretical discourse for its meanings will uncover the nature of the general social milieux in which our theories are generated (Gergen, 1994c, p. 53). Furthermore, a theory is the result of communities of scientists or organisational units having worked together "... to hammer out forms of discourse that will service their localized ends" (Gergen, 1990a, p. 294). A psychological theory, then, is not a reflection of individual scientists each trying to discover truths. It is something which serves the purposes of the psychology community. It is an implement for carrying out social practices, for co-ordinating the activities of psychologists in that community and for making their actions intelligible (Gergen, 1989b, p. 472; 1990b, p. 213). However, such communities are, Gergen believes, not entirely self-serving. Their theories also contribute to society. They furnish the culture with discursive devices that in turn determine the socio-linguistic practices in which such discourse is embedded (Gergen, 1987a, p. 9). Child-care, therapeutic, political, economic and educational practices, and even interpersonal communication, all change when a new form of theoretical discourse becomes available. The aim of a theory is, then, transformative (Gergen, 2001a, p. 419).

1.6.3. PSYCHOLOGICAL PHENOMENA ARE NOT DISCOURSE-INDEPENDENT (A3)

Gergen has less to say about proposition A3 than he has about A1 or A2. There is the suggestion that once psychology has fully appreciated propositions A1 and A2, it would cease to talk about what "exists or occurs" and start to talk about "talk about what exists or occurs". The latter is, of course, an important theme of post-modernism in the social sciences, and Gergen's metatheory is orthodox in this respect. Social constructionism must, he believes, be ontologically mute (Gergen, 1994c, p. 68; 2001a, p. 425).[15] The social constructionist, on pain of inconsistency, is only ever entitled to talk about talk. If what appears to be psychological reality is in fact a construction given by discourse, rather than something reflected by discourse, then how could we ever know this reality, as opposed to merely knowing our own discourse?

Psychologists, however, stubbornly continue to assume that psychology has a subject matter—that situations of a psychological kind occur, and that these situations can be described and explained (Gergen, 1992b; 1994c). This, Gergen maintains, is untenable, because it denies a number of important and inter-related facts: first, that what is taken to be the "mental" is in fact the "social"; second, that the "dualist" assumption of the independence of subject and object is mistaken; third, that socio-historical processes influence our systems of preconceptualisa-tion and linguistic conventions; fourth, that these determine the process of theory construction, and fifth, that the result of such theory construction is to objectify a particular ontology of the person that is not universal, nor even general, but contextually saturated with the effects of social process.

These themes will recur throughout this book. For the moment, it is suf-ficient to provide examples of how Gergen particularises A3. He suggests, for example, that: depression is "...not a state of mind, but an historically situated construction" (Gergen, 1987c, p. 128); without the concept of 'command' or 'obe-dience', "...such 'events' simply do not exist" (Gergen, 1987b, p. 8); mental predicates, such as 'emotion' or 'self', "...are cashed out in terms of the social practices in which they function" (Gergen, 1985a, p. 271); "...each language creates its own domain of relevant facts" (Gergen, 1991a, p. 15); "...the very idea of an 'independent world' may itself be an outgrowth of rhetorical demands" (1991a, p. 23), and that what we take to be psychological entities (such as the in-dividual) and psychological phenomena (such as 'rational behaviour', 'attitudes', 'emotion', 'memory', 'obsessiveness', etc.) all "...lose ontological grounding..." and become "...historically contingent constructions of culture" (Gergen, 1994c, p. 70).

Potter and his colleagues maintain the general (and ambiguous) thesis that the world is not distinct from the processes involved in representing and inter-preting it (Edwards et al., 1995), whilst Shotter reiterates some of Gergen's more specific statements: talk about our 'perceptions', 'memories', 'motives', etc., does not refer to anything real (1993a, p. 182); "...minds, selves, and psyches ex-ist as such only within our embodied discursive practices" (1997, p. 21), and the psyche is constituted in acts of communication (1993a, p. 182; 1998, p. 17). Moreover:

> [T]he entities they [words] denote are known not for what they are in themselves
> but in terms of their 'currency' or significance in our different modes of social life,
> that is, in terms of what it is deemed sensible for us to do with them...They have
> their being *only* within the form of life we (the whole community) conversationally
> sustain between ourselves (1992b, p. 177).

This, Shotter notes, is antithetical to realism: it makes reference to a reality which is not independent of ways of talking and, therefore, of ways of knowing (see also Shotter, 1994, p. 158).

So, crucial to the social constructionist position is the view that a psychological theory, once it is understood, constructs the world of psychological fact. Theories operate as miniature ontologies, specifying the ingredients of the world and how it operates, and different discourses imply quite different ontologies. There is no content to psychological theory apart from what is constructed via the rhetoric of representationalism. Such rhetoric constructs the very phenomena that it is mistakenly thought to be representing.

On many occasions, then, social constructionists are suggesting that the qualities of a psychological situation are not something which it possesses objectively; that these "qualities" are constituted by the linguistic forestructures and social practices of the various lay and psychological communities, and that the "psychological" necessarily implies the implausible notions of individualism and representationalism. There is some justification, however, for a less radical interpretation. Gergen's version of constructionism claims to be ontologically mute. In his words, "Whatever is, simply is" (1994c, p. 72), and although this sentence is itself (vacuously) ontological, Gergen wishes to convey that his philosophical position does not extend to a denial of reality. He would allow that psychological situations might occur and might possess certain qualities (e.g., Gergen, 1997, p. 730), but that they are unknowable, in the traditional bottom-up empirical sense, because what is known is completely determined by linguistic and social practices.

1.6.4. SUMMARY

This concludes the elaboration of propositions A1, A2 and A3 and consequently of thesis A. At the core of these claims is a circularity thesis. The whole process of psychology's theoretical development is, Gergen believes, vitiated by circularity (see also Shotter, 1992a, p. 64; 1993c, p. 461). The meanings of terms in descriptive statements are given by the meanings of terms in theoretical statements (from which hypotheses to be tested are derived). The meanings of theoretical terms are, in turn, arrived at through various linguistic forestructures and social practices used and engaged in by communities of psychologists. So, in arriving at, and in using, such theoretical terms, the ontological question is already begged in favour of the theory. The theory helps itself to its own confirmation. This, of course, is very similar to the theme of Edwards *et al.*'s "Death and Furniture" paper—the realist's dilemma is that in the act of representing, they are "trapped" in discourse.

Such entrapment, such circularity is, in Gergen's view, unavoidable. It is not possible, it would seem, to talk about anything other than talk. The focus of attention must then turn to: "... why, at this moment in history, we account for our experience of ourselves in the way that we do... (Shotter, 1992b, p. 177). The relationship between psychological theory and psychological states of affairs *cannot* be such that "psychological reality" is reflected by psychology's theoretical discourse, when such discourse actually *constructs* "psychological reality". It is this that psychologists are so reluctant to embrace.

1.7. GERGEN'S RATIONALE FOR PROPOSITIONS
A1, A2, AND A3

Gergen's rationale for thesis A and, by implication, for propositions A1, A2 and A3, is provided in his rationale for a social constructionist conception of meaning. Although the details can be found scattered throughout his published works, his 1986 *Correspondence versus Autonomy in the Language of Understanding Human Action* contains a particularly comprehensive account of his position. It is clear that Gergen would now reject the allusions made in that paper to individualism. It is also unlikely that he would now make the ontological claims he then made or, at any rate, unlikely that he would make them without the inverted commas which he uses (though not at all consistently) to distance himself from any material existence implications. Even so, his 1986 paper remains a reasonably accurate statement of his position and he continues to draw on many of its ideas (e.g., Gergen, 2001a). For this reason, it will frequently be referred to in the remainder of this chapter.

In his rationale, Gergen synthesises his findings from a range of disciplines. It consists of four components—one negative and three positive theses.[16] The negative thesis is the rejection of meaning as external reference. The positive theses are: (i) that meaning is indeterminate; (ii) that meaning is contextual, and (iii) that meaning is social.

1.7.1. A THEORY OF MEANING INVOLVING EXTERNAL
REFERENCE IS IMPLAUSIBLE

The first component of Gergen's rationale is directly relevant to propositions A1 and A2. It consists of a justification for his rejection of external reference as a component of an account of meaning. As was noted in 1.6.2, for Gergen, this frequently involves the rejection of the notion of correspondence. About this, he is unequivocal:

> There is no means of arraying all the events in the 'real world' on one side and all the syllables of the language on the other, and linking them in one-to-one fashion, such that each syllable would reflect an isolated atom of reality (Gergen & Kaye, 1992, p. 173).

This is the rejection of a position which, I think, no-one has ever held. Not even the early Wittgenstein suggested that syllables correspond to atoms of reality. It is, however, Wittgenstein's early position that Gergen wants to dismiss. In *Tractatus Logico-Philosophicus*, Wittgenstein (1921/1974) says:

> In a proposition there must be exactly as many distinguishable parts as in the situation that it represents (4.04).

Most of the time, this is what Gergen understands by *external* reference—a concept of correspondence proposed by the early (but rejected by the later) Wittgenstein, one which relied heavily on the (undemonstrable) thesis of logical atomism.[17] Word-world relations have to be spelt out in terms of rigid, simulative correspondence. It is this notion of correspondence which Gergen rejects as untenable. Although he refers generally to correspondence theories, there is no textual evidence that by "correspondence" he understands anything other than this early-Wittgensteinian notion. For example, when discussing the semantic assumptions of many structuralists, Gergen (1994c) claims that:

> If they [the structuralist accounts of the unconscious, universal grammar, etc.] are *pictures* of the structures, then empiricist or realist views of language are correct (p. 39, italics added).

For Gergen, then, a correspondence notion necessarily involves "picturing" or "mirroring".

Gergen's evidence against external reference consists in the repeated failure of correspondence theorists to establish the rules involved in linking language to observations (e.g., 1986a; 1987a; 1987b; 1990a; 1999). This he takes to be unsurprising. What is surprising, he believes, is that they do not recognise the impossibility in principle of identifying those rules. No such rules could ever be explicated, he thinks, because the process of explication would be contextually dependent. In Gergen's opinion, correspondence theorists are no less constrained by social negotiation processes, discursive conventions, rhetorical power and the like, than are psychologists.[18]

Less frequently, Gergen links the rejection of external reference to the thesis of essentialism (1996; 2001c). He maintains that names are treated as though they are derived from the essential properties in nature to which they supposedly refer. For example, the group name "women" presupposes "... an essential entity—a group unified by its distinctive features" and the group name is said to be referential (2001c, p. 174). But social constructionism is, according to Gergen, antagonistic to essentialism—it takes reference to be "... a social achievement and thus inherently defeasible" (2001c, p. 174).

In short, Gergen's thesis is: there are no grounds for a theory of meaning which involves external reference, because external reference involves a correspondence theory of truth and the notion that an entity has essential features. The former relies on words and sentences "picturing" or "mirroring" objects or phenomena and naively negates the role of context in language-use. The latter assumes that there exist in nature characteristics which are language-independent. It is such a defective theory of truth, as well as the thesis of essentialism, which Gergen assumes is the basis of positivist-empiricist metatheory (e.g., Misra, 1993).

1.7.2. THE MEANINGS OF PSYCHOLOGY'S THEORETICAL
TERMS ARE INDETERMINATE

The second component of Gergen's rationale for his social constructionist conception of meaning supplements the first, and is also relevant to propositions A1 and A2. It concerns his view that the referents of psychology's theoretical terms cannot be determined.[19] This, he thinks, is because the meanings of terms generally are not fixed. To ask of a psychological term "What does it mean?" is to fail to recognise this fact.

As support for this indeterminacy thesis, Gergen draws from Continental epistemology.[20] In Gergen's judgement, the indeterminacy thesis is supported by two assumptions which have emerged from this tradition:

(i) that an interpreter must always interpret from within an "horizon of understanding"—the consequence of this being not one, fixed, meaning of a psychological text, but innumerable possible meanings, and

(ii) that the deconstruction of theory demonstrates its figurative (metaphorical) base—the consequence of this being that the meanings of terms are not given by their reference to psychological states of affairs.

Continental epistemology places interpretation and meaning at the centre of the social sciences, and in so doing, turns away from external reference as correspondence with a non-linguistic realm. It is not surprising, then, that Gergen finds that hermeneutic and deconstructionist contributions are highly relevant to social constructionism.[21] Their contribution has been the provision of arguments for the view that theoretical accounts of behaviour are figuratively based, in that they are "... value-saturated products of social agreement" (Gergen, 1992b, p. 22).[22] In a similar vein, Shotter's (1993c) reliance is on Heidegger's notion of *fore-having*—our daily understandings are grounded in particular, concrete contexts, i.e., "... something we have in advance" (p. 460).

Claim (i) is especially associated with Gadamer's (1960/1975) development of a theory that takes hermeneutics beyond Biblical exegesis. For Gergen (1999), Gadamer's work demonstrates that meaning is not fixed, and truth is not ahistorical. Gadamer argues that it is a condition of all interpretation that any knower operates within a contemporary "horizon of understanding", which includes conceptual commitments, pre-judgements, prejudices, and the culture and epoch in which that knower is located. In fact, Gadamer (1960/1975) suggests that:

> An interpretation that was correct 'in itself' would be a foolish ideal that failed to take account of the nature of tradition. Every interpretation has to adapt itself to the hermeneutical situation to which it belongs (p. 358).

Consequently, as a text passes from one cultural and/or historical context to another, new meanings are made which would never have been anticipated by the author, nor by those located in different contexts. The meaning of any text is not, therefore, exhausted by the author's intentions, so there is no possibility of knowing *the* meaning of the text "as it is". Hence Gergen's belief that meaning is indeterminate. Interpretation is always situational or context-specific. Shotter's (1998b, p. 46) views on indeterminacy are, of course, not primarily concerned with the text. An indeterminacy of meaning is the outcome of the various ways of "responding relationally" in the "living moments". It is in these that the making of meanings occurs.

In Gadamer's opinion, this embedment of every text, and of all inquiry, in historical and cultural convention, not only enables the knowing process, it places constraints upon that process (contra Gergen), and therefore upon the products of that process. A consequence of this is that what is meant by "reason", "knowledge" and "truth" must be reconceptualised. "Truth", for example, cannot be knowledge of external, timeless facts, given that it emerges from a process of dialogue between at least two people, each with his or her own "horizon of understanding".

Gergen finds support for claim (ii) in Derrida's deconstructionism (e.g., 1994c; 1999). The themes relevant to Gergen's account of meaning can be found in chapters 1 and 2 of Derrida's *Of Grammatology* (1976). Examine closely, says Derrida, the first principles of any thought-system and it becomes evident that they can be "deconstructed". It can be shown that they are products of a particular system of meaning, not descriptions of external states of affairs. Such first principles are identified by what they exclude. For example, the "mechanistic" metaphor embedded in many psychological theories is said to exclude its allegedly "inferior" binary opposite—the metaphor "teleological". As a result, "intentions", "reasons", "self-determinism", etc. are not "talked about" by the theory. Yet, says Derrida, the defining characteristics of "intentions", for example, are as relevant as the defining characteristics of their binary opposite "mechanistic". The purpose of deconstructionism is not, therefore, to reverse a tradition (Derrida, 1976, p. 37). It is not to licence talk about intentions, reasons, or self-determinism in place of mechanistic metaphors. Deconstructionism advocates, instead, that the binary opposites be replaced by an over-arching concept. However, this new concept must not make the same logocentric mistake as before and search for a signified, for the signified is elusive or indefinite (p. 49). In Gergen's (1994c) words, it is perpetually deferred in that ". . . definitions are supplied by other words . . .", and to ". . . determine what a given utterance means is to be thrust back on an enormous array of language uses or texts" (p. 39).

Binary oppositions are typically regarded by those social constructionists influenced by Derrida as both unavoidable and problematic. They are said to obscure the interdependence between terms; to render the dominance of one term over another as "natural" when those terms are really mutually constituted (e.g., Wetherell & Potter, 1998). Deconstructing a psychological theory will, Gergen believes, reveal the presence of metaphor (such as "mechanistic" or "organismic"). The metaphor, he suggests, guides the theorist in such a way that the actual behaviour of the psychological subject ceases to be of significance in the research process (Gergen, 1986a, p. 145). The implication of this, he thinks, is that because of the dominance of the psychologist's commitment to the metaphor, the theory does not "hook up" to reality—the metaphor turns the psychologist away from the activities of the subject. The theory is not grounded in the subject's behaviour because the metaphor has effectively distracted the psychologist. In this sense it has set limits or constraints on what the theory "talks about". If the metaphor is "mechanistic", for example, the theory is not, Gergen believes, going to talk about intentions, meanings, reasons or motives. Observations will, therefore, be theory-laden. The theory will embrace a metaphor not given through observation (ergo, proposition A1). A literal language (reflecting the world) is rejected and replaced by a metaphoric one.

The same point is made by Shotter (1994). The problem endemic to psychology is that it allows itself to become "entrapped" within a system of terms, statements and beliefs, whose definitions and meanings have become fixed retrospectively. Those within the "discursive or intralinguistic" reality ignore the fact of their "entrapment" and this invites further formulations "in terms of a particular metaphor" (p. 160). It is not the case that "... words *must* have stable, unequivocal, already determined *meanings*" (Shotter, 1993b, pp. 78–79). Words are tools or instruments used in the making of meaning, and until they're used in different particular ways in different particular circumstances, their significance is open, vague and ambiguous (Shotter, 1993b, p. 79).

In summary, indeterminacy of meaning or interpretation is, according to Gergen, a most important challenge to the correspondence assumptions of semantic mapping (1986a; 1999).[23] The relative arbitrariness of language is recognised. If language did "picture" or "mirror" things, there would be no such arbitrariness. In particular, psychological phenomena (if there are such things) do not constrain psychology's "descriptions". To paraphrase Burr (1998), if construction, not objective description. Socio-linguistic practices constrain and construct, and this is what it means to say that language is relatively arbitrary. The constraints do not come from the phenomena under study. "'[W]hatever is' makes no necessary demands on our language ..." (Gergen, 1998b, p. 45). Consistent with structuralist theory (which follows from de Saussure's linguistics), Gergen's position is, then, that such arbitrariness and external reference are incompatible.

If, as Gergen believes, the meaning of a psychological term is not given by its reference to extra-linguistic states of affairs and the term is, in fact, autonomous from, or unrelated to, reality, the question is "How does it acquire meaning?" Gergen proposes two theses which he believes contribute to an answer to this question. The first is that meaning is contextually dependent, and the second is that meaning has social origins within situations.

1.7.3. MEANING IS CONTEXTUALLY DEPENDENT

This third component of Gergen's rationale involves the claim that the context of a term's usage gives that term its meaning.[24] In particular, the meaning of any term in a psychological theory is given by the context in which the term is used.

By "context", Gergen means anything from the immediate particular environment in which terms, propositions, etc. are uttered to a whole cultural tradition (Gergen, 1994c, p. 49, pp. 84–87). For this reason, perhaps, Gergen refers to his account of meaning as "relational". On the one hand, "context" may refer simply to the immediate conditions under which an utterance is employed. He suggests, for example, that context supplements the speaker's action and, in doing so, not only "constrains" meaning but also "creates" it (1994c, p. 265). In this case, context may be equivalent to Wittgenstein's notion of a "language-game". But "context" may also be "sufficiently extended" to include an entire cultural tradition (1994c, p. 49). In this case, it may be equivalent to Wittgenstein's notion of "form of life" (1994c, p. 53).

These contexts are said to be unrelated to the kinds of things which are (mistakenly) thought to give meaning to descriptive terms. Meaning is not given by any event that a term is presumed to refer to, nor does meaning originate within an individual mind. Further, the context of usage "...can also include the syntactic conventions governing [the term's] use" (Gergen, 1986a, p. 139). But there can be no unequivocal articulation of the syntactic conventions governing the use of (say) the term "aggression", as any such articulation would itself be embedded in diverse contexts of usage.

Attempted justifications for the thesis that meaning is contextually dependent can be found in the hermeneutic contributions of Gadamer and others. However, Gergen prefers to invoke the later Wittgenstein and, to a lesser extent, Quine, as support for this particular thesis:

> ...postmodern thought has largely favored some form of Wittgensteinian or use-based (neo-pragmatist) account of language (Gergen, 1995a, p. 77).

Wittgenstein has been identified by some as a "proto-postmodernist" (e.g., Holzman & Morss, 2000), and the value of his later work is thought to lie in his conception of meaning:

> For Wittgenstein's words acquire their meaning within what he metaphorically terms "language games," that is, through the ways they are used in patterns of ongoing exchange.... In effect, the terms acquire their meaning by their function within a set of circumscribed rules (Gergen, 1994c, pp. 52–53).

Shotter (e.g. 1993c; 1994; 2003) also relies heavily on Wittgenstein's "meaning as use" thesis, although Potter and his colleagues do not. Of note is that in *Philosophical Investigations*, Wittgenstein (1953/1967) is concerned to refute

Augustine's view that words name objects.[25] Even in a complete, primitive language, consisting of only four words—"block", "pillar", "slab" and "beam"—such
words, Wittgenstein argues, are not mere names (§§1–2). The meaning of "pillar",
for example, does not consist in the objects the word names, but in the way the
word is used in a language-game (the process of using words in a particular context). In order to discover the meaning of the word "pillar" we must, Wittgenstein
believes, examine the contexts in which people actually use this word. We must
examine, that is, the roles that the word plays in everyday language. Referred to
as the "use theory of meaning", "use", in Wittgenstein's thesis, is characterised
in terms of the circumstances of application within the language-game which the
speaker is "playing" at the time.

In *Word and Object*, Quine (1960) also concentrates on the function of language in particular contexts. He claims that the correct translation between the
words of two languages is one which exploits information about the stimulus conditions under which utterances are accepted (pp. 29–30). The correct translation
would be one which best preserves an overall similarity of usage (p. 31). Consider,
says Quine, the term "gavagai" uttered by a native of a hitherto isolated tribe.
Imagine that having observed the circumstances under which the native utters this
term, the linguist translates it into "rabbit". Clearly, the stimulus conditions which
prompt the utterance "gavagai" are the same as those which prompt the utterance
"rabbit" (pp. 51–52). However, the linguist is not entitled to the assumption that
the native is referring to "... a whole enduring rabbit ..." (p. 52). "Gavagai" could
well apply to "... sundry undetached parts of rabbits ..." or "... rabbit stages ..."
(p. 52). Just what "gavagai" applies to depends upon context, and context, in
Quine's case, refers to the native's conceptual scheme. Reference is, therefore, indeterminate, unless the linguist can discover what the native's conceptual scheme is
(p. 77). But, of course, to do this would be to discover the correct way of translating
the native's language. The conceptual scheme is, then, in principle, unknowable.
Hence, reference remains indeterminate, as does translation. According to Quine,
it would be possible to generate any number of incompatible translation manuals,
each consistent with all observable speech dispositions, but senseless to ask which
is the right manual. So, what constitutes the correct translation is, according to
Quine, empirically undecidable.

The following claim of Quine's (1960) is particularly noteworthy. He suggests
that:

> To the same degree that the radical translation of sentences is under-determined by
> the totality of dispositions to verbal behavior, our own theories and beliefs in general
> are under-determined by the totality of possible sensory evidence time without end
> (p. 78).

This alludes to Quine's (1970) notorious underdetermination thesis. Given two
theories, the outcome of any possible observation will either confirm both theories

equally or disconfirm them both equally. The theories can be empirically equivalent and yet logically incompatible. Which (if either) theory is true is empirically undecidable, and a belief in the truth of either of them must reflect super-empirical values.

Availing himself of Quine's indeterminacy thesis, Gergen (1994c) claims:

> We find, then, no means of ostensively linking terms and precise characteristics of the world. Ostensive definition may work for many practical purposes, but scientific description cannot be grounded or made firm by stimulus meaning. For Quine, scientific theory is "notoriously underdetermined" by what is the case (p. 33).

This, Gergen supposes, is an argument for the contextual dependency of meaning. In conjunction with Wittgenstein's thesis, it demonstrates that language cannot provide context-free description (Gergen, 1986a; 1999).

As further "justification" for his position, Gergen (paradoxically) draws the readers' attention to ethno-methodological research in the social sciences. These studies reveal, for example, that given two different contexts, two different decisions about what constitutes a psychiatric problem will be made. This is taken to indicate that the meaning of the term "psychiatric" varies as a function of context (Gergen, 1986a, p. 140). Gergen implies that this research demonstrates Wittgenstein's and Quine's point—that descriptive terms are indexical; meaning is free to vary across diverse contexts of usage and, in this sense, is arbitrary.

1.7.4. MEANING HAS SOCIAL ORIGINS WITHIN SITUATIONS

The fourth component of Gergen's rationale for his account of meaning is that the conceptual basis for understanding the world is derived from social processes. Social processes involve human interchange concerning "...agreements or rules of interpretation shared within particular communities" (Misra, 1993, p. 407), and from these meanings are generated.

Here Gergen again relies on Wittgenstein's notion of meaning, and he has recently developed a micro-social aspect of this in which an utterance acquires meaning when another person responds to the utterance in some way; when they "...add some form of supplementary action" (Gergen, 1994a, p. 29). This, of course, is the focus of Shotter's research. Like Shotter, Gergen maintains that meaning is located in the relationship between two (or more) people, not within an individual mind, and not within an utterance.

This dialogical theme is also evident in Gergen's frequent recourse to Austin's (1955/1975) notion of performative utterances. That notion is appropriated to support Gergen's thesis that theoretical description is no more than an appearance, and that such "descriptions" instead "...constitute significant forms of social action" (Gergen, 1986a, p. 152).[26]

However, in his 1986 paper, Gergen's justification for the view that meaning has social origins draws also on themes in rationalist and idealist philosophy, themes which he believes have provided a "... threat to the incorrigibility of meaning" (Gergen, 1986a, p. 141). Gergen identifies these themes as:

1. the fusion of object and concept;
2. the determination of "observables" by the conceptual systems that we bring to bear on them;
3. the existence of a system of preconceptualisation;
4. the existence of historically contingent, culturally specific constructions of "emotions", "behaviours" and causal accounts of these phenomena, that all serve a particular social function and,
5. the social construction of scientific "facts" by researchers in an attempt to create order out of an apparent chaos.

Elaborating on these, Gergen begins with pre-twentieth century idealist philosophy. Idealism, he reminds us, argued that the mind is the active generator of a conceptual basis for understanding (what is normally called) "the external world". Idealist philosophers fused what the British empiricist philosophers had incorrectly (according to Gergen) considered to be two independent elements—object and subject.

This idealist fusion entails an "endogenic theory of knowledge" (Gergen, 1982, p. 175) in which mental processes are pre-eminent. Although Gergen continues to reject the endogenic tradition (e.g., 1995b, pp. 18–19; 2001c), it has, in his opinion, rightly informed twentieth century post-positivist philosophy of science. It has helped to rid us of distinctions such as "world" and "mind" or "subject" and "object" (e.g., 1991b, p. 103). The endogenic tradition lives on, he suggests, in the works of Kuhn (1970) and Hanson (1958), who both deny that we see situations as they are. Perception, they claim, is determined to a significant degree by the "paradigm" or "conceptual framework" which the observer brings to bear on the state of affairs to be observed. Also influenced by Kuhn's concept of a disciplinary matrix and by Foucault's reference to a discipline's "gaze", Shotter (1998b, p. 35) maintains that a particular way of "gazing" at a subject matter, the deployment of a particular set of disciplinary practices (as constituted by, for example, modern academic psychology) renders invisible to the discipline various features of the phenomenon of interest. Continuing Gergen's anti-empiricist theme, Shotter's (1997) belief is that "... expression organizes experience" (p. 14).

The implication that Gergen wishes to draw from these aforementioned rationalist and idealist themes and from Kuhn's and Hanson's philosophies of science, is that referred to in 1.6.1—that psychology's theories are not derived from observation. The meanings of terms in a theory are to be found in their relations to all the other terms of the theory, and these meanings "trickle down" to construct the world of "psychological fact". Psychological "descriptions" obtain their meaning from the theory or conceptual framework in which they are embedded and not from causal links between the psychologist (as observer) and psychological phenomena. This thesis is referred to as "semantic holism". It is said to entail the radical incommensurability of theories. The conceptual framework is seen as a semantically closed system and it is believed that, as a consequence of this, the terms of one theory cannot be translated into the expressions of another. Such incommensurability was a central feature of Kuhn's *The Structure of Scientific Revolutions*, although Kuhn later retracted his original formulation (e.g., 1979; 1993).

Gergen also believes that additional support for a non-referential theory of meaning can be found in the social phenomenology of Schutz, and Berger & Luckman, and in recent empirical research in social psychology and the sociology of knowledge. Importantly, for Gergen (1994c, p. 68), these post-positivist contributions place sufficient emphasis on the social to ensure that any system of preconceptualisation, any paradigm, or conceptual framework, need not have the mentalistic flavour which is found in pre-twentieth century idealist philosophy. A paradigm has its origins in the social rather than in the mental; in what is "out there", rather than what is "in here".

Summarising Gergen's rationale for the claim that meaning has social origins within situations: a system of preconceptualisation, arrived at through the internalisation of social processes and constrained by the community's social and historical location, is a semantically closed system. This system is employed in the construction of theoretical discourse, and determines the form and content of that discourse. The origin of the system is social. Therefore, the form and content of theoretical discourse is social. Importantly, the meanings of terms in a psychological theory are given solely by their relations in a socially constituted system (that is, by their internal relations), and these relations exhaust the terms' meanings. There is no external reference.

1.8. CONCLUSION

In sharp contrast to mainstream psychology, most social constructionists judge the categories of cognition, motivation, emotion, learning, social behaviour, etc. to be discursive, and discourse to be central to the constitution of social reality. All human activity is said to be socio-linguistically constituted. Some within social constructionism have extended these ideas to epistemology and semantics. It is thought that these topics must be re-conceptualized as human practices, not as normative theories.

The aim of this chapter has been to outline this extension. Social constructionism—the metatheory—maintains that, given the demise of positivist-empiricist philosophy of science and the advent of ideas from recent Continental and linguistic philosophy, the long-standing traditions and practices of academic and professional psychology must be radically changed. Though the views of Potter and his colleagues, Shotter and Gergen are sometimes disparate, they are united in the belief that much of psychology mistakenly assumes that (a) observation is the foundation for knowledge, (b) true theories mirror reality, and (c) cognition and other cognate categories are language-independent.

The arguments against mainstream psychology have been more thoroughly developed by Gergen than by Potter and Shotter. Gergen's challenge to the positivist-empiricist (alleged) pretension to invariance is embodied in thesis A, which is argued for in his rationale for his social constructionist conception of meaning. This rationale relies heavily on the (assumed) failure of correspondence theories to account for meaning and truth, hermeneutics, deconstructionism, Wittgenstein's identification of meaning with use, Quine's indeterminacy and underdetermination theses, and generally a non-realist philosophy of science. Specifically, Gergen relies on the assumptions that: (i) a notion of correspondence involving "mirroring" or "picturing" is necessary for external reference, and that this is the basis of positivist-empiricist metatheory; (ii) an interpreter always interprets from within a "horizon of understanding"; (iii) theoretical discourse is metaphorical and, therefore, indeterminate in meaning; (iv) meaning is contextually dependent, and (v) the origins of meaning are to be found in socially constituted systems of internal relations. In Gergen's judgement, if putative psychological phenomena do not contribute to the meanings of psychological theories and psychology's descriptions, and if those meanings are indeterminate because of their contextual dependency, then what we take to be knowledge of psychological phenomena is equally contextually dependent.

So, we arrive at social constructionism's central argument: "context" means the immediate milieu, interests, social and linguistic conventions, social processes, cultural traditions, and forms of life. These are not fixed, they can be changed, they vary, they are particular. Expression is given to them in language—in the discursive products (theories, descriptions, facts, bodies of knowledge) of the psychologists who, as social beings, either "carry" or interact with these factors. Consequently, these products are also not fixed; they can be changed; they vary. Witness Gergen's view that "...what we count as knowledge are temporary locations in dialogic space..." (1995b, p. 30). Not surprisingly, this has induced the charge of relativism from the critics of social constructionism. That charge is the subject of the following chapter.

NOTES

[1] Katzko (2002) distinguishes between first-order analyses of social constructionism (the phenomena of interest, or theories of those phenomena) and second-order qualities of constructionism *as a movement* (its motivational and affective features).

2 For other examples of social constructionists' inattention to the implications of their own claims, see Mackay (2003).

3 At times this thesis is taken further and reference is made to *physical* or *natural* reality being discursively constituted (e.g., Edwards, Ashmore, & Potter, 1995).

4 These shudder-quotes are mine. Potter believes that facts are constructed.

5 The difference between discourse and conversational analysts lies in the former's specific interest in how (psycho-)social phenomena emerge from inter-personal conversation, and their frequent use of interview material, newspaper reports, and parliamentary records, as opposed to modes of interaction which occur naturally (Potter, 1996a).

6 I take the term "states of affairs" to be synonymous with "situations", "occurrences", and "facts".

7 See, for example, Gergen (1985a, p. 266; 1987a, p. 2; 1987b, p. 2; 1987c, p. 115; 1989a, pp. 241–242; 1997, p. 724).

8 See, for example, Gergen (1985a, p. 266; 1987b, pp. 2–3; 1988a, p. 31; 1989b, p. 472; 1990a, p. 270; 1990b, pp. 212–213; 1994c, p. 31, p. 33; , 1995a, p. 77; 1995b, p. 26; 1997, p. 724).

9 See, for example, Gergen (1985c, pp. 256–257; 1985b, p. 117; 1986a, p. 141; 1987b, p. 5; 1988b, pp. 285–287; 1992b, p. 23; 1994c, p. 40; 1995c, p. 30; 1997, p. 725).

10 See, for example, Gergen (1985a, p. 266; 1987a, p. 2; 1987b, p. 2; 1987c, p. 115; 1989a, pp. 241–242; 1991a, p. 15; 1999, p. 93; 2001b, p. 806).

11 See, for example, Gergen (1985a; 1987b; 1987c; 1989a; 1994c; 1999; 2001c).

12 Although the doctrine of empiricism may take various forms, Potter's definition is not one of them. Generally, "empiricism" is the thesis that experience is the source of knowledge (Hamlyn, 1967).

13 I use the term "external" to denote that the relation of "referring to" is external to those items which stand in that relation. (The issue of external vs. internal relations is discussed in 5.6.2). When I use only the term "reference" or the adjective "referential", I am referring to "external reference" (the relation between words and the world), not to any notion of "internal reference", nor to reference of the word-word or anaphoric type.

14 In claiming that Gergen rejects *external* reference, I do not suggest that he denies extra-linguistic reality, nor that he rejects referentiality *in toto* (contra Gergen, 2001a, p. 420). Gergen takes reference to be *internal* to "forms of life" or "local communities", and something which enables a localised description if and only if the community has invested it with that function (1994c). I return to this in 3.2.

15 This is not a point endorsed, in practice, by Potter and Shotter. Their central concerns are explicitly ontological.

16 These components are by no means independent and, on occasion, overlap considerably. On other occasions they are inconsistent, and reflect Gergen's sometimes indiscriminate pulling together of disparate views.

17 Russell's (1918) development of Wittgenstein's thesis of logical atomism takes the constituents of facts to be logical atoms which are of two kinds: (i) particulars (e.g., "...little patches of colour or sounds, momentary things...") and (ii) predicates or relations (p. 497) or "...general facts, such as 'All men are mortal.'" (p. 502). One word (and no more) will correspond to a simple object or particular, and combinations of words will correspond to everything that is not simple (p. 520). However, as with all forms of atomism, logical atomism cannot be consistently maintained. The proposal that a term such as "white" is simple, and corresponds to a simple quality "whiteness", is compromised by Russell's attempts to describe, using propositions (such as "This is white", p. 521), what is, on his own account, non-propositional because of its particularity.

18 It is likely that Gergen has in mind here an infinite regress, one which is for ever incomplete and which, therefore, renders knowledge imperfect; describing the social conditions involved in explicating a correspondence theory would then require the social conditions involved in the "first describing" to be described, and so on, *ad infinitum*.

19 See, for example, Gergen (1986a; 1986c; 1987b; 1987c; 1989a; 1990c; 1992b; 1999; Misra, 1993).

[20] Such recourse is consistent with those who view the (alleged) indeterminacy of meaning as the very reason for the social or human sciences being a special epistemological case (see Ch. 4).

[21] Gergen's support has become guarded. He has argued that the conclusion of Habermas' position entails a solipsism which, despite Habermas' attempts, cannot be overcome (Gergen, 1994c, pp. 257–258).

[22] See also, Gergen (1986a; 1987b; 1990a; 1990c; 1992b).

[23] "Interpretation" and "meaning" are terms taken by Gergen (as by hermeneutists generally) to be interchangeable.

[24] See, for example, Gergen (1986a; 1987b; 1990a; 1990c; 1992a; 1992b; 1994c; 1995a; 1997), Gergen & Kaye (1992), Misra (1993).

[25] Henceforth, all references to *Philosophical Investigations* are to sections (e.g., §1). Further aspects of Wittgenstein's thesis are considered in Chapter 6.

[26] The use of Austin's theory is of considerable relevance to Gergen's defence against the charge of relativism. It is considered in Chapter 3.

CHAPTER 2

RELATIVISM AND SELF-REFUTATION

2.1. INTRODUCTION

The claim that social constructionism embodies the doctrine of relativism remains the primary objection to constructionist metatheory (e.g., Brewster Smith, 1994; Bunge, 1993; Burr, 1998; Cerullo, 1992; Chow, 1995; Cromby & Nightingale, 1999; Danziger, 1997; Foster, 1987; Greenwood, 1994; Halling & Lawrence, 1999; Harré & Krausz, 1996; Held, 1998; Liebrucks, 2001; Matthews, 1998; McMullen, 1996; Parker, 1999; Terwee, 1995). Relativism has been variously castigated as: a type of intellectual mischief which presents a special dilemma (Cerullo, 1992); paradoxical (Matthews, 1998); unintelligible (Greenwood, 1989); logically inconsistent (Foster, 1987); self-refuting (Harré, 1992; Kukla, 2000; Terwee, 1995), self-contradictory (Halling & Lawrence, 1999; Maze, 2001), incoherent (Harré, 1992), and philosophically anarchistic (Harré & Krausz, 1996).

Social constructionists, however, deny that their position embodies the kind of relativism which leads to self-refutation and the absurd outcome of "anything goes" (e.g., Edwards et al., 1995; Gergen, 1999; Shotter, 1997). There is, then, an intellectual standoff between the two parties. Is either side right? In this chapter, it is argued that a number of the charges of relativism and self-refutation involve the fallacy of *ignoratio elenchi*. Frequently the critics miss the point because they attribute to social constructionism concepts which constructionists believe should be abandoned. In order to develop this argument, the following discussion will focus on a number of different areas in turn. There is, firstly, a need to determine what the critics mean by their charge of relativism. Secondly, the doctrine of relativism itself requires clarification. This exercise reveals certain confusions in the philosophical literature, and also makes plain that relativism presupposes a number of realist concepts. The consequences of not properly understanding the doctrine and its presuppositions, and of not attending to what social constructionists actually say, are examined. In the final section of the chapter, these consequences are expanded in relation to the charge of self-refutation. Unlike some commentators, I treat the two charges, relativism and self-refutation separately. Not all kinds of relativism are self-refuting. Unfolding the doctrine of relativism in terms of its possible irrational implications is tendentious, hence the sequential manner in which I address these matters.

At times my argument may concede a little too much to social constructionism. It may also at times give the impression that I consider constructionist metatheory to be neither relativistic nor self-refuting. This is not the case. My belief is simply that if the critic does not wish to play into the hands of the social constructionist (and perhaps find his—the critic's—arguments being used as textual evidence to confirm constructionist claims about ideology, that logic is nothing more than a rhetorical device, and so on), then greater care needs to be taken in demonstrating the incoherence of constructionist metatheory. It is futile just to keep proclaiming how ridiculous that metatheory is. Gergen, Potter, Shotter and their cohorts are fully aware that some very unpalatable theories have turned out to be of great merit (if not true!). Paying close attention to what social constructionists actually say counters Gergen & Gergen's (2003) contention that "... many critics of constructionism have not bothered to explore the ideas before falling into an attack mode" (p. 228).

2.2. AN ANALYSIS OF THE CHARGE OF RELATIVISM

Most of the critics have directed the charge of relativism against Gergen's metatheory, and have linked that charge to the notion of truth. They say, for example, that Gergen's social constructionism "... rejects the distinction between truth and falsity" (Liebrucks, 2001, p. 364), that it "... ha[s] given up the quest for absolute truth,..." (Kukla, 1986, p. 480) and this inevitably means "... that psychological knowledge-claims are not true in an absolute sense" (Chow, 1995, p. 260). In Nettler's opinion (1986), "Without an empirical criterion of truth, the predicates employed by proponents of social constructionism are free of reference" (p. 480). Similarly, Cerullo (1992) maintains that "According to constructionist epistemology, the notion of a unitary, objectively-ascertainable truth about social life must yield to the notion that there is a variety of such truths..." (p. 559); that there are no objective, absolute truths about social phenomena.

Greenwood's (1991; 1994) position is similar. He identifies Gergen's metatheory as relativist because it proposes an *in principle* objection to the view that the truth or falsity of a theoretical claim can be determined or evaluated by observational evidence. That is, it denies the epistemic objectivity of psychology's theoretical descriptions (as set out in 1.6.1). Greenwood's (1991; 1994) criticism of social constructionism is also directed at its denial of the linguistic objectivity of psychology's theoretical descriptions. This, according to Greenwood, is to deny the possibility that a theoretical claim may be either true or false, depending on whether the state-of-affairs described actually occurs and has the properties and relations attributed to it (as set out in 1.6.2 and 1.6.3).

In a different vein, it is the social constructionist rejection of objective truth that Terwee (1995) finds acceptable. Terwee justifies his charge of relativism on the grounds that Gergen rejects the view that a theoretical statement can be true relative to context or language-game. That is, according to Terwee, Gergen is right to reject objective truth, but wrong to reject the possibility of a statement being true in the Wittgensteinian sense, that is, true relative to a particular "form of life". It is, then, Gergen's truth nihilism (1.6.2) which Terwee objects to.

In contrast, Harré & Krausz's (1996) charge of relativism does not make the concept of truth focal.[1] Neither does it endorse Terwee's position, despite the fact that both Terwee and Harré rely heavily on Wittgenstein's philosophy of language. In Harré & Krausz's view, Gergen's failure to take up certain non-local considerations, such as the universality of personal identity and extra-cultural discourse, and his denial of the linguistic objectivity of the latter, leaves his social constructionism floundering in "anarchistic anti-objectivism" (pp. 190–191).

A denial of linguistic objectivity is also at the heart of Brewster Smith's (1994) rationale for his charge of relativism. In his opinion, Gergen's account is relativist because it maintains that psychology's constructions, not being descriptions, are reducible to rhetoric and political ideology.

The critiques of Burr (1998) and Parker (1998) address social constructionism generally, but also target the relativism proclaimed by Potter and his colleagues in their "Death and Furniture" paper (Edwards et al., 1995). Burr's (1998) judgement of Potter's relativism is that he sees the world "... as textual and discursive" (p. 19). What is meant by this is unclear. But Burr shares Parker's concern for the practical and political implications of relativising truth: change cannot be argued for if a notion of absolute truth is abandoned; we attend only to difference between narratives, rather than to what we need to know about the world; we are required to abandon our judgements about whatever exists or occurs outside language; such relativism fails to recognise that adopting a "non-position" is to take a position; it involves perspectivism which precludes the most potent weapon the oppressed have—telling what actually happened—and it frequently retreats from its more radical claims (Parker, 1999).

In a still different vein, Mente (1995) regards the relativism embodied in Gergen's metatheory with approval. It is, he believes, pragmatic, therapeutic and intellectually productive because it entails "... a letting go of the idea that truth has an essence" (p. 391). Similarly, Foster (1987) is of the opinion that the relativist, in rejecting the possibility of determinate truth, stands for tolerance, holism, and anti-authoritarian liberalism.[2] Such judgements make the observation that "In the academic world relativism is everywhere abominated" (Barnes & Bloor, 1982, p. 21) appear quaint as the tolerance of relativism increases. This tolerance is evident amongst those who are, nevertheless, critical of social constructionism because of its abandonment of absolute truth. Parker (1999), for example, approves of relativism in psychology because it "... unravels the truth-claims and oppressive practices of the discipline ..." (p. 61). And Cromby & Nightingale (1999) maintain that "... the difficulty is not with relativism *per se* ... relativism is essential to critical thought and academic work" (p. 9), this despite their belief that relativism is the thesis that the "... external world is inaccessible to us in both principle and practice..." (p. 6).

There is, then, diversity and plain contradiction amongst commentators as to what is meant by relativism, why social constructionism is relativist and whether such relativism is abominable, tolerable, admirable or just plain necessary. In the majority of cases the relativism of social constructionism is linked to Gergen's rejection of an absolutist concept of truth. By contrast, some judge Gergen to be correct in rejecting this concept, but either incorrect in failing to appropriate a concept of relative truth, or incorrect in not recognising the universality of certain states of affairs. Finally, for a minority, the admitted relativism of social constructionism is not to be unequivocally condemned but must, indeed, be admired for a range of qualities presumed to be lacking in theories which are not relativist.

Not only is there diversity amongst the critics concerning the charge of relativism, there is also disagreement over whether relativism is *necessarily* linked to a rejection of an absolutist concept of truth. It is important then to postpone, temporarily, the debate between social constructionism and its critics in order to consider the nature of the relativist thesis.

In contemporary academic circles, considering the *nature* of anything is not fashionable. The idea that we can set out the features that something must have if it is to be distinguished from something else (that we can define a particular doctrine or thesis) is judged to be an "essentialist" exercise—a misguided attempt to expose the universal essence of an idea when, in fact, there is no such thing. Whilst I reject the thesis that things have essences, I do not believe that trying to define a term is a fruitless exercise. In Chapter 6, I will argue that despite Wittgenstein's apparent repudiation of definition, definition cannot be avoided and, in this chapter, I maintain that whilst the term "relativism" can refer to a variety of doctrines, all but one of these doctrines are trivial. No doubt my references to truth and my recourse to logic will also be regarded as unfashionable, but as Strawson (2000) recently observed, the 20th century was "... the silliest of the centuries, philosophically speaking" (p. 12).

2.3. RELATIVISM DEFINED

The Oxford English Dictionary (*OED*) defines relativism as:

The doctrine that knowledge is only of relations. Also a name given to theories or doctrines that truth, morality, etc., are relative to situations and are not absolute (p. 552).

A qualification of this definition is provided by Siegel (1992):

Epistemological relativism may be defined as the view that knowledge (and/or truth) is relative—to time, to place, to society, to culture, to historical epoch, to conceptual scheme or framework, or to personal training or conviction—so that what counts as knowledge depends upon the value of one or more of these variables (pp. 428–429).

The distinction between "knowledge" and "truth" is blurred in both definitions. The kinds of things which are true (or false) are declarative sentences or statements. They are the *means* by which a speaker (*S*) expresses or communicates knowledge or, at least, expresses or communicates what s/he takes to be the case. I take it that the connection between "knowledge" and "truth" is: that which is stated truly is knowledge. A further clarification: throughout this book, I'll assume that a "knowledge-claim" is an assertion and also something which is either true or false, and that a statement or knowledge-claim is true if and only if what is stated to be the case is indeed the case. This does not entail certainty (Hibberd, 2002).[3]

From these two definitions, it can be seen that the relativist thesis takes knowledge and truth to be relative to one or more of a number of parameters—scientific communities, time, place, society, and so on. "Epistemological relativism" means that we do not know anything absolutely; that claims of knowledge cannot, in principle, be true or false in themselves, where "in themselves" indicates that they are thus without requiring one or more relations to any other terms, such as their relation to a particular epoch or culture. The thesis is that we cannot arrive at un-relativised knowledge because our knowing is always related to other situations. Knowing is always subject to some kind of conditionality, and so knowledge is not absolute but relative. It is the claim of the relativist that to *really* assert a true statement, or to *really* know something, would require us not only to state the conditions of the statement but to state the conditions of those conditions and so on, in an infinite regress. Hence, it is impossible to know something absolutely, and impossible for there to be statements which are absolutely true.

I shall refer to relativism of this kind as "non-trivial relativism". It and *absolutism* are contrary theses. They are not in contradictory relation because, if either is false, the other *may* be true but could also be false. But both cannot be true, since each affirms something which the other denies. Here, the term "absolutism" is not to be associated with any notions of The Absolute, or with ultimate, immutable or final truths about an unchanging reality, or with "complete truth" in the sense of knowing all there is to know. It simply means that we can know a given situation without knowing the conditions or circumstances under which that situation occurred, that is, without knowing the other situations to which it is related. We can know, and can speak of, separate situations.

The *OED* definition of relativism illustrates that there is variety to the forms that relativism can take, and this is widely acknowledged in the literature. Not only might knowledge be relative, so might other things. There is nothing which restricts relativism to being a thesis about knowledge. Certain forms of relativism are *independent* of any relativism about knowledge. Linguistic conventions, for example, might be, and usually are, relative (sometimes to culture). Time and location are relative. Relativism about meanings is also of this kind because, as I have already intimated, knowledge without language is possible (although the converse does not hold).[4] There is nothing illogical about certain forms of relativism co-existing with statements which are true in a non-relative sense. I shall refer to these forms of relativism as "trivial".

A number of attempts to classify both the non-trivial and the trivial forms of relativism can be found in the philosophical literature (e.g., Edwards, 1990; Feyerabend, 1987; Harré & Krausz, 1996; Hollis & Lukes, 1982; Mandelbaum, 1982; Nola, 1988b; O'Grady, 2002; Sankey, 1994). These taxonomies have been constructed on the basis of *what is relativised* (e.g., knowledge), and not the parameters which something, such as knowledge, is *relative to* (e.g., scientific community, education, society, time, historical epoch, individual). There is substantial variation amongst these taxonomies, but typically the species of relativism proposed are about: (i) perceptions; (ii) concepts; (iii) meanings or, more broadly, language; (iv) truth; (v) rationality; (vi) knowledge; (vii) ontology; (viii) aesthetics, and (ix) morals.[5]

In some of these taxonomies, however, little or no effort is made to determine whether certain kinds of relativism are logically independent of others and, not unrelatedly, whether they are of a kind which can co-exist with absolutism (whether they are trivial or non-trivial). Hollis & Lukes' (1982) and Sankey's (1993) taxonomies exemplify such neglect. But investigating these issues turns out to be of value. Not only does it expose the difference between genuine, non-trivial relativism and a mere thesis about diversity, it also highlights the fact that a non-trivial relativism (that is, one in opposition to absolutism) presupposes certain realist assumptions. As I mentioned beforehand, the anti-realists may object that such an investigation is an essentialist exercise—an attempt to uncover the one and only meaning of the term. This, they might add, is as mistaken as asking the question 'What is therapy?' or Wittgenstein's, 'What is a game?' But I suggest that this investigation *does* uncover the defining characteristics of a non-trivial relativism. The question is: what characteristics are necessary and jointly sufficient for non-trivial relativism, so that the removal of any single characteristic will make that doctrine something quite different?

Firstly, non-trivial relativism must be distinguishable from the innocuous notion of diversity. What is meant here by diversity is that there exist different knowledge-claims about the same state of affairs, different criteria of justification, different methodologies or techniques, different schemes of classification, different states of affairs, etc.[6] Such diversity is, arguably, a function of one or more of the aforementioned parameters—time, place, group interests, ideology, culture, etc. Relativism, by contrast, is the thesis that any knowledge-claim or statement which is true in one scientific community, language or framework, epoch, etc., may be false in another. That is, relativism does not just involve the kind of diversity outlined above. It is more than the obviously true notion that an interpretation of a knowledge-claim is related to the conceptual or linguistic resources of the interpreter or perceiver, or the banal notion that one's view of a particular state of affairs may differ according to one's position in relation to that state of affairs. Clearly, a necessary condition for non-trivial relativism *is* a diversity of schemes of classification, a diversity of knowledge-claims about the same state of affairs, a diversity of criteria of justification, etc. But this is not sufficient, because, if such variations are related to society, culture, time, place, personal conviction, etc., then this (the antecedent) is a fact, an absolute and fully objective (social) fact. Diversity does not, then, entail the relativity of knowledge.

The difference between trivial and non-trivial relativism is that, for the latter, diversity must involve either *contrariety* or *contradiction*. One knowledge-claim or statement must be at least contrary to another, i.e., the truth of one entails the falsity of the other, although the falsity of one does not necessarily entail the truth of the other. This *is* a minimal condition; it is not essential that the two claims be contradictories although they may be. Two knowledge-claims are contradictories if they cannot both be true and cannot both be false, so that the falsity of one entails the truth of the other. *Either* contrariety *or* contradiction is a necessary condition for non-trivial relativism, a condition which I have elsewhere referred to as "disagreement" but now prefer to call "contrariety" (see Hibberd, 2001). Given this condition, there is the potential for the two claims to be inconsistent; to provide a scenario that is equivalent to the "both p and not-p" scenario that prevails when claims stand in a contradictory relation.

To explicate (perhaps belabour) this: imagine that, given four communities of psychologists, each, either explicitly or implicitly, takes just one of the claims below to be the case:
Community A takes it to be the case that:

All cases of primary process thinking involve condensation and displacement (p);[7]

Community B takes it to be the case that:

No cases of primary process thinking involve condensation and displacement (q);

Community C takes it to be the case that:

Some cases of primary process thinking involve condensation and displacement (r), and

Community D takes it to be the case that:

Some cases of primary process thinking do not involve condensation and displacement (s)

Claims p & q are contraries, and r & s are subcontraries, whilst p & s and q & r are contradictories. Claims p & q are contraries because they cannot both be true and might both be false, but if one were true, the falsity of the other would follow. Subcontraries, of course, do not involve contrariety.

Contrariety, as a necessary condition for relativism, might appear to be unnecessarily stringent. Yet, without it the "radical" relativist is not proposing a thesis which is truly in opposition to absolutism.[8] Anything less than either contrariety or contradiction fails to provide the true and not-true (false) scenario and, consequently, fails to provide the paradoxical quality that a non-trivial relativism demands.[9]

Expressed informally, the paradoxical quality of relativism is not simply that the doctrine is self-refuting (for this see 2.7), but that some thing can *be* (as asserted by one individual or group) whilst that same thing can *not be* (as asserted by another individual or group). For example, if "All cases of primary process thinking involve condensation and displacement" is true, then "No cases of primary process thinking involve condensation and displacement" is false, because p implies $-q$ and q implies $-p$. Therefore, if p is the case, by implication, $-p$ is not the case. Two knowledge-claims that are either independent of, or equivalent to, one another are not going to present this paradoxical quality.

Contrariety presupposes a commensurability between the two knowledge-claims. Yet the notion of commensurability is at odds with intuitions about relativism. However, if community A claims p and community B claims q, and a non-trivial relativism requires either q to imply $-p$, or p to imply $-q$ in order for either the p and $-p$ or the q and $-q$ case to arise, this presupposes adequate "translation" for the comparison of two knowledge-claims. Incommensurability would make such translation impossible and the nature of the relation between two knowledge-claims could not be determined. Genuine difference (or similarity) could not be perceived, the paradoxical quality would not be detected, and the challenge to absolutism would not be apparent.

Also presupposed by this condition is the proposition: "'Being' or 'not being' and 'occurring' or 'not occurring' exhaust the possibilities". There is no third possibility; a state of affairs must either obtain or not obtain and cannot do both, which is why $x.\sim x$ is not any state of affairs—it's a nonsense. This claim about how things are is necessary to the bivalent logical system which includes the laws of non-contradiction (nothing can be both x and not x) and excluded middle (anything must be either x or not x).

Neither the contrariety nor the contradiction of two knowledge-claims is sufficient for non-trivial relativism. Two or more psychological communities taking contrary knowledge-claims to be the case is (once again) a fact that does not challenge absolutism. *Taking something to be* the case does not entail that it *is* the case.

A further condition for non-trivial relativism must be an ontological component, in which the world *is*, in at least this one instance, as it *appears* to each community (or culture, individual perceiver, etc.). This is to say that what *is* the case is identifiable with what is *taken to be* the case. I shall refer to this as "subjectivism".[10]

This condition is also associated with Plato's interpretation of Protagoras' doctrine that man is the measure of all things. According to Plato, Protagoras claims that however things appear to someone, things are *for this person* just the way they appear, and if they appear different to someone else, then *for that person* they are truly different (Burnyeat, 1990). Such relativization means that there is no question of, for example, the food being either hot, or not hot, in itself. Consequently, there is no question of one consumer being right and another being wrong about the temperature of the food, because there is no independent fact of the matter concerning *the* temperature of the food. What is the case is taken to be coextensive with certainty. In Protagoras' doctrine, certainty is secured when reality simply consists of how things appear to the perceiver.

Subjectivism alone is not sufficient for non-trivial relativism. It does not entail contrariety, i.e., it does not preclude the possibility that knowledge-claims across communities or individuals may only ever be either independent or equivalent.

In summary, while there is a variety to the forms that the doctrine of relativism can take, not all forms are instances of non-trivial relativism which is truly in opposition with absolutism—one which precludes the possibility that a knowledge-claim may be true in an absolute sense. The requirements for non-trivial relativism are:

(1) that a knowledge-claim is taken to be the case by one community, and either its contrary or contradictory is taken to be the case by another community (*contrariety*), and

(2) that the knowledge-claim, as asserted by the first community, and either its contrary or contradictory, as asserted by the second community, are *both* the case in this actual world (*subjectivism*).

Together, these conditions capture the paradoxical quality of genuine relativism. Moreover, "anything goes" *is* a consequence of such relativism for the following reason: if something can both be and not be, then *every* other proposal is demonstrably true (Copi, 1954). This point of logic appears to have been long forgotten by contributors to the relativism-social constructionism debate. Of course, social constructionists judge it to be not a point of logic at all, but rather a reflection of my problematical engagement with essentialist and foundationalist discourses.[11]

I should also note that condition (1) entails diversity, therefore "diversity" is not needed as an extra condition. It must be reiterated that in identifying these conditions, non-trivial relativism (one truly in opposition to absolutism) presupposes: (i) commensurability between two knowledge-claims, and (ii) bivalent logic. It also takes for granted (iii) that the act of asserting a statement sincerely is the act of asserting it *as* true (of course, it may not *be* true), and (iv) the concept of external reference—the act of asserting something truly, means that the statement or knowledge-claim (the assertion) refers to that something. We use words in an attempt to say something about aspects of the world, and when we do assert what is the case, we propose truly. In short, a non-trivial relativism cannot be articulated without presupposing a number of concepts and assumptions which constitute a realist philosophical system.[12]

From this I conclude that the "relativism versus realism" debate, despite its prominence in the philosophy-psychology literature, is not worthy of serious intellectual consideration. First, genuine relativism leads to the absurd consequence that "anything goes", a consequence which is rejected by realists and anti-realists alike. Second, the diversity which characterises non-trivial relativism is perfectly consistent with the realist view that differences in claims of knowledge, methods, techniques, criteria of justification, etc. are causally related to differences between cultures, epochs, ideologies, etc. Third, genuine relativism presupposes a number of realist concepts.

2.4. EPISTEMOLOGICAL RELATIVISM

With this in mind, certain beliefs about relativism can now be addressed. Although social constructionism's critics (with two exceptions) do not clearly state the particular kind of relativism which they suppose the metatheory to embody, the substance of their criticisms usually reveals the form intended.[13] The majority charge social constructionism with relativism because of its rejection of an absolute conception of truth (2.2). Following Siegel's (1992) definition then, social constructionism is supposed to embody epistemological relativism (*ER*).

Now, given the minimum requirements for non-trivial relativism, the critics' charge does not have the force they intend. In 2.4.1, it will be argued that the only type of relativism which can be properly attributed to constructionist metatheory is a trivial form of *ER*, which is little more than a thesis about diversity. To imply, as the critics do, that social constructionism's *ER* is non-trivial is, at this stage of the argument, to presume a number of theses which social constructionism explicitly rejects, namely those realist assumptions identified towards the end of the previous section.[14] The qualifier "at this stage of the argument" is made because the present concern is with the charge of *ER*, and not with the constructionist's defence against that charge.

In many definitions of *ER*, two distinct theses are involved. Specifically, there is a tendency in the philosophical literature not only to conflate "truth" with "knowledge", but also to conflate "knowledge" with terms such as "justification" or "warranted assertibility". These conflations appear in the Siegel definition. Having stated that *ER* is that knowledge (and/or truth) is relative, Siegel goes on to say that "what counts as knowledge" is relative. However, "what counts as knowledge" could mean "what knowledge is" or it could mean "what is considered to be knowledge", and the latter is not (of course) necessarily knowledge. There is an obvious and crucial difference between what is the case and what is taken to be the case, and the ambiguous phrase "what counts as knowledge" does not discriminate between these two states of affairs.

In Siegel's (1987) more technical definition of *ER*, this ambiguity becomes a clear conflation. *ER* is now defined as:

> For any knowledge-claim p, p can be evaluated (assessed, established, etc.) only according to (with reference to) one or another set of background principles and standards of evaluation $s_1, \ldots, s_n$; and, given a different set (or sets) of background principles and standards $s'_1, \ldots, s'_n$, there is no neutral (that is, neutral with respect to the two or more alternative sets of principles and standards) way of choosing between the two (or more) alternative sets in evaluating p with respect to truth or rational justification. p's truth and rational justifiability are relative to the standards used in evaluating p (p. 6).

Here *ER* is seemingly a thesis about the absence of any context-free way of evaluating a knowledge-claim p. It is not, in contrast to Siegel's other definition, about the relativity of the truth of p, at least, not until the very last sentence of Siegel's definition, where the issue of rational justifiability is conjoined with the issue of truth. Something which is *not* truth, rational justification, is run together with truth.

The same kind of failure to distinguish between an issue concerning justification and an issue about truth is exemplified by Putnam (1981) in his claim that:

> ... if statements of the form 'x is true (justified) relative to person P' are themselves true or false absolutely, then there is, after all, an absolute notion of truth (or of justification) (p. 121).

Similarly, Meiland & Krausz (1982) speak of cognitive relativism as meaning not only that "... a statement is true only relative to a particular conceptual scheme" (p. 8), but also that "... evaluation is relative to a set of abstract principles or concepts" (p. 8). Potter & Edwards (1999) identify epistemological relativism as "... what counts as knowledge in different social and cultural settings ..." (p. 450).

McLennan (2001) refers to non-trivial relativism as the thesis that "... the *meaning* and *validity* of claims are ... culturally or perspectivally relative" (p. 87). In each case, an issue about truth or knowledge is conflated with, or disguised by, something else. In these examples, the process of evaluation, meaning, and what counts as knowledge are confused with knowledge and truth.

The most common conflation is that of justification and truth but, to repeat, truth is *not* the same as justification or evaluation. "Justification" is relational. If a theoretical statement is to be justified, then it is to be justified *with respect to* some criterion or criteria. Nothing is justified *simpliciter* (Kirkham, 1992). The criterion might be truth, but it may also be logically distinct from truth, such as, for example, simplicity, explanatory power, predictive power, usefulness, or coherence with other statements. It is perfectly possible for false knowledge-claims to have explanatory power.[15] In addition, if a conjunction of knowledge-claims, such as $p.r$ is true, it follows that p is true, but if $p.r$ has explanatory power, it does not follow that p has explanatory power (Kirkham, 1992). Truth and explanatory power have different characteristics, and the same applies to the other criteria of justification. Psychologists' rationale for employing certain criteria of justification may be the belief that such criteria are positively correlated with truth, but such a belief has no logical force.

In some accounts of *ER*, then, two distinct theses are confused:

ER_1: Knowledge-claims are justified relative to community, epoch, education, a particular evidential system, etc.

ER_2: Knowledge and/or truth is relative to community, epoch, education, a particular evidential system, etc.

Having pointed out the logical independence of ER_2 (truth) from ER_1 (justification) it can now be argued that relativism about justification (ER_1) is trivial (it presents no challenge to absolutism), for the same reason that justified belief is not knowledge.

2.4.1. EPISTEMOLOGICAL RELATIVISM₁

The relativity of criteria which justify the inclusion of knowledge-claims in a theory presents no challenge to absolutism, and social constructionism's proposed criteria for psychology's theoretical statements, "positions held", "narratives", and "stories" exemplify this. It was noted in 1.6.1 that the social constructionist asserts that observation is not a criterion in the evaluation of statements; that the "worth" of a psychological theory, position or story cannot be assessed by employing the criterion of correspondence with empirical fact. Alternative criteria have been proposed by constructionists at various times: conceptual clarity and coherence (Gergen, 1991a); the ability of the theory to provide the "culture" with a "system of intelligibility" (e.g., Gergen, 1985a); the ability of the theory to add conceptual diversity given the theories already in existence (Misra, 1993); the "generativity" of the theory (e.g., Gergen, 1994c); whether the position held permits better ethical reasons (for acting in a particular way) than others (Shotter, 1997); whether its "verbal resources" are instructive (Shotter, 1993a), and whether the story "works" (Potter, 1996b). Constructionists would not claim that these criteria are fixed, absolute yardsticks, immune to change. Nor would they claim that they are to be construed independently of context or modes of social life (e.g., see Misra, 1993, pp. 403–404).

Contrary to the belief of some, the adoption of such criteria in order to justify its theories, positions, narratives, and what not, does not entail the "anything goes" outcome of non-trivial relativism. One psychological theory or position held might be better than another if, for example, it contributed more to the symbolic resources of the culture. It would be better at achieving this particular goal. If, as some constructionists believe, theoretical statements are to be justified relative to this particular criterion, this does not involve any unrelativised (absolute) epistemological notion, so there is no immediate contradiction on their part. The fact that the relativist about knowledge cannot assert that this is the case without contradiction is of no relevance. Here we are not concerned with the relativity of knowledge. We're concerned with the relativity of criteria used to justify the inclusion of knowledge-claims in a theory or "narrative". The question of whether a defence of ER_1 involves the unrelativised notions of truth and falsity will be addressed shortly. Even if it does, this is not an objection to ER_1; ER_1 is not self-contradictory.

To summarise the argument so far: although constructionism maintains that the significance of a psychological theory or position cannot be assessed by employing the criterion of correspondence with fact, this does not entail that knowledge-claims are contrary or contradictory (condition 1). Nor does it entail that psychological phenomena are as they appear to each community of psychologists (condition 2). ER_1 is a feature of social constructionist metatheory, but it is a trivial form of relativism involving only a thesis about the diversity of criteria of justification. This is a form of relativism which can co-exist perfectly well with absolutism.

2.4.2. EPISTEMOLOGICAL RELATIVISM₂

As has been noted, the majority of social constructionism's critics believe the metatheory to embody relativism about knowledge and/or truth (ER_2), because of its rejection of an absolutist notion of truth. There is no doubt that many of these critics take this form of relativism to be non-trivial. To reiterate: ER_2 is the thesis that knowledge and/or truth is relative to community, epoch, education, particular evidential system, etc. If it is of the non-trivial kind, the same statement or knowledge-claim must *be* both true and not-true (false); the conditions of contrariety and subjectivism must both obtain (2.3).

Social constructionism is an easy target for the charge of ER_2 given its rejection of correspondence theories of truth (1.6.2). But some of the critics making this charge assume that in abandoning such theories, the metatheory must be relativistic about truth (2.2). That is, social constructionism must take truth to be relative to community, epoch, etc. Recall Cerullo's (1992) comment that "According to constructionist epistemology, the notion of a unitary, objectively-ascertainable truth about social life must yield to the notion that there is a variety of such truths..." (p. 559).

This assumption may miss the point. Social constructionists are adamant that their position does *not* entail the "anything goes" outcome of genuine relativism described in 2.3. Presumably, then, they do not subscribe to the notion that both p and $-p$ can be the case. This would be consistent with Gergen's truth nihilism. His metatheory does *not* allow the truth of both p and $-p$; for him *neither* is true; there *is* *no truth* (1.6.2). Although Gergen, on one occasion, suggests mere indifference to any psychological research which is intended to discover truth—"[t]ruth value is of peripheral importance" (1986b, p. 482), on another occasion he mentions a notion of conventional truth (1988a, p. 37), and has recently spoken of "local truths" (Gergen, 2001a, p. 422)—these allusions appear to understate his position. The post-modern desire to reject truth *in toto* is evident in his metatheory. He does not usually vacillate between outright rejection of the whole notion of truth, and a mere relativisation of it. Nor should a reader of Gergen interpret him as merely doubting the truth of psychology's knowledge-claims, in order to imply their falsehood. He is unequivocal: "We are not dealing here with doubts regarding claims about the truth of human character, but with the full-scale abandonment of the concept of objective truth" (1991b, p. 82); "... constructionism offers no alternative truth criteria" (1985a, p. 272); "... concepts of truth and objectivity may largely be viewed as rhetorical devices" (1989b, p. 473), and, "'Truth' as a criterion is simply rendered irrelevant to the acceptance or rejection of constructionist propositions" (1999, p. 228). In Gergen's (1992b) opinion, "One may never exit the language (the system of signifiers) to give a true and accurate portrayal of what is the case" (p. 22). Shotter's position is similar in not allowing the truth of both p and $-p$. The truth of a knowledge-claim is replaced with the criterion of its "making sense" relative to "... a shared form of life, a tradition, or disciplinary matrix; ... all claims to knowledge are grounded in such traditions or matrices, and in nothing else!" (1997, p. 22).

Gergen's recent statements about "truth within traditions" and "local truths" can perhaps be reconciled with the truth nihilism of social constructionism in the following manner. First, take two communities of psychologists with seemingly conflicting views. There may be no *genuine* dispute between them because their views involve reference to diverse contextual parameters in ways which render them incommensurable. The "local truths" are simply affirmations of community preferences based on this "internal" reference. That is, commensurability between two knowledge-claims (a feature identified in 2.3 as presupposed in the articulation of genuine relativism) does not obtain. Second, Gergen (2001a), Potter (1996b) and Shotter (1998) have each endorsed Austin's (1955/1975) concept of performative utterances, and Gergen in particular uses this concept in an attempt to rebut charges of relativism and self-refutation (e.g., 1994c). This will be the subject of the following chapter but, in short, Gergen takes knowledge-claims to be performative utterances. Psychology's discourse may *appear* to be assertoric but it is really not—when uttering what *appears* to be an assertion about some purportedly psycho-social situation, the psychologist is performing an activity, rather like the activity of warning someone about something. Such utterances are neither true nor false. That is, the making of ontological claims is denied. Yet the making of such claims was presupposed in 2.3 as a feature of *genuine* relativism and, along with the notion of incommensurability, it may explain why constructionists contest the charge that their brand of relativism is of the genuine kind, and why they deny the entailment of "anything goes". The critics have not attended to what constructionists actually say.

Now, given the constructionist desire to reject truth, let's remove truth from ER_2. The result is that "what is known" is not "what is true". Knowledge is deflated to "belief" or to "what the community takes to be the case"; belief, knowledge-claims or the affirmations of community preferences become a sufficient condition for knowledge. This is the social constructionists' position. Recall Gergen's claim that knowledge is stored on computer disks and found in journals and textbooks (1.6.2). All that is needed for knowledge are knowledge-*claims* or affirmations, albeit affirmations for which there may be "good reasons", and once again we are left with a trivial form of ER, one that amounts to nothing more than a thesis about diversity.[16]

The critics' charge of ER_2, then, misses its target. To charge social constructionism with the view that truth is relative to community does not deliver the "knock-out blow" which one might expect. The charge involves the fallacy *ignoratio elenchi* because it attributes to constructionist metatheory something which it denies. That metatheory rejects truth *in toto*, and truth nihilism does not licence ER_2. This same fallacy is repeated with the concepts of bivalence and external reference, concepts which were, in 2.3, found to be unavoidable in setting out non-trivial relativism. Gergen's rejection of external reference needs no rehearsal (1.7.1) and his dismissal of bivalence (1994c, p. 297, n. 18) rests upon a rejection of foundationalism which will be examined in 5.6.4. It may well be, of course, that in his rejection of truth, external reference and a bivalent logical system, Gergen is mistaken, but the charge of ER_2 against the metatheory is not the appropriate ammunition with which to destroy that target. Indeed, it plays into constructionists' hands. It confirms for them Gergen's pronouncement that the "mainstream" do not, for ideological reasons, ". . . honor the issues at stake" (Misra, 1993, p. 408).

2.5. ONTOLOGICAL RELATIVISM

Although social constructionists have not *directly* addressed the charge of ER_2, Gergen states clearly that social constructionism is not ontologically relativist (1994c, p. 76).[17] Ontological relativism (*OR*) is the thesis that the way the world *is* is relative—relative to theories, conceptual frameworks, linguistic communities, cultures, historical epochs, individual perceivers, etc. (Nola, 1988a; Sankey, 1993). It entails that the composition of the world *is* different *just because* different perceivers *see* things differently or *just because* language users from different communities use non-translatable vocabularies or languages which are syntactically different.

In dismissing ontological relativism as a feature of constructionist metatheory, Gergen does not state clearly what he takes that thesis to be. For instance, he jocularly characterises his critics as asking (rhetorical) questions, such as:

> "Do you mean to say that if you placed a lighted match into a container of gasoline, the result is undecidable?" ... "Do you mean to say, there is no world out there; we are just making it up?" (Gergen, 1994c, p. 72).

The (imaginary) objections here seem to be that the social constructionist is ontologically relativist because she or he is saying of things or events which we know to exist or occur that they do *not* exist or occur, or that what exists is indeterminate. Confusedly, then, Gergen associates *OR* with, on the one hand, an indeterminacy thesis and, on the other hand, idealism.

Gergen's interpretation of *OR* ignores the fact that the thesis involves conceptual or linguistic frameworks which are said to "do the relativising" or to cause the relativisation of what exists. It is understandable that constructionism's critics might read the metatheory as proposing just this—that psycho-social phenomena (and other matters) are relative to conventions of discourse, theoretical frameworks, "intelligibility nuclei", etc.—given the kinds of claims made by constructionists to elucidate proposition A3 (1.6.3). Claims such as "... the concepts of understanding essentially establish the ontological foundations ... [for] without a concept of "command" or "obedience," [for example] such "events" simply do not exist" (Gergen, 1986a, pp. 146–147), or that "... the 'world as it is' is effectively the world as we unwittingly construe it to be ..." (Gergen, 1988b, p. 287) invite the view that constructionist metatheory takes what exists to be relative to epistemic or linguistic parameters.

This view can, however, be countered on the following grounds. *OR* is implied in ER_2, and so the charge of *OR* against social constructionism is equivalent to claiming that social constructionism takes *truth* to be relative to linguistic community or to some other parameter. That charge, again, attributes to the metatheory something which it denies. If both p and $-p$ are true, the composition of the world *must* be different for community A compared with community B; what is meant by *p* being true is that the state of affairs expressed in *p* obtains, and what is meant by -*p* being true is that the state of affairs expressed in -*p* obtains. Given this entailment, the fallacy of *ignoratio elenchi* committed by constructionism's critics again comes into play. Gergen does not accept that social constructionism makes ontological claims, such as *p*, that refer to states of affairs. Any charge of *OR* presupposes the received view of assertion and external reference (2.3), but these Gergen denies. Recall his claim that scientific language bears "... no determinate relationship to events external to language itself..." (Gergen, 1994c, p. 31). Hence his (inconsistent) use of inverted commas around terms which imply the existence of psychological phenomena, such as "obedience", "envy", "anger", "depression", etc. Gergen wishes to indicate that the normally implied existence is not intended. Further support for this interpretation can be found in the passage containing his "Whatever is, simply is" statement (1.6.3). Here, Gergen (1994c) maintains that:

> Constructionism makes no denial concerning explosions, poverty, death, or "the world out there" more generally. Neither does it make any affirmation. As I have noted, constructionism is ontologically mute. Whatever is, simply is. There is no foundational description to be made about an "out there" as opposed to an "in here," about experience or material. Once we attempt to articulate "what there is," however, we enter the world of discourse (p. 72).

It is evident from this passage that Gergen takes the constituents of reality to be *beyond description*, save for his vacuous non-assertion that "Whatever is, simply is". (If Gergen were to be truly "ontologically mute", he wouldn't be saying anything about what is, not even that it "simply is"). Although expressed less than clearly, this is the essence of Gergen's (1994c) rejection of the charge of *OR*. The critic, he believes, misunderstands the constructionist project. It is concerned with the world of discourse, not with ontology. *If* social constructionism makes no ontological claims, it is not possible for it to embody *OR*.

Again, it may be the case that in his judgement that social constructionism makes no ontological claims and in his rejection of external reference Gergen is mistaken, but the charge of *OR* has, nevertheless, missed its target.

2.6. CONCEPTUAL RELATIVISM

Conceptual relativism (*CR*) is the only cognitive form of relativism which Gergen (1994c) accepts as embedded in most social constructionist accounts, including his own. This, though, is gratuitous. There is an obvious inconsistency in his acceptance of the descriptive claim that *CR* characterises social constructionism whilst rejecting the thesis of external reference, the received view of assertion, a bivalent logic, and so on (see also Hibberd, 2002, p. 689). But, setting this aside, Gergen's pronouncements about *CR* reveal that he, quite correctly, takes it to be a thesis about diversity. This runs contrary to the tendency, in certain taxonomies of relativism, to conjoin conceptual relativism with a thesis either about ontology or about truth (e.g., Hollis & Lukes, 1982; Sankey, 1993).

Conceptual relativism is about conceptual schemes, frameworks or categories of classification. It is alleged to exist when the same phenomena are classified in different ways by different linguistic communities, societies, people, etc. Experience is said to underdetermine what is reasonably believed about the world; conceptual frameworks are not given directly by experience (Hollis & Lukes, 1982). This is consistent with the view that epistemic judgements are in some sense *bound* by conceptual schemes or frameworks which determine what is perceived and consequently restrain or delimit the possible range of claims which a community is able to regard as true or justified. There is a metaphorical boundary within which a community is cognitively trapped. They cannot get outside it in order to assess their own framework or to assess another framework (cf. Popper, 1976).

There are many examples in the literature of various communities classifying, for example, "snow" or "colour" in different ways, and these serve to fuel the claim that *all* concepts are relative to context. Although Hollis & Lukes (1982) caution that such examples only support the claim that *some* concepts are relative to context, they do little to clarify the crucial distinction between a diversity of conceptual schemes and a non-trivial form of relativism. This becomes apparent when, in their discussion of conceptual relativism, they consider the possibility that each scheme *organises* reality. This raises the possibility that p in framework (or community) A may be the case while $-p$ in framework (or community) B may also be the case, and so confuses a thesis about concepts or schemes of classification with an ontological thesis. A relativism about concepts which is *not* conflated with ontological and semantic issues does not imply any consonance between what exists or occurs and the categories or schemes of classification. Also, it *is* possible to show that one conceptual scheme is better than another (contra Sankey, 1993). If not confused with certain other forms of relativism, conceptual relativism is no more than conceptual diversity, and conceptual diversity is not at all sufficient for a non-trivial form of relativism.

Gergen recognises this. He takes conceptual relativism to involve nothing more than: (i) variation in understanding—variation in the ways in which our views are constructed, and (ii) the implausibility of foundationalism—which he takes to involve a reliance on perceived certainties, such as objective truth (e.g., Gergen, 1994c, p. 78), i.e., he takes conceptual relativism to involve issues neither of truth nor of ontology. It is simply a recognition of the multiple ways in which the occurrences in the world are thought about.

With one exception, Gergen's critics, with their emphasis largely on truth, do not identify the relativism of Gergen's metatheory as *conceptual* relativism. The exception is Harré & Krausz (1996). If the term "concepts" is taken to be conceptually cognate with the term "discourse" (and both Gergen and Harré take the term in this way), then the nub of Harré & Krausz's (1996) charge is that Gergen assumes *all* concepts to be relative to context. In their opinion, Gergen fails to discriminate between "inter-cultural domains of discourse" and "extra-cultural discourse", the latter requiring that *some* concepts ("personhood", for example) are not relative to context so that linguistic objectivity obtains. The absence of this distinction, Harré & Krausz believe, results in the "family resemblance fallacy", a target of Wittgenstein's (1953/1967) *Philosophical Investigations*. This fallacy consists in the assumption that there is some essence common to domains of discourse (Harré & Krausz, 1996, pp. 191–192, 196–199). It appears that Harré & Krausz judge that Gergen, in taking the absence of linguistic objectivity to be common across both "extra-cultural discourse where theories confront... an intransigent material world" and "inter-cultural domains of discourse" (Harré & Krausz, 1996, p. 192), commits the family resemblance fallacy.

Whilst Harré & Krausz's observation that Gergen's metatheory is anti-objectivist is correct, it is not correct for the reasons they give. Their judgement not only rests on Wittgenstein's indefinite notion of "family resemblance" (6.5.2), it ignores what Gergen says. Gergen would not accept the distinctions invoked by Harré & Krausz between "domains of discourse" (he would not accept that concepts such as truth and external reference apply to one domain of discourse and not to another). Nor would he accept the ontological thesis which underlies one side of a dualism invoked by Harré—that between the flux of human affairs and the invariance of a material world of types. Gergen's rejection of these notions is illustrated in his critique of the exogenic view of knowledge and its "dualist" foundations and, although Gergen's critique is problematic, it has been a constant feature of his metatheory (e.g., Gergen, 1982; 1994c; 1995b). Harré's apparent disregard of the incoherence of dualism (see 5.6.3) does not explain why he (Harré) rests his argument on the very premises which Gergen rejects instead of exposing the flaws in Gergen's critique of the exogenic tradition, or presenting an argument for the coherence of his own "types of discourse" thesis.

The charge of conceptual relativism can be unfolded differently from that chosen by Harré & Krausz (1996). Social constructionism maintains that meaning is context-dependent; words acquire their meaning through the socio-linguistic conventions appropriated in particular contexts; expressing or communicating anything involves these conventions, and these conventions vary across different communities of psychologists. Let's call this "semantic relativism". From this it can be surmised that the constructionist's position is that the "truths" conveyed are radically dependent upon the local conventions in which the communities' knowledge-claims are set. They are not assertions, in the traditional sense of "assertion", nor are they truths in any objectivist or realist sense of the term "true", and this is why all talk of truth must be dropped. The critic has misunderstood constructionist writings. They are not attempts to "tell the truth" and, according to Gergen & Gergen (2003):

> This misunderstanding is crucial, as *most* constructionists write with the full under-standing that they too are constructing realities and moralities . . . their comments are only entries into what they see as vital conversations. They do not function as fixed truths, but as invitations to new and ever-evolving dialogues and practices (p. 228).

I have argued elsewhere that this "semantic relativism" conflates the distinction between the act of proposing and what is proposed in that act (Hibberd, 2002). To repeat that argument: social constructionism is right to make clear that the use of language is conventional, and that such conventionality is context-dependent. Socio-linguistic conventions *do*, of course, determine what someone describing something says but, given what is said, whether what is proposed is proposed truly depends on whether the world *is* as described, not on the conventions we employ to do the describing.[18] For example, when Gergen and I agree that social constructionism has been influenced (in part) by various ideas in continental epistemology, what we agree on is a certain state of affairs. If we were to discuss this matter further, we would discuss *the issue itself*, not the forms of words, not the conventions, but the situation proposed. We cannot say, as Gergen might wish, that the proposal is "true under that particular set of socio-linguistic conventions" because whilst the *proposing* involves various agreed-upon socio-linguistic conventions, *what is proposed* does not, and it is for the latter that truth is claimed.

However, the idea that we speakers do stand in direct relations to states of affairs, unencumbered by language, is the antithesis of social constructionist metatheory. I return to this in later chapters.

2.7. SELF-REFUTATION

2.7.1. THE CLASSICAL REFUTATION OF RELATIVISM

It has been argued that the charge of ER_2 and the charge of OR against social constructionist metatheory involve the fallacy of *ignoratio elenchi*, and that the kinds of relativism which *do* apply (ER_1 and CR) fail to satisfy the conditions necessary for being in opposition to absolutism. The criticism that social constructionism is relativistic, then, does not have the force which most critics suppose.

The next step in the critics' argument is the observation that relativism is self-refuting. This step has a considerable ancestry. In section 171ab of Plato's *Theaetetus* (Burnyeat, 1990), Socrates, in his defence of Protagoras' "Man is the Measure", drops the qualifiers such as "true for you" and "true for them", and Protagoras is made to speak of truth and falsity in absolute terms. Since then, the objections to relativism have invariably utilised an absolutist conception of truth which is grounded in the bivalent logical system (e.g., Davidson, 1984; Gross & Levitt, 1996; Husserl, 1900/1970; Kirk, 1999; Newton-Smith, 1982; O'Grady, 2002; Passmore, 1970; Siegel, 1987).

The standard attempt to refute relativism takes the following form: In making this claim (that knowledge and/or truth is relative), you are asserting that relativism is true (absolutely). But according to your thesis the truth of relativism is relative to a particular point of view. So, you are saying that relativism is (absolutely) true yet, in doing so, you're disregarding the essence of your assertion which denies the possibility of *any* assertion being absolutely true. Thus your claim contradicts itself. This implies that it is logically impossible for relativism to be the case. Therefore, it's obviously empirically impossible too.

To the absolutist this refutation is conclusive. If social constructionism embodies the doctrine of relativism, then some of its claims must be false, not simply as a matter of empirical fact, but as a matter of logical necessity. This argument may be identified as "transcendental" because it establishes that certain concepts (here, an absolute notion of truth) are necessary for a particular act (here, the act of assertion) (Grayling, 1992). The transcendental argument can be summarised thus:

A: The relativist asserts, "Knowledge (or truth) is relative to conceptual scheme, epoch, culture, etc."
B: So, the relativist asserts that relativism is true.
C: So, the assertion of relativism involves the absoluteness of truth.
D: So, relativism is self-referentially incoherent.

It might be said that to ignore the transcendental argument above is to commit "cognitive suicide".[19] As was noted in 2.3, a doctrine which embodies a contradiction entails, via that contradiction, anything at all.[20]

The castigation of relativism by constructionism's critics (2.2) stems from their acceptance of the transcendental argument. However, when employed against the metatheory, that argument also misses the mark; the constructionists' nihilism about truth is again ignored. They would not take relativism to be true (in any sense). Nor, as has been noted, do they take any of their theoretical claims (or narratives) to be true (in any sense). It follows that premise B attributes to them what they deny. The transcendental argument depends on notions which they believe should be abandoned.

On a different tack, relativism may be judged by the absolutist to be self-refuting, not (only) because of issues about truth, but for reasons to do with the nature of assertion. The transcendental argument rests on the assumption that a commitment to (absolute) truth is embodied in the act of assertion; that to assert something, anything, is to assert it to be true, i.e., *assert* and *assert to be true* are equivalent.

But this too is denied by social constructionism. Gergen's attempt to replace the received view of assertion with an account derived from Austin's (1955/1975) theory of performative utterances was noted in 2.4.2. and will be examined in the next chapter. For the moment, it is sufficient to reiterate Gergen's view that all utterances operate as performatives; that is, when a proposition is uttered an act is performed, an act such as inviting, predicting, ordering or warning. The proposition operates, then, as an "action in the world", and as an action, it has significant social consequences.[21] The proposition does not, however, refer. Although it appears to describe events in the world, it does not in fact describe anything. In sum, the transcendental argument assumes a particular view of assertion which Gergen believes should be rejected.

A somewhat different objection to the standard refutation of relativism has been raised by Edwards et al. (1995) in their "Death and Furniture" paper. Their objection was alluded to in 1.3 but here it requires attention. According to Edwards et al. (1995):

> When relativists talk about the social construction of reality, truth, cognition, . . . and so on, their realist opponents sooner or later start hitting the furniture, invoking the Holocaust, talking about rocks, guns, killings, human misery, tables and chairs. The force of these objections is to introduce a bottom line, a bedrock of reality that places limits on what may be treated as epistemologically constructed or deconstructible. There are two related kinds of moves: Furniture (tables, rocks, stones, etc.—the reality that *cannot* be denied) and Death (misery, genocide, poverty, power—the reality that *should not* be denied) (p. 26).

But this, they argue, presents a dilemma for the realist. Hitting furniture is a semiotically mediated (and, therefore, meaningful) action, as is pointing, demonstrating and describing:

> The very act of producing a non-represented, unconstructed external world is inevitably representational, threatening, as soon as it is produced, to turn around upon and counter the very position it is meant to demonstrate. Furniture 'arguments' perform categorization and relevance via semiosis (p. 27).

Using language to state the realist position is said to undercut or challenge that position; the realist cannot move beyond these acts of representation.

It has been noted by O'Neill (1995) that Edwards et al. refuse to take seriously the fact that some sentences are genuine assertions; that some sentences propose something about the world. Herein lies a commonality with Gergen's metatheory and with Shotter's (2002) dialogical, rhetorical-responsive account of language. The received view of assertion is spurned. Priority is given to the *act* or *practice* of assertion, to the *processes* of representation, and to our supposed entrapment in the particularities of these processes. The fact that in the act of assertion, something is asserted to be the case is (they say) of no consequence.

Social constructionists, then, are unmoved by attempts to employ the transcendental argument against the metatheory. They will have no truck with the notions of truth and assertion presupposed by that argument. But that is not the end of the story.

2.7.2. MACKIE'S ANALYSIS OF SELF-REFUTATION

There are several types of self-refutation, a fact which has received scant attention in the literature, and a consequence of this oversight is manifest in the comments of constructionism's critics.[22] Their comments concerning self-refutation, incoherence, etc., suggest the recognition of only one kind of self-refutation, that is, *absolute* self-refutation or the notion *necessarily* self-refuting.

Mackie's (1964/1985) *Self-refutation—A Formal Analysis* shows that there are at least three types of self-refutation: (i) pragmatic; (ii) operational, and (iii) absolute, and two types of absolute self-refutation, truth-entailing and not truth-entailing. A proposition is absolutely self-refuting only when its form guarantees its falsehood, e.g., "It can be proved that nothing can be proved", or "It is true that nothing is true" or "There are no truths", or "It is not the case that something is possible".[23] In these examples, the standard form of contradiction, p and $-p$, is contained within the proposition, in that, for the proposition to be true, it would have to be false (i.e., not true).

The cases of operational or pragmatic self-refutation are different. The latter involves a contradiction between the way something is presented and what is being presented; e.g., if *I write* that I am not writing, what I write is false. But there are obviously other ways of presenting the proposition "I am not writing" (singing it, for example) which avoid contradiction. Operational self-refutation involves the same kind of contradiction (between the way something is presented and what is being presented) but, in contrast to pragmatic self-refutation, there is no non-contradictory way in which the proposition can be presented. There is, for example, no way to coherently present the proposition "I know nothing". I implicitly commit myself to the claim that I know that I know nothing, and consequently to a denial of what I originally asserted. So, "I know nothing" cannot be coherently asserted, but it may be true. Someone else may be able to say truthfully about me, "She knows nothing". Similarly, "No sentences are intelligible" is at most operationally self-refuting. It cannot be absolutely self-refuting, because whether there are intelligible sentences is a contingent matter (Mackie, 1964/1985).

2.7.3. ASCRIBING SELF-REFUTATION TO SOCIAL CONSTRUCTIONISM

Following Mackie's analysis, a different form of self-refutation can be ascribed to social constructionism. The consequence of this ascription is that Gergen's non-referential account of language is not *necessarily* false.

Gergen's position is encapsulated by the claim that "Propositions do not describe or refer to states of affairs". This claim has the same status as Mackie's "No sentences are intelligible". It is not self-contradictory because its falsity is a contingent matter, not something *guaranteed* by its meaning. But it *is* a claim which cannot be coherently asserted. If propositions do not describe or refer to states of affairs, this proposition does not describe or refer to anything and, so, no theory about *how things are* is asserted. If true, it cannot be put into words.

It is, of course, logically possible that the claim "Propositions do not describe or refer to states of affairs" is not an utterance Gergen would employ in order to state how things are; that he does not want to draw attention to a supposed state of affairs, viz. that propositions do not describe or refer to anything. Gergen could simply be uttering or writing a string of words which (he thinks) do not refer. For example, in saying that propositions do not describe, he may simply be using words to impact on us in some way. This is consistent with Gergen's rejection of truth and the received view of assertion. If so, his position is not self-refuting in any of Mackie's four senses because Gergen has not stated *anything*. In so far as this is the case, we may ignore him.

However, if we assume that Gergen is not negating the possibility of discourse (where how things are thought to be can be put forward, and then denied or accepted), then the charge of operational self-refutation stands. Gergen is attending to some supposed state of affairs—that "Propositions do not describe or refer to states of affairs". But this can be put forward only by using a proposition which draws attention to (refers to) a supposed state of affairs.

So, if Mackie's analysis is right, the claim "Propositions do not describe or refer to states of affairs" cannot be coherently asserted but it may be true. There is a form of self-refutation midway between pragmatic and either kind of absolute self-refutation. The critics may have taken social constructionist metatheory to be *necessarily* false, when in fact it yields something less than absolute self-refutation. It follows that the logical impossibility of Gergen's account has not been established, and that a proposition contrary to Gergen's claim is not a necessary truth.

2.8. CONCLUSION

Although most of the critics of social constructionism are unclear and inconsistent in what they say about relativism and how it is embodied in constructionist metatheory, there is some consensus that the metatheory is relativistic because of its rejection of an absolutist concept of truth.

Analysis of the doctrine of relativism reveals that the only non-trivial form of relativism (one that is truly in opposition to absolutism) is a relativism about truth or knowledge (where knowledge is, at the very least, true belief). This form of relativism involves *contrariety* (either contrariety or contradiction between two or more knowledge-claims) and *subjectivism* (the ontological thesis that the world is as it appears to be). In addition, this form of relativism cannot be described without presupposing: commensurability; a bivalent logical system; that to assert sincerely is to assert as true, and external reference. These (realist) assumptions are unavoidable.

From this analysis of relativism, it is evident that whilst constructionist metatheory does embody a type of epistemological relativism and conceptual relativism, these are trivial; they do not meet the conditions necessary and jointly sufficient for a relativism which challenges absolutism. Importantly, the constructionist's rejection of an absolute concept of truth extends to a nihilism about truth, and to a quite different account of the nature of assertion. In many cases, the critics' charge of relativism and self-refutation against the metatheory is *ignoratio elenchi*; it assumes the legitimacy of concepts which constructionists explicitly reject. Still, no matter how much conceptual ground is conceded to Gergen, his metatheory is self-refuting, it is *operationally*, not *absolutely*, self-refuting. This means that even though Gergen cannot succeed in providing an account of language as non-referential, it does not follow that language is referential. In the next chapter, I consider Gergen's non-referential account of language.

NOTES

[1] This is, no doubt, due to the following: (i) Harré & Krausz's (1996) belief that propositions have no realist truth-conditions; (ii) their (inconsistent) view that truth "...seems hard to come by ..." (p. 69) and is "...unachievable ..." (p. 71), and (iii) their conflation of truth with certainty (e.g., p. 110). The fact that something can be the case without our knowing it is disregarded by Harré (Hibberd, 1995).

[2] As in Harré's case, Terwee's and Foster's rejection of objective truth is a consequence of their conflation of truth with certainty. Terwee maintains that "'True' means a proposition can be proven to be correct in a certain context ..." (personal communication). Foster (1987) characterises relativism as involving the claim that "...we can never know with certainty ..." whether a theory is true or false (p. 94).

[3] I realise that, for some, these are controversial matters. They will be discussed in later chapters.

[4] In contrast to social constructionism, I take it that a necessary condition for language as a social phenomenon is agreement between individuals that certain noises (or other items) be used to refer to certain sorts of situations. This presupposes cognition, in that the individuals know one another as perceiving creatures. Harré & Krausz's (1996, p. 109) judgement that epistemological relativism is a consequence of semantic and ontological relativism incorrectly presumes the opposite—that knowledge is not possible without language. In Chapter 7, it is shown that this false presumption is a residue of logical positivist philosophy.

[5] Non-cognitive forms of relativism, such as aesthetic or moral relativism, are not of concern in this book (although social constructionism has been judged to be morally relativistic).

[6] The recognition of diversity is, of course, important to both realists and social constructionists. However, such is the constructionists' misunderstanding of realist philosophy, they see diversity

as crucial in their opposition to the supposed "universalizing discourse" of realism (e.g., Morss, 2000).

[7] A point of clarification: the quantifiers are not restricted to the communities making the assertions; they are intended to range over the entire world.

[8] While the significance of the issue of "opposition" to relativism is not ignored by Harré & Krausz (1996, p. 209ff), firstly, they provide definitions of "opposition" that, in the absence of any detailed explication, must be either judged as so weak as to render the term meaningless or judged as presupposing the strong definition of "opposition" that they want to avoid. Secondly, they fail to reflect on the significance of the fact that (as they readily acknowledge) bivalence is unavoidably drawn on in describing these oppositions. They do recognise, however, that if their list of oppositions were granted, the forms of relativism allowed would be of the kind that do not seriously challenge absolutism.

[9] The fact that contrariety can provide this paradoxical quality is not made clear in even the more thorough analyses of relativism (cf. Edwards, 1990).

[10] The term "subjectivism" has various meanings; in one place or another it is given individualistic, theological, aesthetic and ethical connotations. Here I am merely saying how I shall use the term in this book.

[11] See Hibberd (2002) for my argument that logical principles are not merely socio-linguistic conventions. I also address this in Chapter 5.

[12] In Chapter 5, I argue that the anti-realist response to this observation—that it simply reveals the verbal conventions which have been appropriated by self-identified realist philosophers—is unsatisfactory to say the least.

[13] The exceptions of which I am aware are Greenwood (1992a), where reference is made to Gergen's support of epistemological relativism, and Nightingale & Cromby's (1999) identification of the *Death and Furniture* paper as a form of "epistemic relativism" (p. 208).

[14] With regard to commensurability, it is more accurate to say that, through his support of post-positivist philosophy of science, Gergen appears to reject this concept (e.g., Gergen, 1994c, p. 43).

[15] That is, if you do not take "explanation" to be a "success-word" (see Stove, 1998).

[16] This is the type of *ER* that Harré & Krausz (1996) settle for as a result of "... dropping the strong demand for truth" (p. 71).

[17] I do not consider the "Death and Furniture" paper (Edwards et al., 1995) to have addressed ER_2.

[18] Maze (2001) makes the same point when he says "The objective question of truth or falsity does not fade away just because we recognize the role of social factors in producing conviction" (p. 401).

[19] The term "cognitive suicide" is from Baker (1987, p. 148). She uses it to refer to any attempt to deny a common-sense conception of the mental.

[20] Unless, of course, a non-bivalent logic obtains.

[21] "Proposition" is the term used by Gergen when discussing scientific description as performative (e.g., 1994c, p. 84).

[22] Although Smith (1997) utilises the Frankfurt School's work on performative contradiction.

[23] In Mackie's analysis, these last two propositions are of the "not truth-entailing" kind. They refute themselves without proposition-forming operators (such as "It can be proved that" or "It is true that") which are truth-entailing.

CHAPTER 3

NON-FACTUALISM

3.1. INTRODUCTION

The case has been made that social constructionism's denunciation of external reference and of the usual view of assertion means that the charges of ER_2 and absolute self-refutation miss their target. Although this aspect of Gergen's metatheory involves *operational* self-refutation, its truth is a contingent matter.

It was noted in the previous chapters that Gergen (2001a), Potter (1996b) and Shotter (1998) have each endorsed Austin's (1955/1975) concept of performative utterances. Gergen in particular uses this concept to provide an alternative to a descriptive or referential account of language, thereby attempting to rebut charges of relativism and self-refutation (e.g., 1994c). He also relies on Wittgenstein's philosophy of language, but it is Gergen's use of Austin's concept of performative utterances which is the primary consideration in the present chapter. It is a concept crucial to Gergen's defence of his metatheory.

In evaluating this concept there is, firstly, a need to make explicit a thesis which, on pain of inconsistency (given his rejection of external reference and the received view of assertion), Gergen should exclude. Also, some philosophical "scene-setting" is necessary. Gergen's account must be understood in terms of the philosophical thesis of *non-factualism*. Austin's theoretical formulations were a development of this thesis, and the progression of Austin's considerations must be traced in some detail in order to understand Gergen's reliance on Austin's theory.

The findings of this chapter are consistent with those of Greenwood (1994), but my approach is different from his in that I make use of material which *Gergen believes* demonstrates his non-referential view of language, in order to show that it does no such thing.

55

3.2. RE-STATING GERGEN'S POSITION

In the reconstruction of Gergen's metatheory (1.5), his primary thesis (A) was identified as:

A. Reality cannot be represented by language. There is no fixed relation between words and the world.

This thesis was said to receive its expression through Gergen's propagation of propositions A1, A2 and A3 (1.6). Proposition A2 in particular—*psychology's theories do not depict, map, mirror, contain, convey, picture, reflect, store or represent reality in any direct or decontextualised manner*—is associated with Gergen's rejection of meaning as involving external reference and a correspondence theory of truth (1.6.2; 1.7.1). I noted in 1.6.2 that although A2 leaves open the possibility that conventional designations can genuinely refer, Gergen rules this out. In his view, there is no connection or link between words and extra-linguistic referents.

Gergen (2001a) has recently objected to his critics' claim that he denies reference. There are, he claims, many places where he has written about referentiality, and he refers the reader to a section of his book *Realities and Relationships*. There, he says, he provides an account of the "... production of empirical truth within communities, and the way in which words can be said to furnish pictures of an independent reality" (2001a, p. 421).

This seems odd. He usually gives the impression that truth must be rejected *in toto* ("... constructionism offers no alternative [to realist] truth criteria" [Gergen, 1985a, p. 272]), thereby precluding any kind of relativist criterion of truth. It also seems odd because of his view that words or sentences cannot picture or mirror objects or phenomena (1.6.2). But if we set these apparent contradictions aside, Gergen's point is that "... description can function *as* picture or mirror, but only within a local game or procedure in which we invest it with this function" (1994c, p. 86).

This point cannot, however, be uncoupled from his many other claims about science *only* being grounded in communities of interlocutors (1.5), or with his view that "... scientific descriptions and explanations of the world are not demanded by the nature of the world itself" (Gergen, 2001b, p. 810). Gergen rejects the concept of "external" reference because he believes that there is a word-world disjunction. He severs the link between words and extra-linguistic referents not only because he thinks it involves the problematical notions of correspondence and essentialism (1.7.1), but because he, along with post-modernists generally, mistakenly believe that what is meant by "external" reference is reference to "ultimate" or "transcendent" reality, and that this requires a speaker or community of language-users to be *non*situated—to have a "God's eye view" of the world. His response is (as noted in Ch. 1) to endorse a notion of *internal* reference, and this he justifies through the selective appropriation of Austin's theory of performative utterances. Before turning to Austin's theory and the intellectual context in which it must be placed, I want to make three points.

First, a notion of *internal* reference cannot be consistently maintained. If reference were internal, it would also be internal to the "discursive paradigm" or "system of intelligibility" in which Gergen is located. In principle, then, he could not speak about other traditions and events external to them. These distinctions could not be made because it would not be possible for him to "referentially" break out of his own paradigm. In practice, of course, Gergen *does* speak about (or refer to) things and processes which are *not* constitutive of the "paradigm" in which he resides.

Second, I suggested above that one reason for the post-modernists' malaise about reference is that they emphasise the language-user as situated or located and, therefore, affected by context. Yet, prominent accounts of external reference typically say little or nothing about the speaker-context, and they sometimes give the false impression that referring is nothing more than a two-term relation between words and things (e.g., Williamson, 1996). Social constructionists, post-modernists, etc. object to this because it ignores the language-user and, in particular, it ignores the language-user as located in a social milieu. But they also rule out an account of external reference which articulates, at the very least, a three-term relation. That is, they rule out the notion that reference of this kind involves language, the situation referred to, and a language-user (the individual or community for whom certain sentences refer to certain situations), where each of these three terms exists independently and each is independently characterisable.[1] This thesis does not involve the notion of statements or propositions as things which, despite their peculiar ontological status, are somehow representative of facts. But it does involve the notion that truths and falsehoods are stated or conveyed by means of words (more precisely, by certain arrangements of words), and that these words are themselves independently characterisable in terms of their physical properties and their location (or occurrence) in space and time. I have offered an in principle reason for rejecting the notion of "internal reference". But when, in this chapter, we consider Gergen's actual justification for this notion (via his use of Austin), we should keep in mind that Gergen is not entitled to "smuggle in" either a two-term or a three-term notion of external reference. He must exclude the possibility that some truths and falsehoods are stated or conveyed by means of words, because that would allow language the kind of referential function he wishes to reject.

Third, it is worth recalling that, in Gergen's opinion, the rejection of a referential function of language is particularly characteristic of post-modernist thought. To repeat the excerpt in 1.6.2, Gergen (1988b) claims that:

> ... as post-modernist thought has made increasingly clear ... , the metaphor of theory as a "map" or "picture" of reality is deeply problematic (p. 286).

This claim is misleading. Certainly a non-referential treatment of discourse is a feature of post-modern inquiry (e.g., Barthes, 1975, p. 33, p. 56). However, the same view can be found much earlier, for example, in Otto F. Gruppe's early 19th century German analytical philosophy of language (see Cloeren, 1975, p. 523). It is present in Nietzsche's (1971) doubts as to whether language can adequately express reality and whether designations and things can ever "coincide". It is also, as we will see shortly, detectable in mid-20th century Anglo-American analytical philosophy. Rejection of extra-linguistic reference is a position peculiar neither to current intellectual trends nor to Continental epistemology. Gergen's claim may be due to his inattention to the history of philosophy, and the intellectual damage which results from such inattention will become increasingly evident as this book progresses. The philosophical tradition which Gergen ignores here is that of non-factualism. In the following section, Gergen's rejection of external reference is expressed in terms common to this area of philosophy.

3.3. NON-FACTUALISM DEFINED

Non-factualism is logically dependent on the concept of factualism. Non-factualism is the thesis that there are certain utterances which have the same grammatical form as statements, but their linguistic function is quite different (Price, 1988). That function is non-referential.

An example of non-factualism is the emotive theory of ethics. An utterance such as "X is good" has the same grammatical form as "X is delusional", but the former, in contrast to the latter, should not be interpreted as descriptive, as fact-stating, as capable of being either true or false. Rather, the sentence should (according to the emotive theory) be understood either as an expression of emotions, attitudes, etc., in the speaker, or as an utterance used to evoke emotions, attitudes, etc., in the listener (Stevenson, 1937/1952).

Other topics which have been given a non-factualist treatment in branches of philosophy are: probability statements; formulae in calculi; definitions; aesthetic claims, and Lockean secondary qualities. Gergen's position is that discourse quite generally, and psychology's statements in particular, must be treated in the same way. Post-modernism has, in this respect, followed some of its intellectual forebears. In generalising the thesis of non-factualism to *all* discourse, it has extended a philosophical tradition.

3.3.1. THE FREGEAN APPROACH TO ASSERTORIC AND NON-ASSERTORIC DISCOURSE

A distinction must be drawn between the thesis of non-factualism and the Fregean theory of fact-stating language. Let us assume that "mood" is a property of certain speech acts, a property which is usually characterised in terms of "force", not in terms of "content". Assertoric discourse is said to be in the indicative mood, and non-assertoric discourse (for example, imperatives, optatives, interrogatives) in one or other of the non-indicative moods.

Frege believed that the truth-value of an indicative sentence was given by its "extension". He allowed non-indicative sentences sense, but he denied that they expressed thoughts or were truth-bearers (Frege, 1919/1967, p. 21). So, for most Fregeans, the indicative mood marks the difference between assertoric and non-assertoric discourse. The Fregean does not, then, deny the distinction between assertoric discourse and discourse of other kinds, but simply wishes to construe the limits of assertoric discourse as widely as possible (Price, 1988). The reason for this is that, in the Fregean theory of meaning, meaning and truth-conditions are inextricable. There is, therefore, some difficulty for those with Fregean sympathies in incorporating non-indicative sentences into a general theory of meaning. In summary, the Fregean position is that only indicatives are assertions and all indicatives are assertions. That is, assertions and indicatives are coextensive.

3.3.2. THE NON-FACTUALIST APPROACH TO ASSERTORIC AND NON-ASSERTORIC DISCOURSE

The non-factualist agrees with the Fregean that not all discourse is assertoric, but wishes to construe the limits of assertoric discourse more narrowly than the Fregean (Price, 1988). The non-factualist claim is that the primary use of language is not that of assertion (as exemplified in the case of emotive theories of ethics).

According to the non-factualist, within the indicative mood there is a taxonomy of non-assertoric speech acts. Fact-stating is restricted to a sub-set of indicatives. That is to say, all assertions are indicatives, but not all indicatives are assertions; some indicatives are assertions and some are not. The non-factualist claims that fact-stating is less extensive than the Fregean would wish (given the latter's commitment to truth-conditional semantics).

3.3.3. GERGEN'S UNIVERSAL GENERALISATION

Gergen's rejection of external reference and of the received view of assertion can now be phrased in terms common to the philosophy of language and linguistic analysis: discourse in the indicative mood (this includes psychology's statements) appears to be assertoric, but is always, in fact, non-assertoric. No indicatives are assertions. Gergen has changed the quantifier *not all* in the non-factualist thesis (not all indicatives are assertions) to *none* (none of them is an assertion); there is no fact-stating. It is this universal generalisation which prompts Brewster Smith's, Greenwood's and Harré's objection that Gergen denies linguistic objectivity (2.2), and Harré & Krausz's charge of "family resemblance fallacy" (2.6).

3.4. AUSTIN'S CONSTATIVE-PERFORMATIVE DISTINCTION

Non-factualism received attention from Austin in his William James lectures, delivered at Harvard in 1955. Initially motivated by the observation that it cannot be said of certain sentences in the indicative mood that they are either true or false, Austin (1955/1975) begins the lectures by employing a *provisional* distinction between constative and performative utterances.[2] Constatives, Austin says, are sentences used in making statements (pp. 1–3). "Sentences" form a class of "utterances" and to make a constative utterance is to make a statement (p. 6, n. 2). Constative utterances, such as "That ship is named the Queen Elizabeth", describe or report or "constate" some state of affairs, or state some alleged fact, and must do this either truly or falsely.

In contrast to constative utterances, some performative utterances have the grammatical appearance of statements (they are in the indicative mood), but are neither true nor false, neither are they nonsense. A performative can as it were masquerade as a statement of fact, as being descriptive or constative, when in fact it is an activity of another sort; it *does* something rather than *says* something (pp. 4–6).

According to Austin, an example of a performative utterance is: "I name this ship the Queen Elizabeth"—as uttered when smashing the bottle against the stem (p. 5). Here, the speaker is not describing herself as naming the ship. She *is naming* the ship. To utter, "I name this ship . . ." is to name the ship; she *is performing the act.*

At this point, then, Austin thinks that the constative-performative distinction is grounded on the fact that neither truth nor falsity is predicated of performative utterances such as that above (p. 6). Performative utterances, Austin suggests, are either "happy" or "unhappy", but are not and cannot be true or false (p. 14ff). A performative is "unhappy" if the utterer is, for example, not entitled to name ships, or if the formula is uttered incorrectly, thereby rendering the act of naming the ship unaccomplished. In these instances the act "misfires". It is also "unhappy" when the act is achieved, but the utterer, in so doing, is insincere. To say "I promise . . ." when you have no intention of keeping the promise is, according to Austin, an example of an act that is "hollow" rather than one that completely "misfires" (p. 16). To say "I promise" when your act is insincere or "hollow" is not, according to Austin, to speak a false utterance. Such an utterance can only be false if the speaker is *describing* herself as making a promise but, Austin maintains, she is *not* doing this.

Austin is, however, unable to classify some utterances either as constative or as performative. For example, he maintains that neither "true" nor "false" can be appropriately predicated of sentences like "The present King of France is bald" or "The United Kingdom is triangular". Consider also the utterance "There is a bull in the field". This, he says, may or may not be a warning, for the speaker may simply be describing some scenery (p. 33). So, in order to prevent performatives from being identified as constatives, Austin invokes the *explicit performative* speech device.

3.4.1. THE EXPLICIT PERFORMATIVE FORMULA

The explicit performative formula is central to Austin's theory. An explicit performative sentence is an utterance containing a verb in the first person singular present indicative active, preceding a performative. The verb is the name of the kind of act the speaker would (ordinarily) be performing in uttering that sentence. An example of this is, "I warn you that there is a bull in the field". Austin claims that:

> ... any utterance which is in fact a performative should be reducible, or expandable, or analysable into a form, or reproducible in a form, with a verb in the first person singular present indicative active (grammatical) ... Thus: "Out" is equivalent to "I declare, pronounce, give, or call you out" ... "Guilty" is equivalent to "I find, pronounce, deem you to be guilty." ... Unless the performative utterance is reduced to such an explicit form, it will regularly be possible to take it in a non-performative way ... (pp. 61–62).

It is important to consider Austin's clarification that, although an explicit performative sentence has the appearance of being "constative", in uttering an explicit performative the utterer is *not asserting* that he is performing an act of the sort named by the explicit performative verb; instead in uttering the explicit performative sentence he *is performing* an act of the sort named by the explicit performative verb. It is the job of the explicit performative formula to *make explicit* (which is not the same as stating or describing) the action which is performed by the utterance (pp. 60–61). "I predict that ... " is not a case of me reporting my own speech in the first person singular present indicative active, but an instance of me making explicit what action is being performed (that of predicting) by my utterance.

However, Austin again finds reason to be dissatisfied with this distinction between primary (or implicit) and explicit performatives. There remain anomalous utterances. For example, "I state that ... " meets the grammatical criterion for an explicit performative but the utterance is, at the same time, the making of a statement and is either true or false (p. 91).

The consequence of this, and other anomalies, is a shift in Austin's theory. The explicit performative formula is relinquished as a grammatical *criterion* for distinguishing between constatives and performatives, although explicit performative utterances continue to feature prominently in his account.

3.4.2. A THEORY OF SPEECH ACTS

By lecture VII, Austin had judged it necessary "... to make a fresh start on the problem" (p. 91). Perhaps *all* utterances can be categorised according to the kind of act they perform? In lecture VIII, Austin introduced the thesis that there are three types of act standardly performed when one says anything: the locutionary, the illocutionary, and the perlocutionary.

A locutionary act is an act of "saying something" (p. 94). A sentence is used to convey a meaning, meaning being made up of "sense" and "reference" (p. 93). For example, when I tell you "The School of Psychology is undergoing an external review", I perform a locutionary act:

> ... which is roughly equivalent to uttering a certain sentence with a certain sense and reference, which again is roughly equivalent to "meaning" in the traditional sense (p. 109).

However, in performing a locutionary act, I also and *eo ipso* perform an illocutionary act (p. 98).

An illocutionary act is an act performed in saying something. A sentence is used with a certain "force", such as informing, ordering, warning, etc. (p. 99). For example, in performing the locutionary act of saying "The School is undergoing an external review", I may perform the illocutionary act of warning. Additionally, to perform a locutionary act, and therefore to perform an illocutionary act, may also be to perform a perlocutionary act (p. 101).

A perlocutionary act occurs when in performing the illocutionary act of warning you that the school is undergoing an external review, the speaker, either intentionally (p. 101) or unintentionally (p. 106), "... produce[s] certain consequential effects upon the feelings, thoughts, or actions of the audience, or of the speaker, or of other persons" (p. 101). For example, I might succeed in performing the perlocutionary act of getting you to consider submitting a proposal to the review board.

In proposing this later theory, Austin wishes to reject the idea of the purity of performatives. He wishes to abandon the either/or dichotomy of performative and constative utterances (p. 150). The distinction, he claims, involves an artificial abstraction. Every genuine speech-act is now admitted to have features of both kinds (p. 147). There is, Austin maintains, "... no necessary conflict between (a) our issuing the utterance being the doing of something, (b) our utterance being true or false" (p. 135). Austin's point is that whilst stating is performing an (illocutionary) act, and the notion of a "statement" an abstraction, the question still arises: was what I stated true or false? (pp. 139–140).

Despite this shift from mutually exclusive *classes* or *types* of utterances to *aspects* of utterances, Austin at times writes as though the former view has been retained. For example, in retaining the notion of an *explicit* performative utterance, he maintains that the relationship between performative utterances and illocutionary acts is such that "... when we have an explicit performative we also have an illocutionary act ... " (p. 132). But what he now means by the phrase "performative utterances" is those *aspects* of particular speech-acts:

> With the performative utterance, we attend as much as possible to the illocutionary force of the utterance, and abstract from the dimension of correspondence with facts (p. 146).

Similarly, the constative utterance is judged to be an abstraction from the illocutionary aspects of the speech act, where we concentrate on the locutionary force of the utterance (pp. 145–146). The doctrine of the performative-constative distinction should, in Austin's opinion, be regarded as a special case of the doctrine of locutionary and illocutionary speech acts in just this sense (p. 148).[3] This, then, is the extent of Austin's non-factualism.

3.5. GERGEN'S ALTERNATIVE TO EXTERNAL REFERENCE AND TO THE RECEIVED VIEW OF ASSERTION

3.5.1. THE APPROPRIATION OF AUSTIN'S THEORY

We may now observe how Gergen brings Austin's account to bear on the status of metatheoretical and psychological claims. First, it is worth noting that in his appropriation of Austin, Gergen cannot allow, as Austin finally did, that many speech acts have both a performative and constative aspect. Gergen cannot allow a performative utterance (or one which has an illocutionary force) a *dual* role, in which, in uttering the performative, something is said that is either true or false. No matter how Gergen might interpret Austin, and no matter which of Austin's theories is utilised (performative-constative or speech act), a performative utterance (either primary or explicit) cannot be constative, nor can it have a constative aspect. Nor can Gergen allow a performative to *cause* a constative to be uttered. To do so would require a recognition of the constative, i.e., referential, function of language—the thesis Gergen denies. These constraints are being belaboured because if Gergen doesn't do this, he will have provided no reason at all for believing that the notion of external reference and the received view of assertion are fundamentally mistaken.

Gergen's appropriation of Austin's work occurs from 1985 onwards (e.g., 1985b; 1987a; 1989a; 1989c; 1994c; 1999; 2001a). As an extreme non-factualist, Gergen (1989a) construes language in general, and psychological statements in particular, in the following manner:

> ... words about mental states operate as Austinian performatives ... They are not reflections on some other world; their significance is achieved in their very doing. In daily life, then, statements about mental conditions operate more like smiles and embraces than mirrors or maps (p. 257).

The passage above clearly indicates that Gergen takes "statements about mental conditions" to be purely performative utterances.

We are familiar with Gergen's claim that psychology's theories function as vehicles which "enable" psychologists to co-ordinate their activities with one another and that it is these activities which enable words to "take on their meaning" (1994c, p. 49, pp. 87–88).[4] Psychological claims, as "actions in the world", are (Gergen says) the *acts* of psychologists, and, through this human co-ordination of action, psychology involves the *making of meaning* (1997, p. 726). This is important because it parallels the logical positivist notion that philosophy is not concerned with the pursuit of truth, that philosophy cannot in principle consist of systems of true propositions because philosophy is an activity. It is, says Schlick (1931/1979), "... *the activity of finding meaning*" (p. 220). But let's return to Gergen's use of Austin's theory. It can be unfolded in the following manner: if psychological statements are performative utterances, then the speakers (psychologists) are performing acts, namely "describing", "predicting", "explaining", "warning", "recommending", etc. Psychological statements do not describe, predict, and so on.[5] They are not constative.

Gergen is aware of the constraints on his appropriation of Austin. Importantly, Austin's constative-performative dichotomy is disclaimed on the grounds that:

> ... all those arguments lodged against the correspondence view of truth (and the picture theory of language) simultaneously serve to undermine the assumption of the constative—of truth bearing propositions (Gergen, 1994c, p. 85).

It seems that, in returning to his rejection of a correspondence theory of truth, Gergen has in mind this argument:

A: There is no correspondence relation between constatives and states of affairs.
∴ B: There are no constative utterances.
∴ C: There can be no constative-performative dichotomy.
∴ D: All apparently constative utterances are purely performative.

Gergen's belief that any notion of external reference necessarily involves correspondence relations was noted in 1.7.1. But the absence of picture-like correspondence relations does not in fact preclude certain combinations of words, at the behest of some speaker or group of speakers, referring to certain states of affairs. However, Gergen, given his rejection of external reference, cannot treat constative utterances as anything other than *pure* performatives. Unlike Austin, Gergen cannot allow speech acts to have this dual, concurrent role. So, it appears that the first step in Gergen's (1994c) "alternative way of conceptualising the constative" (p. 85) is to eliminate the constative.

Gergen's reconceptualisation makes use of Austin's distinction between the "happy" and "unhappy" performative utterance. A performative is "happy" when it "... fits appropriately or congenially into a conventional state of affairs ..."; it is "happy" if it fits the "procedure", where "procedure" is taken to mean some form of social convention (Gergen, 1994c, p. 85). This is consistent with Austin's view that performatives must not be evaluated in terms of a "true-false" dimension, and it is congruent with the contextualism of Gergen's account of meaning (1.7.3). It is worth quoting the following passage from *Realities and Relationships* at length:

Thus, when we say that a certain utterance is "accurate" or "inaccurate," "true" or "false," we are not judging it according to some abstract or idealized standard of correspondence; pictorial accuracy is not at stake. Rather, we are indicating its degree of felicity or infelicity in particular circumstances. The proposition that "the world is round and not flat" is neither true nor false in terms of pictorial value—its correspondence with the objective world. By current standards, however, it is more felicitous to play the game of "round-world-truth" when flying from Cologne to Kansas and more felicitous to "play it flat" when touring the state of Kansas itself.

It follows that description can function as picture or mirror, but only within a local game or procedure in which we invest it with this function. We can develop a local ritual in which a correspondence view is vindicated; however, this vindication is not a function of the mimetic capacity of words but a historically and culturally situated agreement (1994c, p. 86).

The excerpt, as a whole, obviously shows signs of Wittgenstein's influence, but it is also, Gergen believes, an endorsement of Austin's final position (1994c, p. 86 and n. 17, p. 297). Gergen claims that as a result of successfully functioning within one particular set of circumstances, an utterance can develop the capacity to function within another "game" (1987a, p. 7), "performative activity" or "form of life" (1994c, p. 86). To use the Gergen vernacular: take theorising, describing, explaining, predicting or verifying to be activities or games derivable from an original form of life. Assume that a particular performative utterance is felicitous within that life-form. It has functioned successfully in co-ordinating a relationship. Through this success it can then come to function as, for example, a description or prediction within the rules of another, derivative, game (Gergen, 1987a, p. 7; 1994c, p. 29).

What does this mean? We cannot say that the felicity of a performative utterance causes a constative to be uttered, because Gergen has ruled out constatives. Perhaps, then, Gergen means that a felicitous performative comes to function (or be used) as a description or prediction. Vague though this formulation is in the excerpt above, it seems to allow language a referential function. Elsewhere, it is quite clear that, contra Austin, Gergen intends the referential function to be "internal" (or localised) to "specific communities of scientists" (1995b, p. 27); that internal referential relations only contribute to "the making of meaning". Recall again Gergen's (1994c) comments, cited in 1.5:

... because disquisitions on the nature of things are framed in language, there is no grounding of science or any knowledge-generating enterprise in other than communities of interlocutors (p. ix).

In 1.7.4, reference was made to "a semantically closed system", and it appears that Gergen has in mind something of this kind.

To summarise the argument: Gergen's appropriation of Austin's theory is necessarily selective because of the former's rejection of external reference, but it is a misappropriation. He interprets Austin as finally coming to the view that the constative is a species of performative. But, on the contrary, Austin's view was that the performative-constative distinction should be regarded as a case of the doctrine of locutionary and illocutionary speech acts. At no stage in the development of Austin's thinking did he repudiate the Fregean notions of sense and reference, or the concept of truth. Secondly, Gergen merely *tells* us that reference is "internal" or "local" or "situated". He has yet to say (given his rejection of external reference) what this is supposed to mean.

3.5.2. GERGEN'S EXAMPLE OF THE PERFORMATIVE FUNCTION OF WORDS

An attempt is made by Gergen to demonstrate what he means by the localising of "description" in the context of performative activity. Gergen's example is similar to one which appears in §2 of Wittgenstein's *Philosophical Investigations*. Gergen is employed by, and working with, a wall plasterer, Marvin.[6] When Marvin requires Gergen to provide a wet mixture of plastering compound and water, Marvin utters the word "skosh". When a drier mixture is required, he says "dry-un". Of this "language game", Gergen (1994c) comments:

> In effect, "skosh" and "dry-un" became part of a relational dance in which we were engaged—words around which we coordinated our actions in order to achieve a perfect finish...If Marvin and I were exposed to a series of mixtures after two weeks of immersion in this procedure, with very little error we could have agreed on which were "skosh" and which "dry-uns". If I said "dry-un cumin up," this would also inform Marvin of what he might predict at that moment. The prediction could have been confirmed or disconfirmed. In effect, by virtue of their function within the relational form, such terms as "skosh" and "dry-un" developed the capacity to function within the game of description and verification. The words themselves do not describe the world; but because they function successfully within the relational ritual, they come to serve as "descriptors" within the rules of that game (p. 87).

One truism in this passage is (as Gergen says): "Words take on their meaning only within the context of ongoing relationships" (1994c, p. 49). The agreement between Marvin and Gergen *is* the establishment of a "local" convention which functions against a background of human social practices. Obligation and representation are two such practices which come immediately to mind.

However, this scenario does not at all preclude external reference. To elaborate: what does Marvin intend by the utterance "Skosh"? Let us suppose that when Marvin says "skosh" he is not telling a joke, nor uttering an expletive, nor being either ironical or metaphorical, and that to consider what Marvin intends by "skosh" is to consider the sense or meaning of "skosh" that Marvin intended "skosh" to have.

If "skosh" is a performative, then, according to Austin, it can be expanded into an explicit performative sentence which is equivalent in meaning. Hence:

M1: Skosh,

means the same as

M2: I (hereby) order you to send me up a wet mixture.[7]

This should be unobjectionable to Gergen. He has himself told us that by the expression "skosh", Marvin means "wet mixture", and he describes the context in which such a command is uttered (making the expression "send me up" appropriate, or felicitous, in that context). Also, while "skosh" doesn't mention the speaker, the import of the utterance is, in part, determined by who the speaker is—Marvin. Gergen could have chosen not to obey the command for that reason. That the second command mentions Marvin (as the speaker), but the first command does not, does not at all indicate that the two commands are not equivalent in meaning.

Following Grice (1957/1967) and Schiffer's (1972) development of Grice's theory, M1, and its equivalent M2, can be further explicated: Marvin meant that Gergen was to send him up a wet mixture by (or in) uttering "skosh" if and only if Marvin uttered "skosh" intending thereby to bring about a certain state of affairs— to have informed Gergen of his need for wet mixture.[8] Thus:

M3: My primary intention in uttering this sentence is to inform you, by means of recognition of intention, that I need some wet mixture.

It would be incorrect of Gergen's critics to claim that Marvin is asserting (constating) that he is ordering Gergen to send him up a wet mixture. The possibility that, in uttering an explicit performative, one is constating that one is performing an act of the kind named was rejected by Austin. Austin's position can be defended with the following argument, adapted from Schiffer (1972) and Searle (2002).

Let us accept Austin's belief that the explicit performative formula makes explicit "... what precise action it is that is being performed by the issuing of the utterance ..." (1955/1975, p. 61). If it were true that in uttering "I (hereby) order you to send me up a wet mixture", Marvin was asserting (constating) that he was ordering Gergen to send him up a wet mixture, then it would not be possible for Marvin to make explicit by the explicit performative formula the *full* illocutionary force of his utterance. To make explicit the fact that "I (hereby) order you to send me up a wet mixture" performs an assertoric speech act, Marvin would have to say "I (hereby) assert that I (hereby) order you to send me up a wet mixture". To make explicit the assertoric force of this new assertion, a longer explicit performative would be needed, and so on, *ad infinitum*, without Marvin ever having made explicit the full illocutionary force of his utterance. Yet, commonly, we *do* use the explicit performative formula to make explicit the act we are performing in the issuing of an utterance; "I promise", "I predict", etc. Performatives, that is, are ordinarily used *without assertoric force*. In uttering an explicit performative, the speaker is not asserting (constating) that he is performing an illocutionary act of the kind named.

In short, the utterance "I (hereby) order you to send me up a wet mixture" is *not* uttered with assertoric force. Marvin is not *saying* that he is performing the speech-act of ordering Gergen to send him up a wet mixture. This is why Austin claimed that an explicit performative was not constative—the speaker does not mean that he or she is performing an act of the sort named by the explicit performative verb.

However, this does not entail that Marvin is not saying *something else*. It is a general principle of conversation that saying something may entail the communication of something else (Cole & Morgan, 1975). Although Marvin is issuing a command to Gergen that has no assertoric force, he clearly intends Gergen to come to know something. That is, information is being conveyed to Gergen. We cannot say that Marvin meant that (was constating that) he was ordering Gergen to send him up some wet mixture because this would be a case of constating (leading to the infinite regress). But we can say that what Marvin meant, in part, by "skosh" was "I need some wet mixture".[9] Marvin's communication of this need is simply disguised. "I need some wet mixture" and "An intention of mine in writing this book is to..." are not of different logical forms. Yet, it would be false to suggest that the latter utterance is not uttered to inform you of, or declare to you, my intentions. Assuming, then, that Marvin was not mistaken about his need for wet mixture, a simple matter of fact has been conveyed to Gergen. It has been conveyed, in part, because Marvin and Gergen have agreed that the term "skosh" stands for a certain state of affairs, Marvin's need for wet mixture.[10] The "local" nature of this agreement is of no relevance to Gergen's rejection of external reference. The *establishment* of a socio-linguistic convention is invariably "local". Use of the convention may spread, but seldom (if ever) does the convention become "universal"; different languages have different conventions for *saying the same thing*. So, the "situated" or "local" setting up of conventions does not entail that we cannot describe things as they are. Again, Gergen's conflation of the distinction between act and content comes into play (2.6). Marvin's performative action, in the form of the utterance "skosh" rests on an agreed-upon convention, but what is being said through that act is not conventional. If Marvin was not mistaken about his need for wet mixture, what is said is a fact, one which is conveyed to Gergen. Moreover, it will forever be a fact. In a thousand years time, it'll still be a fact that at a particular time, in a particular place, this particular Marvin needed a wet mixture of plastering compound and water.

Thus, Gergen's example has not excluded the possibility that some truths and falsehoods are stated or conveyed *by means of* words. This is not to claim that performatives are derived from assertoric discourse. But the realist thesis that external reference is, at least, a three-term relation in which the referent is "uninterpreted reality" is consistent with Gergen's example. Marvin is ground-ing the word "skosh" in his extra-linguistic need for a wet mixture of plastering compound and water.

Let us assume for a moment, though, that the argument above is wrong-headed. Let us accept Gergen's post-modernist denial of the subject, and accept his denial that a particular need or *psychological* state of the speaker was com-municated. It is still feasible that Marvin's performative was conveying a *social* state of affairs—as in, for example, "You are obliged to send me up a wet mixture because I am paying you handsomely". External reference and the received view of assertion would not have been excluded.

3.6. DO ALL SPEECH-ACTS EXPRESS STATES OF AFFAIRS?

In failing to rule out the possibility that Marvin has conveyed some state of affairs, Gergen has not excluded the possibility that performatives are, in part, reflexive statements about their speakers, that truths and falsehoods are conveyed *by means of* statements and, thus, that language is referential. More, Gergen has not excluded the factualist possibility that *all* speech-acts express states of affairs and, therefore, *all* speech-acts have components that are fact-stating, that communicate information, albeit perhaps in some disguised manner.

This is not a currently fashionable view of language and one that Greenwood (1994) holds back from in his argument that performatives exploit descriptive forms of language. By this Greenwood means that a performative serves a social function *because* other forms of language are descriptive. For example:

It is in fact remarkably hard to excuse one's behavior *without* offering a description of one's debilitating or distressing psychological state, or of situational impediments or extenuating circumstances (Greenwood, 1994, p. 48).

But Greenwood goes on to say that this is "... in contrast to the relative ease with which we can apologise without offering any description: by just uttering 'I apologize' or 'I am sorry'" (1994, p. 48). The situation is, then, that whilst Greenwood objects to the social constructionist view that *all* discourse is of the pure performative kind, he believes that *some* utterances, such as "I am sorry" are pure performatives in that they can be uttered without the use of the descriptive form of language.

Yet, if the arguments in the preceding sections are correct, it is possible to expand "I apologise" into the explicit performative, "I (hereby) apologise to you". The speaker of this utterance would not be constating that he was apologising, but he may be constating or conveying something else, such as "I need to inform you that I feel bad about what has happened". The communicating of some truth (or falsehood) is simply disguised.

3.7. CONCLUSION

In 1.5, the basis of Gergen's metatheory was identified as the thesis that reality cannot be represented by language; that there is no fixed relation between words and the world (thesis A). This thesis must be accepted if: (i) "represented" is taken to mean "an agreement or correspondence with" reality, and (ii) "fixed relation" is taken to mean "natural connection", rather like the natural connection that exists between clouds of a certain kind standing for rain. On this, realism and social constructionism can agree. But Gergen is mistaken in believing that (i) and (ii) constitute *the* "realist view of language" (1.7.1). His attempt to demonstrate that language cannot be used to state (extra-linguistic) facts or falsehoods—in which various arrangements of words are *conventional* signs employed by individuals and communities *as a means of* stating or communicating what that individual or community takes to be the case—is unsuccessful. Gergen's own example of a "local game of description" or "performative activity" is, in fact, quite consistent with a realist account of language. This conclusion concurs with Greenwood's (1994) claim that social constructionism fails to provide any good reason for believing that all performatives are *pure* performatives. So, there is nothing to suggest that Gergen's "alternative" to a referential account of language *is* an alternative at all.

The comment was made in 3.2 that the non-factualism of social constructionist metatheory is not a post-modernist invention; that the development and acceptance of non-factualist theories has been a recurring feature of *analytical* philosophy through the nineteenth and twentieth centuries. Particularly noteworthy is the fact that logical positivism, the *bête noire* of social constructionism, incorporated a non-factualist view about certain types of proposition. Yet constructionists always present social constructionism as having nothing in common with positivism, and as the necessary correction to such misguided philosophy. Gergen, in particular, does not consider the possibility that his attempt at a non-referential treatment of language is, in some respects, consistent with the logical positivist treatment of language. Nor does he recognise the similarity between his view that theoretical statements are neither true nor false but constitutive of "performative activity", and Schlick's view that the propositions of philosophy are neither true nor false but "the activity of finding meaning". Nor does Gergen seem to be aware of the resemblance between Schlick's tactic in defending the verifiability principle—to maintain that it is not an assertion—and his own tactic in defending social constructionism against the charge of self-refutation—to maintain that discourse generally is not assertoric. This is also the strategy sometimes employed by Potter (e.g., Edwards et al., 1995) and Shotter (e.g., 2002). Yet, these social constructionists believe that the relationship between social constructionism and logical positivism is antithetical; that social constructionism is offering theoretical possibilities which are contrary to the allegedly implausible philosophies of science that have preceded it. The content of the present chapter suggests something else and, after examining the extent to which psychology endorses the "antithesis" belief, the remainder of this book will consider that "something else".

NOTES

[1] It may involve a fourth term—a third party (either a definite or indefinite individual, group or community). The language-user, in using language, intends to draw some situation to the attention of this third party.

[2] All references to Austin's lectures are from the 2nd edition of *How To Do Things With Words*.

[3] This is the position that Strawson arrived at after initially maintaining (in 1950) that the only purpose served by utterances that appear to ascribe truth to some statement is to perform an illocutionary act. By 1964, Strawson had concluded that to make such an utterance is both to assert something and to perform some illocutionary act (Kirkham, 1992, p. 29).

[4] This is at odds with another claim, made in the same paragraph, that theoretical language is "constitutive" of these activities (Gergen, 1994c, p. 87). This conflation between "enabling" (which involves a causal process) and "constituting" (which does not) is discussed in Chapter 5.

[5] There is, of course, a truism involved in saying that theories do not, for example, make predictions—only people do that.

[6] This anecdote is re-told in Gergen (1999).

[7] The parenthetical "hereby" precludes the utterance from being a statement about how one habitually behaves, or about the historic present (Austin, 1955/1975, pp. 57–58).

[8] Gergen's likely objection to this expansion is considered in the final paragraph of this section.

[9] This does not imply reference to some inner "mental" state.

[10] A more general and intricate analysis of intentionality and performatives is provided by Searle (2002).

CHAPTER 4

THE RECEIVED VIEW OF LOGICAL POSITIVISM AND ITS RELATIONSHIP TO SOCIAL CONSTRUCTIONISM

4.1. INTRODUCTION

In 1.1, it was noted that the central aim of social constructionism is to provide a viable alternative to the positivist-empiricist philosophy of science. This aim is largely a consequence of the constructionists' belief that positivist-empiricist philosophy has failed as a metatheory for psychology. This belief is consistent with the current, vigorously anti-positivist movement in Western intellectual thought.

The previous chapter shows how Gergen's attempt to achieve this aim fails. Gergen's metatheory is not at all a viable alternative to positivist-empiricist philosophy, and the question arises whether it is any kind of alternative at all. It was suggested in chapter 3 that Gergen has extracted the non-factualist aspects of Austin's thesis and cemented them to a general non-factualist line of thought. Given logical positivism's qualified non-factualism, as exemplified in Schlick's view of philosophy, this would indicate an affinity with Gergen's metatheory.[1] Gergen may have unwittingly developed the non-factualist component of logical positivism and taken it to an extreme. If correct, this alone would refute the generally accepted notion that logical positivism and social constructionism lie at opposite extremes of the philosophical spectrum.

It is important, then, to be clear about what this accepted notion is. If it is to be argued that this notion is mistaken, establishing its content is essential.

Accordingly, the present chapter seeks to identify the perceptions of commentators about positivist-empiricist metatheory, their judgements of its role as a metatheory for psychology, and their beliefs about its relationship to social constructionism.

4.2. TERMINOLOGICAL INEXACTNESS: POSITIVISM, LOGICAL POSITIVISM, AND LOGICAL EMPIRICISM

First, some terminological vagueness needs attention. Textual evidence indicates that most psychologists and philosophers use either the term "positivist" or the term "empiricist" inclusively to refer, at the very least, to logical positivist and logical empiricist philosophies of science.[2,3] Some psychologists have adopted the label "empiricist" (e.g., Gardner, 1985; Gergen, 1994c; Madsen, 1988), or even "modernist" to refer to logical positivism and logical empiricism (Gergen, 1992b; 2001b), but the term most frequently used is "positivist" (e.g., Tolman, 1992).

Undoubtedly, the temporal and intellectual proximity of 20th century logical positivism to logical empiricism and 19th century positivism is a partial cause of this terminological inclusion. These three philosophies of science are not, of course, distinct. For example: (i) the belief that metaphysics should be eliminated, together with a commitment to empiricism, is common to the positivism of the nineteenth century and logical positivism (Weinberg, 1936), and (ii) Carnap's programme of logical syntax was a feature both of logical positivism and of logical empiricism (Coffa, 1991).

However, the three philosophies are not identical. The influence of symbolic logic on logical positivism distinguishes it from positivism. The logical positivists accepted the dicta of Russell and Whitehead in *Principia Mathematica* that neither mathematical nor logical propositions are based on experience. They took the view that such propositions cannot be changed or refuted by experience, and so are valid *a priori*, that is, valid independent of experience. In addition, neither positivism nor logical empiricism, unlike logical positivism, endorsed the verifiability principle *as a criterion of meaning*. This criterion—that the meaning of a proposition is its method of verification—was considered by many logical positivists to be the cure for semantic neglect, a disease which they believed to be responsible for the disarray in epistemology. The criterion illustrates the importance which the logical positivists attached to the analysis of language and meaning, an emphasis that was shared not at all by positivism, and only to a certain extent by logical empiricism. The emergence of logical empiricism is associated with the abandonment of the verifiability principle (as a semantic, though not an epistemic, criterion) and the migration of many logical positivists either to America or to England (Hacking, 1983; Passmore, 1967). The label "logical empiricism" was adopted to refer to the more charitable versions of logical positivism that began to emerge during the late 1930s (Passmore, 1966).

These distinctions are obscured by the use of the term "positivism" or (less frequently) "empiricism" as a blanket label for logical positivism and logical empiricism. The two philosophies are grouped together, firstly, on the basis of resemblance—they are similar in some respects—and, secondly, on the basis of historical connection or continuity—because many of the logical positivists later became logical empiricists.

To add to this confusion of nomenclature, there was never unanimity among the logical positivists about the most appropriate name for their movement. (Nor, of course, were they ever in total agreement about philosophical issues). Certain members, both of the Vienna Circle and of the Berlin School, preferred labels such as "consistent empiricism" (Schlick, 1938, p. 342), "scientific empiricism" (Carnap, 1936, p. 422, ftn. 2) or "logistic empiricism" (Reichenbach, 1938, p. v).

In the present chapter, the term "positivism" will be used because of the preference for it amongst psychologists. The term, however, is to be understood only as a shorthand label for a set of characteristics thought to be shared by logical positivism *and* logical empiricism. These characteristics are generally supposed to be in contrast with those of social constructionism. However, it is the more precise belief, viz. that social constructionism is antithetical to *logical positivism*, which subsequent chapters in this thesis will address.

4.3. THE FAILURE OF POSITIVISM AS A METATHEORY FOR PSYCHOLOGY

Amongst historical, philosophical, and theoretical psychologists especially, there is concern that residues of positivism's conceptual principles and methodological practices linger in social and psychological science (Bickhard, 2001; Gardner, 1985; Leahey, 2004; Tolman, 1992).[4] The concern arises because of substantial agreement that positivism has failed as a metatheory for psychology.

Firstly, it is claimed that over the decades, philosophical analysis has shown the central tenets of positivism to be false (e.g., Bickhard, 2001). In Gergen's (1987d) opinion, for example:

> Deeply debilitated are the assumptions of induction, verification, falsification, decontextualized theory, meaning, operationism, word-object isomorphism, the criterion of coherence, the cumulative character of science, and so on.... we are now in a phase of "post-empiricist" analysis (pp. 21–22).

Secondly, it is claimed that psychology's appropriation of positivist philosophy of science also reveals positivism to be defective.[5] The inability of positivist doctrines to formulate an account of the nature of psychological theories and certain research practices is frequently lamented (e.g., Camic, Rhodes, & Yardley, 2003; Margree, 2002; Tolman, 1992). To cite just a few specific examples: it is said that positivism fails as a research paradigm for feminist methodology (McGrath, Kelly, & Rhodes, 1993), special educational needs (Vulliamy & Webb, 1993), subjectivity (Bornstein, 1999), ethical psychotherapy (Bickhard, 1989), clinical practice (Keeley, Shemberg, & Zaynor, 1988), psychological practice (John, 1994), psychoanalytic practice (Zeddies, 2001), psychoanalytic theory (Domenjo, 2000), pedagogics (Heshusius, 1986), human action (Falconer & Williams, 1985), developmental psychology (Bickhard, Cooper, & Mace, 1985), language development (Marjanovic, 1990), qualitative research (Avis, 2003; Guba & Lincoln, 1994), and meaning and human interaction (Denzin, 1982; Schermer, 2001).

This failure of psychology's appropriation of positivism is judged to be a natural consequence of positivism's inability to accommodate certain phenomena which are characteristic of social and psychological life.[6] These phenomena have been variously identified, but it is helpful to consider D'Agostino's (1992) claim that "reflexivity", "indeterminacy" and "contestability" are three prima facie reasons for an epistemology specific to the social sciences.

In the literature, *reflexivity* has two interpretations. The first is that the researcher (by extension, social science) is a constituent of the system which she or he studies (Steier, 1991). Therefore, the researcher is saying something about herself in the content of her research. There is, then, no distinction between "subject" and "object" or "knower" and "known". An understanding of the objects of study is not, then, independent of the researcher (Gergen & Gergen, 1991). It was evident from chapter 1 that this is a recurring theme in constructionist writings.

The second interpretation is that human beings, as objects of study in the social sciences, are self-interpreting autonomous subjects, unlike the objects of study in the natural sciences. Human subjects, once aware of the social influences on them and aware of various social scientific ideas, are no longer naive. As reflective social agents, subjects may act to alter the conditions of their social lives, after these conditions have been identified as causally efficacious in the explanation of a particular phenomenon. They can, that is, retrospectively invalidate the generalisations that result from social scientific investigation (Bohman, 1991; D'Agostino, 1992).

Whilst the first interpretation of reflexivity focuses on the researcher and the second on the object under study, both allude to a mutual interplay between psychologists and the objects of their research. It is believed that positivism cannot accommodate the amorphous relationship between researcher and subject. Also important, however, is a supposed consequence of that interplay. The claim is that it seriously compromises the validity of the scientific conclusions which emerge from the research, and that this, too, is something that cannot be reconciled with positivist philosophy.

The phenomenon of *indeterminacy* is said to follow from the second interpretation of reflexivity. The self-interpreting autonomous human subject, characterised by intentions and beliefs, renders social phenomena not merely complex but impervious to controlled experimental manipulation. Determinate outcomes cannot be predicted, human action cannot be fully analysed, and uncertainty about the nature and degree of social phenomena necessarily prevails. Predictive success requires determinacy, and it is judged that positivism cannot be reconciled with indeterminacy and its consequences.

Finally, it is claimed that theoretical concepts invoked in the social sciences are, because they are subjective, *contestable*. Concepts which result from social scientific research are dependent on the concepts of researchers who are themselves agents and products of social processes. Therefore, so it is claimed, such concepts are not purely descriptive, they have an evaluative dimension. Normative biases necessarily abound in what is portrayed as "scientific explanation", and evaluative judgements replace the descriptive concepts which positivism presumed to exist independently of any values.

Setting aside the question of whether the social sciences require a metatheory different from that of the natural sciences, the received view is that a philosophy or metatheory for psychology must accommodate all of these phenomena, and positivism fails to do this. It misconceives social scientific practice, and the results of that practice, because it misconceives the characteristics of the researcher, the characteristics of the subject under study, and the nature of the relationship between them.

4.4. THE RECEIVED VIEW

The folklore surrounding logical positivism in particular is such that the differences between it and social constructionism, outlined in Table 4.1, appear clear and substantial.

It is not surprising then that social constructionist metatheory is widely supposed to be antithetical to the positivist or empiricist philosophy of science (e.g., Attewell, 1990; Burr, 1995; Capaldi & Proctor, 2000; Cobb, 1991; Fishman, 1988; Gerrod Parrott, 1992; Harré, 2002b; Lyddon, 1991; Neimeyer et al., 1994; Osbeck, 1993; Paranjpe, 1992; Peeters, 1990; Potter, 1992; Shotter, 1993b; Steier, 1991; Unger, 1989). Gergen, as we know, shares this supposition. Social constructionism, for him, is a radical departure from an empiricist philosophy which has been shown to be defective (e.g., Gergen, 1990a; 1990c; 1991a; 1991b; 1992a; 1992b; 1994c; Misra, 1993). Moreover, this view is not at all peculiar to psychologists. It has been prevalent throughout the social sciences and philosophy for some time (e.g., Lincoln & Guba, 1985; Spector & Kitsuse, 1977; Suppe, 1974). Even when a possible alliance between positivism and social constructionism is acknowledged, its potential significance is dismissed on the grounds that both took different routes to the same anti-realist destination (e.g., Martin, 2003).

TABLE 4.1. Perceived differences between logical positivism and social constructionism

Logical positivism	Social constructionism
1. A prescriptive philosophy of science and so it misconceives actual scientific practice.	1. Specifically concerned to provide an account of the various practices of scientific communities.
2. Driven by an objectivist ideology.	2. Rejects the possibility of objective social science.
3. Embodies a denial of the subject as individual.	3. Recognises the subject as social, not individual.
4. Deems logic as an abstract, formal system essential to scientific inquiry.	4. Views logic as rhetoric—rejects all analytic distinctions which presuppose a binary logical system.
5. Takes theories to be axiomatic, formal systems.	5. Theories are little more than the discursive practices of particular scientific communities.
6. Subscribes to a naive empiricism—observation statements are derived solely from uncontaminated sense-data.	6. Observation statements are not epistemically prior to theoretical discourse.
7. Involves verificationism and operationism.	7. These characteristics signify the mistaken belief that referential relations between words and the world can be established.
8. Mechanistic, dualistic, deterministic, naturalistic, individualistic, reductionist, atomistic, absolutist, physicalist, quantificationist, foundationalist and inductivist.	8. Any assumptions which involve these characteristics are flawed and prohibit an understanding of social life.

However, the comments of a few indicate some disagreement with the received view. Tolman (1992), for instance, observes that the logical positivists are phenomenalists; that phenomenalism is a subjectivist epistemology (which ultimately collapses into solipsism) and that Gergen elaborates "... the subjectivist conclusion" (p. 38).

Terwee (1995) states that social constructionism is located in "... the empiricist tradition" (p. 193), on the grounds that both conclude that there is no truth. Unfortunately, Terwee's sweeping reference to the 'empiricist tradition' is left unclarified. It is not clear whether he is referring to logical positivism in particular, to positivism in general, or to neither. Further, if the 'empiricist tradition' has concluded that there is no truth, it is not at all clear why it continues to be "... motivated by the quest for objectivity ..." and absolute truth (Terwee, 1995, p. 193). Notwithstanding these obfuscations, Terwee judges Gergen's social constructionism to be not entirely at odds with its intellectual antecedents.

To take just one more example, Greenwood's (1994) view is that social constructionism "... repeat[s] many of the errors of traditional empiricist assumptions about linguistic objectivity" (p. 39), in that both presume that if theoretical descriptions are not linked to observable states of affairs by ostensive or operational definition, then those descriptions are not objective.

4.5. CONCLUSION

A survey of the psychological literature, though not exhaustive, reveals substantial consensus amongst theoretical psychologists concerning (i) the features common to logical positivism and logical empiricism, and (ii) the differences between positivist philosophy of science and social constructionist metatheory.

Among the few dissenters, Tolman and Greenwood, and possibly Terwee, are, however, quite correct in their linking of social constructionism with these earlier intellectual traditions. Those connections can be elaborated, and this is my aim in the remainder of the book.

NOTES

[1] Affinities between Gergen's constructionism and James' pragmatism have also been noted (Hastings, 2002), as have similarities between the former and behaviourism (Roche & Barnes-Holmes, 2003), and between the former and Hegelian dialect (Mather, 2002).

[2] Some psychologists may intend that "positivism" also refer to 19th century positivism and possibly earlier contributions, such as those of Bacon and Hume.

[3] There are exceptions. Chow (1992) and Daniels & Frandsen (1984), for example, use the term "positivist" to refer only to logical positivist philosophy of science.

[4] Bickhard (2001) also regards Machian positivism as having an ongoing influence in psychology.

[5] Again, there are occasional exceptions. Some commentators are content with a "modified positivism" remaining in psychology (e.g., Alliger, 1992; Chow, 1992), or the reconciliation of positivism with other traditions such as empiricism and hermeneutics (e.g., Saugstad, 1989).

[6] Proponents of this view may hold one of two positions. The first recognises the *Natur-* and *Geisteswissenschaften* distinction. The aims and methods of social scientific investigation cannot be those of the natural sciences, and consequently social science requires a metatheory different from that of natural science. Others, such as Gadamer (1960/1975), reject this, arguing that any metatheory must attend to the fact that all understanding involves an act of interpretation. Consequently, a metatheory appropriate to the social sciences is also appropriate to the natural sciences. Social constructionism's concern lies with the social sciences and they appear to accept the distinction above. However, much of their thinking has been influenced by post-positivist epistemological critiques of the *physical* sciences, Kuhn's (1970) *The Structure of Scientific Revolutions* being a case in point.

CHAPTER 5

CONVENTIONALISM

5.1. INTRODUCTION

My intention now is to challenge the common view in psychology that social constructionism is antithetical to positivist philosophy of science.

By "antithetical", I mean that social constructionist metatheory and logical positivism share nothing which is central to each. I aim to demonstrate that social constructionism, and the *bête noire* of social constructionists, logical positivism, are partially equivalent with respect to central tenets. There are, of course, differences, but social constructionism resembles some of the lesser known but important aspects of logical positivism, aspects that, surprisingly, are inconsistent with the logical positivists' adherence to empiricism. In doing so, constructionism perpetuates some of the philosophical errors of the positivist movement. Ironically, some of psychology's current metatheoretical commitments evolve directly from the positivism it affects to despise.

The first part of this book demonstrated that social constructionism's rejection of the possibility of an objective psycho-social science was arrived at largely via a consideration of language. The present chapter addresses a prominent feature of Gergen's beliefs about this subject: that language conventions form "linguistic frameworks" or "forestructures" which (among other things) generate "scientific facts" (1.7.4). This idea does not appear in Potter's research (although he too takes facts to be constructed), whereas Shotter (1994) acknowledges the existence of "frameworks", but adheres to Wittgenstein's belief that we can become bewitched by the interpretative constraints they impose. Neither Potter nor Shotter develops or fully endorses this feature of Gergen's metatheory.

In Gergen's metatheory, the ontological status of these "linguistic frameworks" is not simple. They consist of *a priori* elements, but they are said to be contingent upon the social conditions under which the terms (which comprise the frameworks) are employed (1.7.3). This medley, in which *a priori* elements coexist with the *a posteriori*, has an interesting precedent which is discussed in this chapter. The following chapter will deal with the *a posteriori* aspects of constructionism's contingency thesis with which we are more familiar: that language acquires meaning through its use in socio-linguistic practices.

Conventionalism is the subject matter both of this and of the following chapter because *both* socio-linguistic practices and theoretical frameworks (or systems) are said to have a purely conventional status. The doctrine of conventionalism, then, should be understood more broadly than is usually the case. Historically, the doctrine has developed from attempts to determine the status of certain *theoretical propositions*. Three consequences of this are: (i) that conventionalism is typically identified as a thesis about the status of theories in science (e.g., O'Hear, 1995), (ii) that the notion of a (theoretical) "framework" or "system" typically accompanies conventionalist accounts, and (iii) that conventionalism is sometimes confused with instrumentalism. But, understood more broadly, conventionalism is, in part, the thesis that the meaning of some or all linguistic terms (depending on the extremeness of the thesis) is not given *at all* by the features of the world to which the terms purportedly refer. Reference does contribute to the terms' meanings, but reference is said to be to something other than the *supposed* referents. Reference is to other terms, or to certain norms or practices, or to the precepts of the stipulator, and this is said to make reference *internal* rather than *external*. Conventionalism, then, is not the same as instrumentalism, which is a theory about theories. Signifying is logically prior to theorising about theories. Conventionalism is primarily a theory about meaning, and only derivatively a theory about theories.

When applied to theoretical propositions, conventionalism holds that the meaning of some or all of the terms and relations within a theoretical framework (or system) are wholly determined by other terms and relations in that framework, and/or reflect certain norms, practices or precepts of the scientific individual or of the scientific community. For this reason, they are said to be non-empirical. The claim is that propositions which consist of these terms and relations are conventions. They do not convey, or purport to convey, information about the world or, more specifically, about the subject of each proposition, i.e., the thing that each proposition is apparently *about*. They cannot, then, be true (in any realist sense of the word). Nor, of course, are they amenable to verification. This, so it is believed, makes them implicitly analytic.[1] A consequence is that *any* network of conventions (set of propositions) can be generated, and then "applied" to *any* set of states of affairs.

The aim of the present chapter is to demonstrate that the *a priori* elements of Gergen's relational account of meaning exemplify this conventionalism, and also to show that they are the culmination of a conventionalist doctrine which (i) evolved throughout the 20th century, and (ii) was clearly evident in logical positivist philosophy. Social constructionism has not effected the supposed radical break from its philosophical foe. Quite the contrary. Gergen's metatheory generalises the logical positivists' restricted conventionalism to all propositions, and in the process commits (in spades) the philosophical errors made by the logical positivists in *their* adoption of conventionalism.

Greenwood's (1992b) defence of scientific realism is suggestive of connections between social constructionism and later logical (scientific) empiricists, such as Braithwaite, Hempel, Feigl, and Kimble. In focussing on the earlier logical positivist movement (4.2), I take the conventionalist accounts of Schlick, Reichenbach and Carnap to be representative of that philosophy and, therefore, appropriate for comparison with Gergen's metatheory. My own suspicion is that, philosophically, Neurath has more in common with many social constructionists, including Gergen, but Neurath was by no means "a moderate" in logical positivist circles. If there are connections to be discovered, as I claim there are, they will be of greater import if they are between the "moderates" of logical positivism and the "radical" of social constructionism.

The material of the present chapter is closely related to the material of Chapter 7 which, in part, examines two ideas which form the basis of Gergen's conventionalism. That involves unfolding the Kantian aspects of Gergen's metatheory, and it is no accident that, in tracing the development of conventionalism (in the present chapter) we begin with Kant's epistemology.[2]

5.2. CONVENTIONALISM'S INTELLECTUAL ANCESTRY

5.2.1. THE CONTEXT: KANT AND J. S. MILL

Kant's influence on the doctrine of conventionalism stems from his rejection of the empiricist claim that the source of all knowledge is experience of things through the senses. Some knowledge, Kant maintains, is *a priori*. The testing ground for his distinction between *a priori* and *a posteriori* knowledge is necessary truth.

Necessary truths, according to Kant, consist of: (i) laws of thought; (ii) axioms of geometry; (iii) arithmetic truths, and (iv) metaphysical principles. These instances of *a priori* knowledge are prior to experience in that either or both of the categories (or concepts), space and time, are necessary for the sensory intuition of these truths (Caygill, 1995, p. 36). These categories are formal elements of the subject-side of the knowing relation, and provide a "framework" in which uncategorised sensation is ordered or arranged. Space and time are not empirically derived concepts, they are *a priori* necessary conditions of sense experience.

Kant further states that *a priori* knowledge is of two kinds—analytic and synthetic—and that necessary truths are synthetic, in that the predicate of the proposition is not completely characterised by the proposition's subject. This is illustrated in his account of Euclidean geometry. Euclidean geometry is, according to Kant, a body of synthetic *a priori* knowledge about the nature of space. It is grounded in intuition, because the truths of Euclidean geometry are not accessible to investigation through the senses. They are known by a faculty of *a priori* intuition, which is the necessary condition for the possibility of the sensory intuition of appearances. But a statement such as, "the sum of the internal angles of a triangle is equal to two right angles", is not analytic. It does not (merely) give us information about the meanings of terms, in the way that "All bachelors are unmarried adult males" does. In the latter, the predicate is semantically "contained" in the subject-term of the proposition; in the former, it is not. "The sum of the angles of a triangle is equal to two right angles" is, then, a synthetic *a priori* truth. It gives us information about empirical reality, and "empirical reality" in Kant's epistemology is appearances or phenomena which are, of necessity, already categorised or ordered in being experienced. It is *appearances* which are the objects of empirical sensory intuition, and which constitute knowledge, not some thing-in-itself, for such a thing is unknowable. The categorised objects of knowledge are, for Kant, phenomena, and these must conform to the propositions of geometry. According to Kant, then, geometry determines the characteristics of space synthetically, and yet *a priori*. The properties of space could not be determined in this way if space were not a pure *a priori* form of human sensibility—a necessary category of sense experience.

Kant's objection to empiricism was denied by J. S. Mill in *A System of Logic* (1843). Mill (1843) claims that all "necessary truths" are in fact generalisations supported by induction from experienced uniformities (Bk. II, Chaps. 5–7). They are, then, empirical claims, and certainty cannot be claimed for them. If experience is the cause of such truths being known, such truths must refer to the situations or things experienced. It is obvious, Mill says, that the definitions of Euclidean geometry are not about non-entities. It is also obvious that in nature, objects such as lines, angles and figures are not exact instances of the definitions of Euclidean geometry. Euclidean geometry is about *ideal* lines and *ideal* circles. But without the experience of real objects, we could not conceive of such ideal entities. The definitions of Euclidean geometry are, in Mill's words, "...some of our first and most obvious generalisations concerning those natural objects" (Ch. 5, Sec. 1, p. 148). Similarly, he takes numbers to be numbers of something, and the inductions of arithmetic to be generalisations from experienced properties of things (Ch. 6, Sec. 2, p. 169).

At this early stage of conventionalism's development, it is apposite to recall that Gergen: (i) dismisses British empiricism on the grounds that it mistakenly assumes independence of subject and object, and (ii) maintains that post-positivist philosophy of science has benefited from pre-twentieth century idealist philosophy because the latter recognises a system of preconceptualisation which implies the *dependence* of object on subject (1.7.4). There is, then, some sympathy on

Gergen's part for a Kantian view where categories of understanding (the a *priori*) are projected onto what is experienced, and the resultant claim that the object of experience is constituted by the qualities of the *a priori*.

5.2.2. THE EMERGENCE OF CONVENTIONALISM: HILBERT'S INVESTIGATION OF EUCLIDEAN GEOMETRY

Conventionalism emerged from a simultaneous resistance to Kant's dictum that not all knowledge is derived from experience and a rejection of Mill's thorough-going empiricism. The conflict between Kant's argument for *a priori* knowledge and Mill's argument for *a posteriori* knowledge through induction is the precursor to the conventionalism which emerged in Hilbert's research into the axioms of geometry. A number of implications of Hilbert's research resonate with current philosophy of science generally, and Gergen's metatheory in particular.

Hilbert (as cited in Bernays, 1967) initially limited his investigations to one class of necessary truths—the axioms of geometry. In correspondence with Frege, Hilbert argued that the complete set of axioms constitutive of Euclidean geometry is an autonomous, formal system (Frege, 1903/1971, pp. 6–21). That is, the terms and relations contained in the axioms are *completely defined* by the axiom-structure as a whole. In the remainder of this book, I will refer to this feature as the "condition of internal reference". The axioms have meaning, but their meaning is determined within the framework. The set of axioms is said to be *implicitly analytic*. An internally consistent system of axioms, such as Euclidean geometry, states in full the characteristics of relations such as "between" and terms such as "point" or "straight line". Hilbert's view (as cited in Baker, 1988) was that the meaning of these relations and terms, independently of their being part of that system, is of no relevance. *Their application or connection to reality is of no consequence.* Hence, the system's autonomy.[3]

There are three implications of Hilbert's formalism. First, if each type of geometry (e.g., Euclidian, Lobatschewskian, Riemannian) is a formal, autonomous system, generated by different sets of axioms, then the relations and terms in these systems have different definitions. A Euclidean straight line, for instance, is different from a Lobatschewskian or Riemannian straight line. Geometrical systems are not, then, competing theories of space. They are not in fact about space. They are simply different definitional systems, different "ways of talking" (Baker, 1988). All are equally valid. One geometrical system is no better than any other.

This first implication anticipates aspects of what is now referred to as an incommensurability thesis (Baker, 1988). Any pair of theories are said not to share a common language and to fail, therefore, in intertranslatability. Gergen's apparent acceptance of an incommensurability thesis, his rejection of external reference, his emphasis on the particularity of meanings as a function of language-game and linguistic framework, and his subsumption of matters epistemological under a relational view of meaning have much in common with Hilbert's interpretation of formal systems. There is irony in this, of course, because post-modernists generally are highly critical of formalism (Rosenau, 1992).

This similarity extends to a second implication of Hilbert's treatment of geometry, one which is a precursor to the semantic holism, outlined in 1.7.4. Given Hilbert's condition of internal reference (the meanings of all terms and relations are defined by the axiom-structure), whatever is logically derived from the structure must also have its meaning defined by the structure. That is, meaning "trickles down" from the axiom-structure to its derivatives. This anticipates the semantic holism to which Gergen subscribes.[4] In its extreme form, the condition of internal reference is extended to observation statements. Meaning does not "trickle up", it "trickles down" to these statements and, for this reason, observation statements are said to be "theory-laden". Apart from the formalism of Hilbert's account, the discrepancy between Hilbert and Gergen is simply one of generality. Hilbert restricts his account to the axioms of geometry, Gergen extends his to all language.

A third implication of Hilbert's account is that the geometric axioms provide neither *a priori* nor *a posteriori* knowledge. Contra Kant and Mill, Hilbert's view is that Euclidean geometry is not *about* the nature of space (regardless of whether the "nature of space" is taken to be a "phenomenon" or an actual thing). This is critical. Frege (1903/1971) had argued that axioms presuppose knowledge of the meanings of primitive terms, but Hilbert's position was that the axioms are arbitrary stipulations which presuppose nothing as known (Frege, 1903/1971, p. 11). This is a radical claim, but one which Hilbert stressed in his conceptualisation of the axiom-structure as a formal, autonomous system. If a structure such as Euclidean geometry is internally consistent, it can be understood without reference to worldly things. Therefore, it conveys no knowledge. It is an empirical question whether paths of light rays, for example, are characterised by a particular geometrical system. But, Hilbert maintains, such a question is irrelevant to an understanding of that particular geometry. The formal system is separate from its applications. The importance of this point is that it illustrates a turning away from the *genesis* of knowledge and, perhaps as a result, the term "empirical" was subsequently used by logical positivists to mean "the application of some formal system to reality", as well as referring to the origins of knowledge.

It will become evident that this emphasis on understanding the semantics of terms and relations within an axiom-structure anticipates aspects of logical positivism, in particular the positivists' "linguistic turn". Moreover, despite the fact that Gergen grounds psychological theories in the social milieux in which they are generated, thereby precluding their autonomy, he does conceptualise them as divorced from reality, and he accepts (though not without some ambivalence) that any system of propositions must be internally consistent (e.g., Gergen, 1987d, p. 22; 1991a, p. 21; 1994c, p. 69; Misra, 1993p. 403).[5]

5.2.3. POINCARÉ'S THEORY OF THE STATUS OF GEOMETRICAL AXIOMS

The next stage in the development of conventionalism occurs with Poincaré. In *La Science et l'Hypothèse* (1902), Poincaré reasons that the axioms of geometry are neither synthetic *a priori* intuitions nor experimental truths. Thus, he arrives at the same conclusion as Hilbert, at about the same time. The importance of Poincaré, however, is: (i) that he was the first to use the term "convention" to designate the status of such axioms; (ii) that he extended his conclusion to scientific principles—he took conventionalism beyond the confines of geometry, and (iii) that his influence on Schlick, in particular, was substantial.

Poincaré (1902/1952) reasons that the axioms of geometry are not, as Kant had proposed, synthetic *a priori* intuitions simply because alternative geometries are conceivable. Second, they cannot be, as Mill had proposed, empirical truths because the axioms concern ideal lines and circles; geometry is an exact science, not one amenable to constant revision, as is an experimental science (pp. 48–50). Therefore, Poincaré concludes, the axioms must "...reduce to definitions or to conventions in disguise" (p. xxii). As to the origins of these conventions, they are, Poincaré says "...the result of the unrestricted activity of the mind, which in this domain recognises no obstacle" (p. xxiii). They are subject to the internal constraint of consistency (p. 50). However, contra Hilbert, they are not arbitrary. Experience guides our choice of convention.

Poincaré's formalism regards conventions or definitions in disguise as having no truth-value.[6] We may believe Euclidean geometry to be the true description of physical space but, in fact, to ask whether it is true:

> ... has no meaning. We might as well ask if the metric system is true, and if the old weights and measures are false; ... One geometry cannot be more true than another; it can only be more convenient (1902/1952, p. 50).

This restricted truth nihilism foreshadows the all-inclusive version which characterises Gergen's metatheory, and is a feature of Poincaré's account for precisely the same reason. The various geometries, he says, are neither true nor false because they are not answerable to reality. They are not subject to any external constraint.

However, Poincaré (1902/1952) goes on to say that, as conventions, these geometries are "rigorously true" (p. 50). By this he means "certain because they are definitions in disguise" (p. 50, p. 136). The suggestion is that these definitions are implicitly analytic. Poincaré concedes Kant's point that the axioms and theorems do not have the same form as that of an analytic definition, such as "a triangle is a three-sided figure" or "all wives are female". It is not always possible to demonstrate the analyticity of a theorem by showing that either the subject or predicate term is definitionally embedded in, or constituted by, the other term. However, the definitions of primitive terms and relations are given by the axiom-structure as a whole and in this sense they are implicitly analytic. This notion of analyticity signals a similarity with logical positivism, and is also evident in aspects of Gergen's metatheory (5.5.1).

In sum, conventionalism begins with the proposal by Hilbert and Poincaré that the axioms of geometry do not convey what is known (no matter whether knowledge is *a priori* or *a posteriori*). The claim that axioms are conventions introduces a third possibility and, in the history of the philosophy of science, it ended the forced choice between the positions of Kant and Mill, that is, between rationalism and empiricism.

5.2.4. POINCARÉ'S APPLICATION OF CONVENTIONALISM TO SCIENTIFIC PRINCIPLES

Could Hilbert's and Poincaré's account of the status of the axioms of geometry be generalised to other classes of necessary truth? Poincaré (1908) believed not. Conventionalism concerning the laws of logic was, he argued, self-refuting, because any proof of the internal consistency of a set of axioms must fall outside the scope of conventions about the use of symbols (Bk. 2, Chs. 3–5). The status of such a proof was, in Poincaré's judgement, as Hilbert had demonstrated—a synthetic *a priori* truth. Whilst Kant's position concerning the axioms of geometry was false, conventionalism did not, so Poincaré believed, extend to logic and mathematics.

However, he provided an argument to "show" that it does apply to principles in the physical sciences. This marks another significant step in the history of the philosophy of science. Although this new form of conventionalism (about scientific theories) was first introduced by Édouard Le Roy in 1900, Le Roy's account was too radical to be taken seriously.[7] Poincaré's account, by comparison, is restrained, considered and scholarly in attention to detail.[8] It made credible the idea that the physical sciences consist, in part, of "definitions in disguise".

Poincaré (1902/1952) arrives at this generalisation from a comparison of geometry and science.[9] Geometry is concerned with certain *ideal* solids, removed from the natural solids of reality, but one cannot ignore the fact that experiment has played a considerable role in the genesis of geometry (p. 70). So too with scientific principles. Whilst there are certain principles (such as the principles of inertia and dynamics, and the law of acceleration) in whose genesis experiment has played a role, this does not mean, Poincaré thinks, that such principles have the status of empirical propositions. If they did, they would be approximate and provisory, but they are not. As with the axioms of geometry, what characterises scientific principles is their absolute value (absolute, at least, in the minds of the scientists). Such principles consist of ideal, invented definitions of the relevant terms because the scientist needs to produce a law " . . . to which our mind attributes an absolute value" (p. 138). Though constrained by the logical requirement of consistency as well as by experimental facts (p. 27), the scientist transforms an empirical generalisation into a disguised definition or convention (pp. 138–139). It is, for example, "... by definition that force is equal to the product of the mass and the acceleration... " (p. 104). This principle (of dynamics) is a convention of sufficient generality as to render it "... no longer capable of verification" (p. 166). It is not an empirical proposition, it is "... a principle which is henceforth beyond the reach of any future experiment" (p. 104), and, therefore, quite unlike an empirical proposition which, he says, lacks generality and is constantly subject to revision.

This disjunction between the particular and the general makes anomalous Poincaré's (1902/1952) later claim that we will have realised the limits of a convention's applicability when it "... ceases to be useful to us—*i.e.*, when we can no longer use it to predict correctly new phenomena" (pp. 166–167). This anomaly is addressed in 5.6.3. For the moment, it is noted that Poincaré claims that a principle can correctly predict new phenomena, or be disconfirmed by experimental evidence, and yet not be an empirical proposition. This may be compared with Gergen's favourable citing of empirical evidence which "confirms" aspects of his argument (e.g., Gergen, 1985a, p. 267; 1997, p. 726), despite his claim that "descriptions" are performative utterances which do not convey, or purport to convey, information about the subject of the proposition.

The crucial aspect of Poincaré's account, then, is that scientific principles have the same status as sets of geometrical axioms. They have their origins in experience of the world, but they are not empirical or true because, like the axioms of geometry, they are based on ideals. Empirical propositions, by contrast, are either true or false, because they are about independently existing states of affairs. In Poincaré's account, a scientific theory consists of both types of proposition.

Given this, Poincaré (1902/1952) has no objection to simultaneously accepting two contradictory theories. It is, he says,

> ... quite possible that they both express true relations, and that the contradictions only exist in the images we have formed to ourselves of reality (p. 163).

Thus, if two theories contradict one another, it might be because the scientist's convention in one theory is different from a convention in the other, not because there are two contradictory *empirical* propositions. Because these images (conventions) are "rigorously true" (in the sense defined above), reconciling contradictory theories is not an issue for Poincaré, just as it is not for Gergen (e.g., Misra, 1993, p. 403).

5.2.5. CONCLUDING REMARKS

The preceding sections bear on the claim that logical positivism has features in common with social constructionism. Firstly, as the following section will show, logical positivism was influenced by Kant, Hilbert and Poincaré. Secondly, despite obvious differences, there are also links between the works of these philosophers and Gergen's metatheory. Herein lies a connection between logical positivism and social constructionism.

5.3. THE CONVENTIONALISM OF THE LOGICAL POSITIVISTS

The conventionalism of Hilbert and Poincaré influenced logical positivism to a significant degree.[10] This influence occurred in the presence of other important determinants: Russell and Whitehead's *Principia Mathematica*, Einstein's general theory of relativity, Wittgenstein's *Tractatus Logico-Philosophicus*, and certain ideas from Frege, were all contributing factors.[11] Additionally, there was the influence of Kant. While it is true that logical positivism embodied a movement away from Kantian idealism (Scriven, 1969, p. 197; Smith, 1986, p. 3), that movement occurred only slowly, as the following comments from Maria Reichenbach (1965) reveal:

> Those philosophers who followed Einstein in his reasoning had therefore to emancipate themselves from Kant. This emancipation did not occur in one radical step but gradually. Such transitional points of view are presented in the writings of some of the philosophers of science in the earlier part of the twentieth century, for instance, in those of Moritz Schlick and Rudolph Carnap. The same is true of Reichenbach *RAK* [The Theory of Relativity and A Priori Knowledge] (p. xiv).

Although the anti-realist aspects of logical positivism were commented on during the 1930s and 1940s (e.g., Passmore, 1943; 1944; 1948; Stebbing, 1933; 1933–34), the piecemeal nature of the positivists' dissociation from Kant has been underestimated. This has contributed to the illusions about logical positivist philosophy. One notable consequence is the popular, but quite false, belief that a realist philosophy is necessarily positivist (cf. Brand, 1996; Lovie, 1992; Ussher, 2002). Another consequence is that similarities between logical positivism and social constructionism metatheory have remained unnoticed. Gergen (1994c) exacerbates this in his (false) claim that there is no connection between his own metatheory and Kant's epistemology (see Ch. 7).

5.3.1. SCHLICK

Schlick continued Hilbert's and Poincaré's development of conventionalism as an alternative to Kant's *a priori* knowledge. He began this project in *Allgemeine Erkenntnislehre* (first published in 1918), and it informs his view of the status of scientific theories.

Conventions, according to Schlick (1925/1974), are implicit definitions and these differ from concrete definitions (pp. 69–72, p. 355]. The latter will always involve "... pointing to something real" (p. 37) as when, for example, the concept of "point" is explained by pointing to a grain of sand.[12] This makes such concepts empirical. Implicit definitions, by contrast, are non-empirical. Of these, Schlick (1925/1974) says:

> [They] have no association or connection with reality at all; specifically and in principle they reject such association; they remain in the domain of concepts. A system of truths created with the aid of implicit definitions does not at any point rest on the ground of reality. On the contrary, it floats freely, so to speak, and like the solar system bears within itself the guarantee of its own stability. None of the concepts that occur in the theory designate anything real; rather, they designate one another in such fashion that the meaning of one concept consists in a particular constellation of a number of the remaining concepts (p. 37).

In Schlick's system, then, there are two types of definition: (i) concrete definitions in the empirical domain, and (ii) implicit definitions, in the conceptual, non-empirical domain. The concepts of a theory *acquire* content only to the extent that a system of implicit definitions bestows meaning on them (1925/1974, p. 34). Following Hilbert, Schlick's claim is that because meaning is given to concepts from within a definitional system or framework, their content is non-empirical.

In his discussion on the "empirical or real sciences", however, Schlick's (1925/1974) distinction between concrete and implicit definitions is not clearly maintained. For instance, Schlick takes time measurement to be an example of an implicit definition, having initially identified it as a "concrete process" (pp. 71–72). Units of time are defined in terms of the periods of rotation of the earth about its axis. This, he claims, is an implicit definition chosen from a number of alternatives. It is selected because the laws concerning the rotation of the earth appear in a very simple form. This, according to Schlick, is no different from choosing Euclidean geometry rather than some other geometry in order to define concepts such as "line", "point", etc. Euclidean geometry is suited to our everyday experiences and, thus, is used as the geometry of everyday life. The choice of definition or axiomatic system is made, then, for reasons of simplicity, and is not necessarily "the best possible definition" (p. 72). At this point, the definition is no longer " . . . tied to one or another concrete process . . . " (p. 72). So, the definition is chosen for pragmatic, functional, utilitarian reasons, not because units of time have characteristics of a kind designated by their definition.

The pragmatism evident in Poincaré's conventionalism is manifest in Schlick's account of implicit definitions. However, Schlick does not appear to endorse Poincaré's view that experience has a role in our *choice* of convention (even though Poincaré maintains, anomalously, that the chosen convention is without any content which reflects or refers to such experience). In his example of time, Schlick (1925/1974) suggests that the *only* reason we would not accept the Dalai Lama's pulse beats as marking off equal periods of time (and, therefore, providing an implicit definition) is because such a definition would be impractical (p. 72). It would be reliant upon the constant good health of the Dalai Lama. If this were the *only* reason, then the periodic process of the earth's rotation would not be a better definition than the Dalai Lama's pulse rate on *ontological grounds*. Schlick's observation that using the Dalai Lama's (possibly irregular) pulse beats would be impractical, presupposes an independent notion of regularity (of equal time units). This illustrates the ambivalence of the logical positivists about the direct experience of reality. In this case, experience or knowledge of the earth's rotation is not denied, but the causal consequence of that experience—that it informs our definition of time units—is.

The details of Schlick's position display the anomaly which is evident in Poincaré's account. Schlick (1925/1974) claims that an uninterpreted system of conventions or implicit definitions, devoid of empirical content, "coincides fully" with a network of empirical propositions that are coordinate (correspond) to the system of facts:

> ... we can find implicit definitions such that the concepts defined by them ... will then be connected to one another by a system of judgements coinciding fully with the network of judgements that on the basis of experience had been uniquely coordinated to the system of facts ... (p. 70)

Here, by "coincide fully", Schlick means "to agree with" or "to correspond to", not merely "to exist or occur simultaneously with". The unanswered question is how implicit definitions with no empirical content could agree with or correspond to empirical propositions—what do "agree with" and "correspond to" mean in this case?

Setting aside, for the moment, the incongruity of Schlick's *implicit-concrete* distinction, it parallels the *necessary-empirical* distinction invoked by logical positivism in its characterisation of scientific theories. A theory is said to consist, in part, of a system of propositions not amenable to verification because the terms and relations of the theory are autonomous, non-empirical, and mutually dependent for their meaning. The *system* has the same status as an implicit analytic statement in that, if taken as a whole, it is analytically true. To apply such a system to reality involves, as the example of time suggests, a choice of definitional system from "... the infinite wealth of relations in the world ..." (such as the Dalai Lama's pulse beat), and then to "... embrace this complex as a unit by designating it with a name" (Schlick, 1925/1974, p. 71). This seems to suggest that the distinction between necessary, analytic propositions and empirical propositions is not absolute. However, for Schlick, the fact that any axiomatic system can be fully understood, independently of any knowledge of that system's application, is proof of the distinction.

Schlick, then, endorses Poincaré's thesis that components of a scientific theory have the same status as the axioms of geometry. It is significant, however, that whilst

Poincaré was not prepared to apply conventionalism to mathematics and logic, Schlick is. This marks another step in the generalisation of the conventionalist thesis. Poincaré had applied conventionalism to scientific principles, and Schlick, presumably wanting to provide a *general* account of necessary truths, applies it also to mathematics and logic.[13]

To achieve this, Schlick has first to dismiss Poincaré's claim that the propositions of logic and mathematics cannot be conventions, by showing that the status of Hilbert's proof (that a system of axioms are internally consistent) is not a synthetic *a priori* truth. The proof, Schlick says, *seems* to appeal to intuition but, in fact, it does not. No synthetic element is introduced, in Schlick's opinion, because intuition is not a basis for the validity of mathematical propositions but *a means of understanding them*. The role of intuition is psychological, not epistemological (Schlick, 1925/1974, p. 356). Synthetic *a priori* truths are to be explained in terms of conventions, that is, intentions, decisions, or stipulations to use symbols in various ways, in order to understand whatever needs to be understood.[14]

In the light of this objection, Schlick develops an account of logic and mathematics which is consistent with his conventionalist treatment of other necessary truths. In Schlick's (1932/1979b) opinion, a conventionalist account of logic constitutes "... a perfect understanding of the nature of logic and its relation to reality or experience" (p. 345). This "perfect understanding" involves giving up both a view of logic as consisting of psychological laws (psychologism), and a view of it as the laws of nature or of "Being". In his reflections on the work of the Vienna Circle, Kraft (1953) captures the result of these renunciations in the following passage. Logic is said to provide:

> ... the foundations of conceptual order. Logical relations are merely conceptual relations, they are not factual relations within the empirical world, but only relations within the symbolic system. Classes, e.g., are nothing real but only conceptual syntheses. And you cannot find in your environment peculiar negative facts, along with positive facts, corresponding to the concept of negation. Since logical relations are purely formal, they can be ascertained without any regard to the specific meanings of propositions, the concrete states of affairs. Consequently they cannot assert anything about reality (pp. 20–21).

This last statement is consistent with Schlick's (1932/1979b) claim that:

> The application of logic to reality consists in its application to propositions about reality—but in applying the logical rules in this way we are not asserting anything about reality (p. 345).

Further:

> ... no fact can prove or disprove the validity of logical principles, simply because they do not assert any fact, and are, therefore, compatible with any observation" (p. 223).

From this it is clear that, in building on the work of Hilbert and Poincaré, Schlick admits into his treatment of logic the central theme of the conventionalist thesis: the non-empirical status of certain kinds of proposition. The principles of logic, Schlick (1932/1979c, pp. 234–235) claims, do not express knowledge. They assert no fact at all, being concerned only with symbols, not with reality.[15] Even when applying a logical principle to real existents, Schlick maintains that no new facts are conveyed to us. So, applying the principle of excluded middle (either p or not-p), the statement "My friend will either meet me tonight or not" is one that, according to Schlick, speaks of reality because it speaks of my friend and a possible meeting, but it asserts nothing about my friend and our meeting. It conveys no information about this situation, *or about any other situation*.

Furthermore, the shift in emphasis in current philosophy of science, from the referents of terms in a proposition to the speech-act in uttering the proposition, is evident in Schlick's (1925/1974) analysis of negation. Negation, he claims, refers to a specific linguistic act, "A is not B", asserted in a particular context, one where a proposition is judged to be false (pp. 63–64). Schlick does not treat negation as ontological, whereby the utterance "A is not B" expresses the fact that situation A does not have property B. He does not, as Kraft made clear, acknowledge the existence of negative facts.

It does not follow from the claim that logical principles are non-empirical that they are conventional. Yet, this appears to be Schlick's position; he makes no clear distinction between conventions and tautologies. Schlick does not distinguish the assertion that the propositions of logic are conventions of symbolism (à la Hilbert and Poincaré) from official logical positivist doctrine, that such propositions are (i) tautologies that have no application, and are (ii) the *consequence* of such conventions rather than the conventions themselves (à la Wittgenstein).[16] Again, Schlick's comments on negation exhibit confusion. He maintains that "... the principle of non-contradiction is merely a rule for the use of the words "not", "none" and the like ... " (1925/1974, p. 337). That is to say (if Schlick is to be consistent), the principle is a convention. If it is "merely a rule" for the use of certain words, choosing another rule is always possible, and the principle is *not* (contra Schlick's own positivist credo) a tautology! Schlick's distinction between conventions and tautologies is, at best, very hazy. This haziness may be a consequence of: (i) Schlick's (1925/1974) view of deduction—specifically, that what follows from a set of conventions must itself be a convention of symbolism (p. 166); (ii) Russell's identification (in the *Principia*) of arithmetical equations (later identified, by Wittgenstein, as conventions or rules of grammar) with propositions of logic (tautologies) (G. P. Baker, 1988, p. 144); (iii) the many passages in the *Tractatus* where the features of logical propositions are precisely those proposed by Hilbert, Poincaré and Schlick as the features of conventions (e.g., 5.551, 5.552, 5.5521, 6.11, 6.111, 6.113, 6.1222, 6.124, 6.126, 6.3), and (iv) the fact that, post-*Tractatus*, Wittgenstein did not consistently maintain his distinction between tautologies and rules of grammar in relation to geometrical and metaphysical propositions (Baker, 1988, pp. 144–145).

5.3.2. REICHENBACH

In *The Theory of Relativity and A Priori Knowledge* (*RAK*), published in 1920, Reichenbach's intention was to *modify* Kant's notion of synthetic *a priori* judgement in order to make it consistent with relativity theory. Reichenbach maintains that there are two distinct meanings of *a priori* which can be traced to Kant: (i) necessarily true or true for all time, and (ii) constituting the concept of object. The first meaning, he maintains, must be dispensed with. The second meaning is, he suggests, consistent with relativity theory. *A priori*, according to Reichenbach (1920/1965), "...means 'before knowledge', but not 'for all time', and not 'independent of experience'" (p. 105). The significance of this is far-reaching, for it is this notion of *a priori* which Gergen unwittingly employs in his account of psychological theory (5.5.1). It also illustrates the *gradual* emancipation from Kant on which Maria Reichenbach (1965) had commented.

Reichenbach justifies his position by invoking Einstein's conceptualisation of the measurement of length. In Reichenbach's (1920/1965, pp. 96–97) opinion, Einstein showed that what we measure as length is not the relation between the bodies, but their projection into a coördinate system.

In *RAK*, there are a number of synonyms for the term "coördinate system": "principles of coördination", "system of reference", and "constitutive principles". The "laws" of probability, the principles of time and space, and the Euclidean metric are all coördinate systems. They involve, according to Reichenbach (1920/1965, p. 54), non-empirical statements which serve as prescriptions. They are general rules laid down before the terms and concepts of the would-be theory have a well-defined subject matter. Once established, they enable us to conceptualise a certain state of affairs in a particular way (pp. 54–55), for without them, there are no conceptual categories (p. 55), and there is no possibility of "defining" the reality (that is, our experience) that confronts us (p. 50). In Reichenbach's view, the principles of coördination:

> ... define the individual elements of reality and in this sense *constitute* the real object. In Kant's words: "because only through them can an object of experience be thought." (p. 53).

The principles of coördination account, then, for the "ordering" of perceptual data which results in knowledge (p. 56). In fact, Reichenbach suggests that they may justifiably be called "order principles" (p. 52), and that it is in these principles of coördination that the object of knowledge is defined (p. 56, p. 104). The thrust of Reichenbach's criticism of empiricist philosophy is that it fails to recognise the difference between these *principles of coördination* and the *axioms of connection*, the latter being individual empirical laws such as the laws of physics (p. 54, pp. 93–94).

For Reichenbach, then, support for Kant's second meaning of *a priori* is found in Einstein's theory of relativity because, in this theory, the relation of length is relative to the coördinate system selected for the purpose of obtaining knowledge. The new method of the theory of relativity assumes that what used to be taken as "geometrical length" is not an absolute property of a body, but a property of a body *and the chosen system of reference*. The relation between bodies manifests differently depending upon which system is chosen (Reichenbach, 1920/1965, p. 97). Hence, Reichenbach's claim that the principles of coördination "define the individual elements of reality" and "constitute the real object".

This is what it means to say that conventionalism has explained away Kant's synthetic *a priori* judgements (Reichenbach, 1920/1965, p. 47, p. 57). Reichenbach's principles of coördination are conventionalist frameworks which are "before knowledge," but not "for all time" and not "independent of experience". The outcome of rejecting Kant's first meaning of *a priori* is that the *a priori* system or framework loses its fixed and absolute status. The only acceptable notion of *a priori* is now assumed to be relativist. Euclidean geometry, for example, may be *a priori* in the context of everyday life, but Riemannian geometry is *a priori* in the context of the general theory of relativity.

Noteworthy, too, is Reichenbach's belief that the distinction between an axiom of coördination and an axiom of connection collapses when the system of reference becomes part of what is known. The old view that the measurement operations involved in determining length are independent of nature is, in Reichenbach's (1920/1965) opinion, false because the chosen system of reference becomes " . . . a special property of the object . . . " (p. 100). It is no longer an axiom of coördination " . . . *but has become an axiom of connection*" (p. 100).

Feigl (1969, p. 18) declares that Reichenbach rejected Poincaré's conventionalism. This is misleading, and may have contributed to the illusion that logical positivism was consistent in its commitment to empiricism. It is true that both in *RAK* and in *The Rise of Scientific Philosophy* (1954), Reichenbach explicitly rejects Poincaré's position. The substance of his rejection is that:

> . . . mathematicians asserted that a geometrical system was established according to conventions and represented an empty schema that did not contain any statements about the physical world. It was chosen on purely formal grounds and might equally well be replaced by a non-Euclidean schema (Reichenbach, 1920/1965, pp. 3–4).

And in the footnote attached to this passage, Reichenbach notes that:

> Poincaré has defended this conception. . . . If he had known that it would be this [Riemannian] geometry which physics would choose, he would not have been able to assert the arbitrariness of geometry (ftn. 1, p. 109).

Firstly, Poincaré did *not* assert the arbitrariness of geometry. As was pointed out in 5.2.3, his claim was qualified in two respects. Secondly, the issue between Poincaré's conventionalism and Reichenbach's is whether the axioms of geometry are empirical propositions. Poincaré's position was that they are not (5.2.3) but, as previously noted, Reichenbach says that they *become* empirical propositions *after* coördinative definitions have been established. This is reiterated in his later work. Riemannian geometry is said to be applicable to astronomic dimensions while Euclidean geometry is not, but the applicability of these systems is an issue only after sets of coördinate definitions have been laid down (Reichenbach, 1954, pp. 132–140). This is the distinction between Poincaré's and Reichenbach's conventionalism. In the former, the axioms of geometry retain their conventional status, while in the latter, they become synthetic statements. It is an important difference between the two, but their commonalities are sufficient to falsify Feigl's claim that Reichenbach's account does not have a conventionalist component akin to that of Poincaré. Both insist that conventions or principles of coördination are non-empirical components of scientific theory; that is, they have no descriptive or referential function, and cannot be true or false. Both maintain that any system of principles or definitions can be discarded and replaced by another system, and that, when this occurs, knowledge undergoes change.

5.3.3. CARNAP

Carnap's propagation of conventionalism is evident in *The Logical Structure of the World* (the *Aufbau*) (1928). This book was originally entitled *Theory of Constitution* as if to make plain the Kantian nature of Carnap's project. In the *Aufbau*, Carnap (1928/1967) attempts the logical construction of concept formation. Although it is in principle possible to reduce all concepts to the immediately given (p. vi), the logically prior aim of science is the formation of a constructional system (section 179), such a system being achieved through convention or—Carnap's preferred term—postulation (see sections 1, 2, 67, 179). The system is said to be strictly formal, in the manner of Hilbert, yet not independent of experience. It displays the step-by-step derivation (construction) of various kinds of concepts (or objects) from elementary experiences. This is consistent with Reichenbach's concept of *a priori*. Carnap's system is not "independent of experience", but it is "before knowledge":

> ... each constructional step can be envisaged as the application of a general formal rule to the empirical situation ... These general rules could be called a priori rules, since the construction and cognition of the object is logically dependent upon them. ... However, the rules are not to be designated as "a priori knowledge", for they do not represent knowledge, but *postulations*. In the actual process of cognition, these postulations are carried out unconsciously. Even in scientific procedures, we are rarely conscious of them and they are rarely made explicit (Carnap, 1928/1967, Section 103).

This expresses the now familiar conventionalist thesis that: (i) *a priori* knowledge can be explained in terms of general, formal rules or conventions, and (ii) that knowledge of the objects of science (the immediate data of sense, according to logical positivism) could not occur without this *a priori* framework in place to make sense of, interpret, or give meaning to sense data.[17]

The formation of a constructional system as the logically prior aim of science was a consistent theme throughout Carnap's philosophical contributions. In the years between the publication of *The Logical Structure of the World* (1928) and *Logical Syntax and Language* (1934/1937), this theme was given expression in Carnap's claim that the pure syntax of a "non-natural" or constructed language would suffice to define the various terms and relations of that language. In order to demonstrate this, Carnap constructed two such model languages. From these, he deduced that: (i) all languages consist of a syntactical structure composed of formation—and transformation—rules, and concepts that characterise the language; (ii) transformation—rules consist of axioms and rules of derivation which determine the conditions under which sentences are derivable from others, and (iii) each syntactical structure provides a method of definition that, although general to all languages, gives rise to definitions of concepts that are *relative* or *limited* to the finite set of premises of the language. The definition of the logical concept "consequence" was, for example, more complex in Carnap's second model language than in his first (Kraft, 1953, p. 53). The key point is that, as with Reichenbach's principles of coördination, Carnap's *a priori* constructional system is relativised in that the meaning of "logical consequence", and of other logical concepts, is relative to the model language constructed. Hence, Carnap's *principle of the conventionality of language forms*, more commonly referred to as the *principle of tolerance*. The principle is that neither truth nor falsity can be predicated of the various language forms. They are equally legitimate because their genesis is stipulation and convenience.

After *Logical Syntax and Language* (1934), Carnap revised his position. Whilst retaining his notion of a constructional system, he no longer thought that the definitions of logical concepts contained in the language system are given *only* by syntactic rules. Now, semantic rules also contribute, and logical truth must be taken to mean "true given the semantic rules contained within the constructed object language" (Kraft, 1953, p. 62).

The importance of semantic rules for Carnap's conventionalism is evident in *Meaning and Necessity* (1947). Here, he is concerned to demonstrate that a language which refers to abstract entities neither embraces a Platonic ontology nor violates empiricism. A scientist or philosopher wishing to use such a language "... has to introduce a system of new ways of speaking, subject to new rules; we shall call this procedure the construction of a linguistic *framework* for the new entities in question" (Carnap, 1947/1991, p. 86). Take, for example, a linguistic framework concerning propositions: "... the system of rules for the linguistic expressions of the propositional framework . . . is sufficient for the introduction of the framework" (p. 88).

Importantly, Carnap maintains that there is only one kind of legitimate question to be asked of this constructed language form. It is the *internal* question concerning the existence of such entities *within the framework*. The question, "Are there propositions?" cannot, Carnap (1947/1991) believes, be taken in an external or ontological sense for ". . . then it is noncognitive" (p. 88), and cannot be answered at all because:

> To be real in the scientific sense means to be an element of the system; hence this concept cannot be meaningfully applied to the system itself (p. 86).

"Are there propositions?" must be treated as an internal question, one which can be answered only through logical analysis based on the rules for the use of the expressions within the framework. The answer, of course, will be analytic, i.e., logically true (p. 87). To take the question externally would be to fall into the metaphysical nonsense either of the realist, who would, Carnap thinks, answer in the affirmative, or of the idealist, who would answer in the negative. In fact:

> . . . the question of the admissibility of entities of a certain type or of abstract entities in general as designata is reduced to the question of the acceptability of the linguistic framework for those entities (p. 93).

Reiterating the pragmatism of Schlick's conventionalism, Carnap takes framework acceptability to be determined by pragmatic criteria. Efficiency, fruitfulness and simplicity are decisive factors affecting the philosopher's choice of linguistic system. In short, the issue of the material existence of the system of entities is replaced by a decision, based on pragmatic criteria, to use or not use a particular language form.

Carnap is adamant that this decision should never license the ontological conclusion that the referents of the linguistic system are real *simpliciter*. His attitude, he says, is always ontologically neutral (Carnap, 1963, pp. 17–19). The chosen system is (presumably) efficient, fruitful or simple, and the only conclusion justified is that these qualities ". . . make it advisable. . . " to accept the linguistic system (Carnap, 1947/1991, p. 87). In short, the conventionalist, Carnap believes, has the right attitude because he accepts the framework without believing in the material existence of the entities named in the framework. He realises that he is merely using a particular language. He knows that the framework is not truly a network of assertions, i.e., empirical propositions; he knows that it does not imply any assertion about reality (p. 93). Carnap's judgement is that the critic of this position conflates the "acceptance of a system of entities" with "an internal assertion" (p. 93). The critic may, for example, ask for evidence that numbers are real. But this is to presume (falsely, for Carnap) that numerals are words which designate entities. Such a presumption reveals an intolerance to alternative linguistic forms.

Friedman (1999) observes that, notwithstanding Carnap's influence, many of his acolytes did not "... come to conceive their enterprise as a purely pragmatic exercise in language planning having no theoretical or ontological implications whatsoever (p. 233). Yet a descendant of Carnap's conception certainly characterises social constructionism, though without his formal-logical method. Recall Potter's and Shotter's repudiation of traditional epistemology and their derision of metatheoretical debate (1.3; 1.4): "... whether ... one should adopt an overall realist or constructionist position or approach is irrelevant" (Shotter & Lannamann, 2002, p. 587). Note, too, Gergen's (2001a) belief that the ritual of scholarly argumentation is futile because of its "realist" commitments (such as the goal of truth), and his preference for alternative forms of communication.

This connection between Carnap and social constructionism is perhaps through the philosophies of Goodman and Rorty (Hacking, 1999). As with Reichenbach, Carnap's view was not simply a logical positivist phenomenon only later to be renounced. Carnap's notion of a constructional system or framework is retained throughout the transition from a syntactic to a semantic, pragmatically oriented, conventionalism. Carnap was instrumental in developing conventionalism into the thesis it is today. Recognising the importance of non-empirical, linguistic systems is still assumed to be the antidote to the metaphysical confusions of realism and idealism.

5.3.4. Summary

The development of conventionalism by the logical positivists can now be summarised:

(1) Each of the leading members of the logical positivist movement advanced the conventionalism of Hilbert and Poincaré, albeit through different formulations.

(2) Their rationale was a *defence* of empiricism. If an account of necessary truths in terms of implicit definitions or conventions could be given, the possibility of synthetic *a priori* knowledge could be eliminated.

(3) Such an account must, however, avoid the implausible implication of Mills' empiricism, that a proposition such as $5 \times 4 = 20$ is empirical, and thus either true or false. This proposition is certain and cannot be empirical. No doubt experience originally occasioned the construction of implicit definitions, frameworks or systems and mathematical propositions. But the *genesis* of knowledge is not what is involved in this second meaning of "empiricism". What is involved is the fact that empirical propositions are uncertain, and that their truth can only be determined by new experience of the material world.

(4) The "necessary truths" of logic and mathematics are conventions concerning the use of terms.

(5) Certain concepts in scientific theories, such as "time", "length", or "proposition", also have an *a priori* conventional status. Again, this is not inconsistent with empiricism, because *a priori* knowledge does not mean "independent of experience" or "for all time". It means "before knowledge".

(6) These framework propositions reflect the norms, practices or precepts of the scientist or scientific community, in that they designate rules for the use of the terms in the framework, not features of the world to which they purportedly refer. The meanings of the terms and concepts employed in these propositions are contextual, in the sense that they are relative to the system in which they are employed. This means that the propositions are analytically true, i.e., true given the linguistic framework employed.

(7) The choice of frameworks is not arbitrary. It is not determined by the features of the events under investigation, but involves a practical decision, and is determined by pragmatic criteria such as simplicity and fruitfulness.

At this point, I can do no better than cite from Friedman's *Reconsidering Logical Positivism* (1999):

> Our understanding of logical positivism and its intellectual significance must be fundamentally revised when we reinsert the positivists into their original intellectual context, ... [W]hen we take due account of ... [this], we see that their central philosophical innovation is not a new version of radical empiricism but rather a new conception of a priori knowledge and its role in empirical knowledge.... For the underlying idea of a relativized a priori constitutively framing the empirical advances of natural science is still, in my opinion, of central philosophical significance (p. xv).

The received view of logical positivism (outlined in 4.4) involves an obfuscation of the facts. Many in psychology, and in the social sciences generally, are plainly unaware of these aspects of positivist philosophy.[18] As a result, significant facets of the positivist project have been misconceived.

5.4. FROM LOGICAL POSITIVISM TO SOCIAL CONSTRUCTIONISM VIA KUHN'S ACCOUNT OF SCIENCE

Friedman's (1999; 2002) judgement about the contemporary significance of a relativized *a priori* is motivated by Kuhn's account of science and his notion of "paradigms". Similarities between Kuhn's account and Carnap's conventionalism have recently been uncovered (Earman, 1993; Irzik & Grünberg, 1995; Reisch, 1991). The conventionalism of the logical positivists generally, and of Carnap in particular, far from being rejected by Kuhn, became pivotal to his historical and sociological account of knowledge. The result was a social emphasis which overlaid the conventional system, a feature not manifest in preceding versions of the thesis.

Because of its relative recency and enormous appeal, Kuhn's account is well-known. It is sufficient to make only the following comments. A Kuhnian "paradigm" is said to impose an intelligible order on "known facts". It consists, in part, of general metaphysical principles, laws, theoretical assumptions and methodological prescriptions which give content to a scientific community's "... conceptual categories ... " (Kuhn, 1970, p. 64). The meanings of terms embedded in the various components of the paradigm "trickle down" to the observational sentences formulated by the scientist. The imposition of the paradigm enables theoretical and experimental "problems" to be solved and provides guidelines for the solution of other "problems". It is a way of conceiving natural phenomena, in the sense that the business of "normal science" is a collective "... attempt to force nature into the preformed and relatively inflexible box that the paradigm supplies" (p. 24).

The Kuhnian paradigm, then, is a convention, albeit one on a much larger scale than envisaged in Poincaré's account, or in Schlick's conceptualisation of concepts and implicit definitions. Kuhn's paradigm is an extensive web of assumptions and prescriptions which, once taken up by a scientific community, guide and justify intellectual views, scientific behaviour and the meanings of various concepts. And, just as Poincaré's "definitions in disguise" can be exchanged for another coherent system if the system "... ceases to be useful to us—*i.e.*, when we can no longer use it to predict correctly new phenomena" (Poincaré, 1902/1952, pp. 166–167), so too can one paradigm be exchanged for another if the new paradigm "... permit[s] predictions that are different from those derived from its predecessor" (Kuhn, 1970, p. 97). In Kuhn's account, this requires the two paradigms to be logically incompatible. Logical incompatibility is synonymous with incommensurability (e.g., pp. 97–98). Theories are said to be incommensurable when many of the terms of one theory cannot be translated into the expressions of the other. The incommensurability thesis accompanies Kuhn's conventionalism just as it accompanied the conventionalism of his predecessors.

The same can be said for semantic holism. In Hilbert's formalism, it is evident that the concept of semantic holism is pertinent irrespective of whether the analytic-synthetic distinction features in an account of theory. The distinction does not feature in Kuhn's account (or in Gergen's). But the all-embracing nature of Kuhn's paradigms (as conventional systems), to the extent that they are said to determine the process of observation, entails an extreme semantic holism. Semantic holism extends to all scientific propositions in Kuhn's account, and thereby precludes the analytic-synthetic distinction.[19]

Conventionalism, then, did not end with the demise of logical positivism and logical empiricism. However, in many philosophical and psychological communities, especially in those which adopt a nominally "anti-positivist" stance,

Kuhn's account of science is believed to be radically different from those philosophies of science.[20] In this respect, social constructionism, as we have seen, is no exception.

5.5. CONVENTIONALISM IN GERGEN'S METATHEORY

Gergen regards Kuhn's philosophy as a major contributor to the refutation of logical positivism and logical empiricism, and he accordingly incorporates components of it into his own metatheory. In general, Gergen endorses Kuhn's account, but there are some aspects which he does not support. He rejects Kuhn's view (inexplicable, given Kuhn's account of the paradigm's predominance) that anomalies are entirely unexpected phenomena marking the beginning of a scientific revolution (Gergen, 1994c, p. 15). Further, Gergen believes that Kuhn's philosophy not only lacks the necessary linguistic emphasis, but also presupposes individualism; that, despite providing a sociology of science, Kuhn ignores the *predominance* of the social and the socio-linguistic.[21] Notwithstanding these differences, Gergen's debt to Kuhn is clearly evident, and he readily acknowledges it (p. 13). The critical point is that the differences between the two are not of the kind which would preclude the continuation of the conventionalist thesis. And this is what occurs; in Gergen's account of the status of psychological theories and logic, twentieth century conventionalism is retained.

5.5.1. PSYCHOLOGICAL THEORIES AS CONVENTIONS

Among Gergen's many claims concerning psychological theories, the following are particularly pertinent:[22]

(1) Mental predicates (in a psychological theory) are defined in terms of other mental predicates (1985b, p. 122).

(2) A psychological theory, then, consists of a closed system of definitions (1987c, p. 123; 2001a, p. 421).

(3) Mental predicates reduce to a set of extended tautologies; language about the mind is analytic in character. It is equivalent to mathematics in that its propositions are intelligible without "necessary linkages to events outside" (1985b, p. 122; 1987c, p. 119; 1994c, p. 8).

(4) All reasonable propositions declaring a functional relationship between the stimulus world and the psychological domain, or between the latter domain and subsequent action, are true by definition (1987c, p. 122; 1988a, p. 38).

(5) Psychological theories are essentially products or extensions of existing language conventions. These conventions determine when certain statements should be used and not used and, because knowledge is expressed

in the written or spoken word, what is known is determined by these conventions (1987c, p. 120, p. 122; 1988a, pp. 37–45).

(6) Therefore, these language conventions form a linguistic forestructure for the subsequent generation of "scientific facts" (1988a, p. 36; 1994b, p. 415).

(7) The significance of facts or anomalies is largely achieved because of the form of intelligibility by which they are constituted (1994c, p. 14).

(8) To make clear the linguistic conventions is to foreshadow virtually all that "can be known" (1987c, p. 121).

First, a small but important digression of which more will be said in later sections (5.6.2; 7.3). Claims 5–8 illustrate Gergen's inconsistent use of inverted commas. On some occasions, such as in claims 6 and 8, Gergen removes the implication of success (cognitive achievement) by putting inverted commas around words such as "facts" and "knowledge". On other occasions, such as in claims 5 and 7, the implication of success is left in. This inconsistency leaves the reader with no clear indication of what he means by these words. Potter is similarly lax. He seems to think the distinction between reality and "reality" unimportant (see Potter, 1996b, p. 98).[23] In this respect, these constructionists continue the tradition of Popper, Lakatos, Kuhn and Feyerabend (see Stove, 1998).

I noted at the beginning of this chapter that neither Potter nor Shotter has expounded on these *a priori* elements of conventionalism. Shotter (1993a) does, however, make some claims which are allied to propositions 5–8 though, unlike Gergen, he sometimes admits a notion of falsity. A function of descriptions, Shotter suggests, is that they "lend" structure to the vague events which occur in this open and unstable world (p. 181). He may consider the following to be an example. Take the descriptions offered by those realists "ensnared in Cartesian language" (see Shotter & Lannamann, 2002). These realists speak frequently of an independence between subject and object. Their language holds them captive to the idea that the subject-object relation is real and, in this respect, "lends structure" to the hazy, formless world in which we live. In Shotter's opinion, there can be no metalanguage which we "stand outside" and use at will, but our forms of communication do have a shaping function. Moreover, the "lent" structure is grounded in the background circumstances of our lives. So, like the logical positivists' concept of *a priori*, the "lent" structures are not "independent of experience", nor are they "for all time", but they are "before knowledge".

Also relevant is Potter's (1996b) belief that facts are constructed (p. 3); that scientific practice involves making facts, not discovering them (p. 30) and that descriptions are not determined by events (p. 6). Realists, idealists, relativists, etc., are all judged by Potter to employ different rhetorical constructions in an attempt to make their version of reality appear the more credible, but descriptions, he says, do not imply truth (p. 8). Potter makes no mention of "language conventions", "linguistic forestructures" or "lent structures", but he endorses the constructionist view that knowledge is made, not discovered. And, when reading Potter, one is again reminded of Carnap's (1963) view that employing different forms of discourse do not commit the speaker to anything ontologically.

Now, to return to the less rudimentary claims of Gergen. Propositions 1–4, exhibit the features of conventionalism noted in Hilbert's and Poincaré's treatments of the axioms of geometry. Whilest Gergen's system is socio-linguistic, not geometric, it is, he says, equivalent to mathematics (claim 3) in that it is an analytic and autonomous system.

There are also similarities between Gergen's conventionalism and that of the logical positivists. First, Gergen's focus is the conventionality of language (claims 5, 6 and 8). This is consistent with the linguistic emphasis which characterises logical positivism's conventionalism and, in particular, it is consistent with Carnap's notion of linguistic frameworks.[24] The conventionalism of the logical positivists and of social constructionism is without the mentalistic emphasis which characterised 19th century philosophy.[25] It is also notable that, like Schlick, Gergen does not clearly distinguish between conventions and their products (5.3.1). Claims (5) and (6) assume the distinction between conventions and the products of such conventions (e.g., linguistic forestructures, theories, knowledge-claims). Nonetheless, the latter are themselves given conventional status. Claim (8) implies this and, elsewhere, Gergen (1994c, p. 53) intimates that if we analyse the products of these conventions, their conventional nature will be uncovered.

Secondly, both versions of conventionalism contain the claim that theoretical propositions are characterised by autonomy and analyticity. In particular, Gergen's view of theoretical propositions as non-empirical, "semantically free-floating" (Gergen, 1987c, p. 118; 1989c, p. 71; 2001a, p. 421) and analytical, echoes Schlick's metaphor that a system of truths generated from implicit definitions is one that "floats freely". The difference between social constructionism and logical positivism in this case is one of *quantity*. The former takes autonomy and analyticity to characterise *all* theoretical propositions, the latter takes them to characterise only *some*. The analytic-synthetic distinction is no part of Gergen's metatheory, nor is the related logical positivist dictum that meaning is given to sentences in one of two possible ways, either through implicit or through ostensive (concrete) definition.

Thirdly, Gergen's account is consistent with the logical positivists' notion of *a priori*. Although Gergen takes the condition of internal reference to be characteristic of linguistic frameworks, they are also, in his opinion, contingent upon social contexts which involve relational facts about communities of psychologists (1.7.3). This seems to reveal some confusion concerning the ontological status of these frameworks; *a priori* elements are said to coexist with socio-linguistic states of affairs. Recall again, though, Reichenbach's appropriation of Kant's second meaning of *a priori* (5.3.2), "before knowledge," but not "for all time" and not "independent of experience". Gergen's concept of a linguistic framework matches Reichenbach's appropriation. The framework is not independent either of the social milieux experienced by the psychology community or of other states of affairs (i.e., it is not "independent of experience"), but it is logically prior to any knowledge-claims which are made (i.e., it is "before knowledge"). This does not render this notion of *a priori* feasible, but it does provide a superficial remedy for an apparent contradiction.

Fourthly, the view of Reichenbach and Carnap that a system of conventions enables the ordering or conceptualisation of the object of knowledge is the very function that Shotter (1993a) contemplates when speaking of descriptions which "lend structure" to the world, and that Gergen has in mind in claims 5–8. This is affirmed in the following passage from *Realities and Relationships* where Gergen suggests that:

> ...we gain substantially if we consider the world-structuring process as linguistic rather than cognitive. It is through an a priori [sic] commitment to particular forms of language (genres, conventions, speech codes, and so on) that we place boundaries around what we take to be "the real" (1994c, p. 37).

Fifthly, Shotter's view that vague events are "lent" their structure by language and Gergen's "world-structuring process" are both akin to the logical positivists' conceptualisation of a system's *application to reality*. Gergen (1994c), too, speaks of the application of the framework to "...events outside the nucleus" (p. 8). Although he would reject Reichenbach's notion that, upon application, the propositions become empirical, there is, nevertheless, agreement that the conventional system or framework is applied to reality, in the sense of being "put onto" reality (p. 8). Further, Gergen believes that "...the nucleus does not require these linkages [to reality] in order to be understood or compelling" (p. 8). This, of course, epitomises the views of his conventionalist predecessors that the meaning of the system is determined from within and, hence, is intelligible without any reference to states of affairs.

Sixthly, in Gergen's account of knowledge, semantics and epistemology are logically prior to ontology (claims 5–8). This is also an assumption of logical positivism.[26] A statement by Reichenbach (1954) is particularly striking in this respect: "We must not say 'the two rods located at different places are equal', but we must say that we call these two rods equal" (p. 132). Reichenbach sees this as the solution to the "problem" of indeterminacy, in which the ability to discover what is the case is impeded by the effects of the observational process on the object of study (pp. 131–132). The solution, he thinks, is to regard an ontological matter as purely semantic. The received view, that positivism ignores indeterminacy (4.3), is not only false, it obscures the fact that logical positivism's and social constructionism's attempts to deal with this so-called "problem" are similar. Both insist on replacing the study of situations with the study of language. Of course, the use of language *is* situational and studying language-use *is* a legitimate intellectual pursuit, but the thinking seems to be that because we cannot ascertain *with certainty* answers to ontological questions, let's hedge our bets and attend instead to something "closer to home".[27]

5.5.2. LOGIC AS CONVENTIONS OF DISCOURSE

Other similarities between Gergen's metatheory and logical positivism can be found in Gergen's treatment of logic. About this subject, he says:

> The criteria of logic, comprehensiveness, and the like do not render science rational; such criteria are essentially moves within various domains of discourse—rhetorical devices for achieving discursive efficacy. This does not mean that anything goes— at least in practice. Conventions of discourse are often sedimented, restrictive, and wedded to social practice in compelling ways (1994c, p. 14).

Something similar characterises Potter's thinking. When issues of logic are spoken about by realist theoretical psychologists, they are, he says, merely engaging in rhetorical strategies. These lend an air of authority to their claims and make logical issues *appear* asocial (e.g., Edwards et al., 1995; Potter, 1992).

There is, firstly, an obvious and important difference between social constructionism and logical positivism on the matter of logic. Logical positivism takes symbolic logic to be essential for the precise formulation of concepts, propositions and rules concerning their use and, following Russell, it is said to *replace* traditional or classical logic. Russell's (1946/1984) denunciation of the latter cannot be passed over:

> I conclude that the Aristotelian doctrines with which we have been concerned in this chapter are wholly false, with the exception of the formal theory of the syllogism, which is unimportant. Any person in the present day who wishes to learn logic will be wasting his time if he reads Aristotle or any of his disciples (p. 212).

Social constructionism goes further and accords logic no substantive role at all. Logic is reducible to language. It is nothing more than an elaborate language-game involving "warranting conventions" which function as rhetorical devices for argumentative strategies (Gergen, 1994c, p. 14).

This difference signals an important similarity, however, and one which follows from logical positivism's and social constructionism's indifference to ontology generally. Neither accepts the traditional view of logic. Specifically, neither accepts that the subject matter of logic is not language (discourse, semantics or grammar) or rules determining the use of symbols, but is instead the *general* features of states of affairs and the relations of entailment between those states of affairs which language conveys (e.g., Anderson, 1962; Cohen & Nagel, 1934/1963, pp. iii–vi; Cohen, 1946, pp. vii–ix). Gergen would endorse Schlick's view that the propositions of logic make no assertions about what exists or occurs and, thus, are uninformative. He would also accept: (i) that Carnap's constructed language shows logical concepts, such as "consequence", to be defined solely in terms of "language form", and (ii) an implication of this—that the logical concept "consequence" does not denote an objective relation of entailment between real situations.

A further point of resemblance is evident in Gergen's attempt to ground the "warranting conventions" of logic in pragmatic criteria. Like the conventionalists before him, he avoids complete arbitrariness, maintaining that the conventions emerge "for good reason". In Gergen's metatheory these "good reasons" have to do with the interests of the scientific community, in that the forms of discourse are said to service its localised ends (e.g., Gergen, 1990a, p. 294).

Associated with these points of agreement is the similarity between Gergen's treatment of negation and that of Schlick. This highlights their subordination of logic to language. In Gergen's (1994c) alternative to Kuhn's account of paradigm change, he argues that the dominant discourse sets in motion and exacerbates "discourses of negation" (pp. 10–11). Conventions (of negation) serve the intentions of those wanting to displace the dominant discourse. Now, although Gergen's account of conventions is, in this respect, different from Schlick's, there are similarities in that both treat negation as *nothing more* than (i) a linguistic act which occurs as a counter to what is asserted to be the case, and (ii) a convention or rule to be used to determine, either the use of the word "not" (Schlick), or when certain statements should be used (Gergen). Gergen maintains that negation is a convention operating "within discourse", and like Schlick, he does not treat it ontologically; he does not accept negative facts. That is, neither treats negation as some state of affairs (of the form, "a situation s is not of the type in which x is y") being conveyed by language.

5.6. THE INCOHERENCE OF CONVENTIONALISM

There can be no objection to a psychological metatheory retaining the ideas of its intellectual forebears when those ideas are clear and cogent, but "framework" or "system" conventionalism, which has been part of much of 20th century philosophy of science, cannot be maintained consistently. With respect to the logical positivists' conventionalism, some critique has been provided (e.g., Baker, 1988; Coffa, 1991; Friedman, 1999; Passmore, 1943).[28] The over-riding judgement is that the distinctions upon which their conventionalism rests (implicit vs concrete, necessary vs empirical, pure vs applied) are not made good. Social constructionists, of course, repudiate such distinctions and assume constructionism to have successfully avoided them. In the remainder of this chapter I shall question this and provide objections to the "framework" conventionalism in Gergen's metatheory.

First, the fundamental error of conventionalism. It has to do with the condition of *internal* reference, and this was addressed in 3.2. The notion that the meanings of terms and relations are given solely by a closed, autonomous system or framework cannot be maintained consistently. It requires making a distinction between the framework and an external domain of things, and this requires getting outside the framework and seeing it in relation to something else. But, given internal reference, such a distinction cannot be made. It is not possible to "break out" of the system, whether that system be narrowly geometry or, more broadly, the discursive practices of communities of psychologists. *How to* "break out" is not a genuine problem for the thoroughgoing conventionalist—there is *no way* to get out.

5.6.1. THE CONDITION OF CONSISTENCY RESTS ON AN EMPIRICAL CLAIM

To recapitulate: a defining characteristic of conventionalism is that the meanings of terms and relations in a system derive from within that system; this is the condition of internal reference. This condition is as evident in Gergen's account as it is in the conventionalism of Hilbert's geometrical axioms. In each case the thesis is that definitions, systems, or frameworks are intelligible *without recourse to worldly things*.

For this condition to be satisfied, it is necessary that the condition of consistency also be satisfied. Networks of axioms, implicit definitions, postulations and linguistic frameworks must not contain a contradiction. If there were an internal contradiction, the claim that such frameworks are conventions *would be refuted* because the intelligibility of the system or framework could not obtain. Without recourse to worldly things, the internal consistency of the system is required to render its terms and relations intelligible.

It might be objected that this presupposes a notion of consistency which the conventionalist does not accept. There is, however, no evidence to suggest that the conventionalist means by "consistency" something other than what is ordinarily meant—the absence of both asserting that some state of affairs does obtain and that it does not. They do not employ any other notion of consistency. For instance, Schlick (1925/1974) means by "consistent", "free of contradiction" (p. 356), and Gergen (1994c) is no different:

> In the present analysis, I have paid my dues to traditional analytic demands, striving to achieve an internal coherence in the case of constructionism . . . (p. 69).

These examples are not exhaustive but, in the absence of any conventionalist alternative, it is reasonable to suppose that they rely on a system-independent sense of "consistency". What is meant by "consistency" applies universally, and what is meant involves recourse to the factual—the fact that the meanings of terms and relations are not self-contradictory.

To return to the main point: if there is no recourse to worldly things, the absence of contradiction is essential for the intelligibility of the framework; if a framework is intelligible yet self-contradictory in any respect, then the meanings of its terms and relations cannot be given from within that framework. So, to avoid self-refutation, a conventional system or framework must not contain a contradiction. This, for the conventionalist, is a necessary truth. However, according to logical positivist strictures, necessary truths have the status of conventions. (Schlick's dismissal of Poincaré's objection that conventionalism applies to logic and mathematics involved just this point). And Gergen, to be consistent, must say that the statement "All linguistic frameworks are internally consistent" is itself a convention, not an empirical hypothesis. So, given that logical positivism and social constructionism ground conventions in pragmatism and self-interest, it would follow that the statement "It is a convention that conventions be consistent" would itself have to be underpinned by these considerations.

Such a conclusion is hardly satisfactory, and this points to the implausibility of internal reference as the sole provider of meaning. Firstly, the statement "It is a convention that conventions be consistent" is empirical because, in order to decide its status, we would have to conduct an empirical investigation of linguistic usage. Secondly, the conventionalist is obliged to explain why an alternative "convention" has not been chosen, and the only facts that such an explanation is entitled to draw on are certain pragmatic criteria, not the facts of any other aspect of the world. No such explanation has been forthcoming.

5.6.2. CONVENTIONALISM AND THE FALLACY OF CONSTITUTIVE RELATIONS

Some framework conventionalists conceptualise knowledge as something constituted by an *a priori* system. Gergen, for example, maintains that different systems result in different facts (e.g., claims 5–7). Here there is a commitment to a *constitutive notion of relations*. What is known is said to be constituted by the deployment of an *a priori* system in the fact-making process. At this point, a digression from the topic of conventionalism is needed, to make clear what I mean by "knowledge" and "fact", and then to explain this notion of constitution.

The word "knowledge" requires the general notion of "what is" or "object" because, in knowing, *something is known*. That "something" is an event, a fact, an occurrence, a situation, or a state of affairs. Knowing also involves one or more knowers: a large community, a small group, or an individual. Knowing is, then, a relational situation; *a* knowing *x* is itself an occurrence, a fact. Regardless of the complexity of either term (the knower and the something known), or of the interconnections between them, if there *is* a relation, *there are these two terms and not one*.[29] Whatever is known, some fact, is not constituted in the process of knowing; the fact has an independent existence. This is why "knowledge" is a success-word (5.5.1). Knowledge implies discovery; it is a cognitive achievement. Critics of this view may wish to consider whether this normative characterisation of knowledge precludes a descriptive theory which accounts for this normativity.

On the subject of facts, they are (as I have just implied) states of affairs (e.g., Armstrong, 1997). They are not lexical items; they are not statements, descriptions, or assertions (knowledge-claims). Not all statements state facts, but to state a fact is to state what is the case. My stating a fact, in a particular time and place, is itself a fact, but it is not the fact referred to in the act of stating truly. A fact is not constituted by being truly stated, nor is it constituted in intersubjective agreement. Facts don't change when theories change; facts sometimes contradict theories. Facts are independent existences, sometimes known and sometimes described by language-users, but there are many facts of which we are ignorant. The activities of scientists can result in the discovery of a fact but these activities are not *part of* the fact. It is a point of logic that if *x* results in *y*, *x* cannot be part of *y*.

Of course, people can use these two words ("knowledge" and "facts") to mean what they please, provided that they make clear what they *do* mean, otherwise usages which differ from the above are simply *a misuse of language*. Such misuse is now common, particularly among constructionists, who would have no truck with the content of my previous two paragraphs. They would also make the *ad hominem* claim that the manner in which I have set them down is dogmatic and authoritarian (e.g., Edwards et al., 1995; Gergen, 2001a; Raskin & Neimeyer, 2003; Shotter, 1998a).

However, usages which differ from those above presume that it is a mistake to draw the boundaries in the way I have. The question is: what happens when the boundaries are drawn differently? The latter occurs, for instance, when Hacking uses the word "knowledge", without inverted commas, when referring to a body of assertions (e.g., 1999, p. 170), when Danziger does likewise (e.g., 1990, Ch. 1), and when Liebrucks (2001), again without inverted commas, speaks of knowledge as that which is produced (e.g., p. 372).[30] The consequence of drawing the boundaries in this way is that what is captured by the ordinary meaning of the word "knowledge" (and by standard philosophical analyses of the concept of knowledge) is ignored; that is, that knowledge excludes ignorance, error, and mere opinion (e.g., Friedman, 1998; Kvanvig, 2003; Williams, 2001). It involves *discovery*, not *production*. Similarly, with the word "fact".

Now if constructionists (or others) are of the opinion that we cannot sometimes discover what is the case, I have two suggestions: (i) they find two words other than "knowledge" and "fact" to refer to whatever is, on their view, socially produced, and (ii) they apply their opinion consistently and acknowledge that in their own research into the social factors affecting the research process, *they* are not sometimes discovering what is the case, and that we are none the wiser about these factors than we were 2,500 years ago!

Conceivably, one reason for the practice of using the word "knowledge" in place of "knowledge-claim" or "assertion" is that we do not always know whether our assertion *is* true, for instance, we can know some situation without knowing that we know it.[31] This, of course, may well be the case. But that is an epistemic point which makes no difference to the ontological point that *if* you know something, you know *what is the case*. Something has been discovered, or grasped, or perceived. It has not been produced. The great problem with using "knowledge" in place of "assertion" is that the uncontroversial claim that our *assertions* are constructed or produced quickly slides into the nonsensical claim that *knowledge* is constructed or produced. I repeat my earlier point: to claim that knowledge is constructed involves a misuse of language.

Now to the notion of constitution. The constitutive notion denies independence to what is known. This is the *sine qua non* of idealism, whereas the notion of independence is the *sine qua non* of realist philosophy. To say (as realists do) that objects, attributes, or situations exist or occur independently of mind, language, or the imposition of concepts, is to say that the former are not constituted by the latter.

Whether some relations are constitutive, or none, is controversial (even amongst realists). The position I take here is that a relation which connects two entities is not intrinsic to either (see also Mackie, 1967, p. 178). This is not at all to dismiss the concept of construction. In the constructionist literature, the word "constitution" is used ambiguously—either to mean "the making of", or to mean "the components of". The first meaning is synonymous with "construction" and implies a causal process. The second meaning involves an identity thesis, in the sense of "being composed of" (Koslicki, 2004). When I use the term "constitution", I do not mean "construction". Institutions are produced through the interplay of individuals and social groups. In this case, a segment of reality is constructed. Similarly, the practical interventions of psychologists in the research process may affect research outcomes, but do not constitute them.

Why is a constitutive notion of relations erroneous? If we consider a situation of the form *aRb*, where *a* is an entity that is in relation *R* to the entity *b*, the error can occur in claiming that either:

   (i)   *aR* constitutes *b*, or
   (ii) *Rb* constitutes *a*, or
   (iii) *R* constitutes *a* and *b*.

To claim that *aR* constitutes *b*, is to claim that *b* is a component of *aR*, that *b* is a part of, identical with, or necessarily related to *aR*. In (i) and (ii) the error consists in an entity being confused with the features or qualities of another entity and relation.[32] In (iii) the error consists in a relation being confused with the features and qualities of the two entities that are related. These are errors because there is a failure to recognise that relations are not intrinsic to the items which stand in those relations; the relation *R* holds between *different real things* (*a* and *b*). Importantly, recognising this:

> ... implies that each of these [*a* and *b*] is an independent thing, or thing with an existence and character of its own, and that it cannot be properly described in terms of the other thing or of the relation between them (Anderson, 1930/1962, p. 42).

The constitutive notion is, then, fallacious. It denies a difference between things, or between relations and things, through the constitution of one thing or relation by another (Anderson, 1930/1962; Holt et al., 1912; Perry, 1925).

Consider, for example, the (relational) situation of a book being on a desk: something's being a book is not constituted by its being on a desk; something's being a desk is not constituted by its having a book on it, and neither book nor desk is constituted by the relation of being upon. Books and desks exist independently of one another, and sometimes come to stand in this relation.

Less obviously the same error appears in all representational theories of cognition (Anderson, 1930/1962; Maze, 1991; Michell, 1988). According to the representationalist, external events are known only via internal (to the mind or brain) representations of those events. But, in "explaining" knowledge, the representationalist *presumes* the knowledge which he or she attempts to explain. Knowledge of a thing or situation (*s*) is required in order to say that the cognitive representation (*m*) represents (is in relation *R* to) *s*. A "solution" to this problem is to say that the representation's reference to *s* is contained within the representation itself. Expressed symbolically, *m* is said to constitute *Rs*. This is *not* a solution. The relation of representing (*R*) is mistakenly treated as though it were part of the character of *m* itself. Again, to suggest that some thing can have the relations it stands in *inside itself* conflates relations with properties or qualities.

The rejection of a constitutive notion of relations entails a rejection of *internal* relations and, for this reason, might be considered controversial. An internal relation is said to be one where the existence of the relation is entailed by the existence of the terms (Armstrong, 1997, p. 87). For instance, it could be said that the relation of representing (*R*) is entailed by the existence of the cognitive representation (*m*). A more common example is the relation of resemblance ("identity in certain respects"). Monozygotic twins are said to stand in an internal relation of resemblance because this relation is entailed or necessitated by the qualities of each twin.

The concept of internal relations may be accepted by some because they accept a notion of "necessary truth". Thus, in the twins example, the relation of resemblance might be said to be necessary (and so "internal") just because of what is meant by "monozygotic twins". However, I do not recognise "necessary truth" as something other than "contingent truth".[33] If no possible circumstance could make a proposition false, then this is so not because there is something over and above certain facts. In this sense, then, every proposition has "contingency". Furthermore, relations such as resemblance or entailment are real.[34] "Entailment", for example, is an ontological relation between certain situations. Similarly, the relation of resemblance between entities is real and, therefore, neither an abstraction nor something inherent in the terms which stand in that relation.

Another argument offered in support of constitutive (internal) relations runs as follows: take the relation of fatherhood (R) where a is the father of b. Only one man can father a particular child. So the relation "father of" is said to be a constitutive relation because the relation R and b uniquely determine a. Rb is said to constitute a in that identifying the relation and the particular b "... says something about a.... One and only one man can be a, once the relation R is defined and a b specified" (van Sant, 1959, p. 28). The relation "author of" is thought to be constitutive for the same reason. Again, a notion of necessity is contained within these examples: given Rb, necessarily a.

There are two points to make about this. First, it is true that once the relation "father of" and the particular child have been identified, the particular man can be determined. But this is an epistemic point—it refers to what *we can determine*. The ontological point is that the man, as a man, is not constituted by being the father of a boy. Using ordinary language, we might *say* that he is constituted *as a father*, but this is not true. In this case, our language-use is misleading because it ignores the logic of the situation. "Father of" is a relation, not a property or quality. As a relation, it holds between two independent entities, each consisting of various properties and relations. The relation "father of" does not belong to either of them.[35] The second point is that neither the relation "father of", nor the relation "author of", are relations of necessity. They are complex causal relationships, apposite to the concept of construction, not constitution.

To expand on this last point: if, as I maintain, relations have only an external or extrinsic character, they do not "... penetrate, possess, and compromise their terms..." (Perry, 1925, p. 319). This does not mean that relational situations cannot make a difference to their entities. It does not mean, for example, that the situation of a book being on a desk may not, over a period of time, be a partial cause of the pages of that book turning yellow. It simply means that relations are not internal to the entities or situations that stand in *those* relations; the relation of *being upon* is not internal to either the book or the desk. To take another example: research suggests that the relational situation of patient and psychotherapist can affect the patient's brain chemistry, in a manner similar to certain drug treatments. The claim is that the relational situation of patient-therapist interactions does, over a period of time, make a difference to certain aspects of the patient. Most, if not all, constructionists would construe this as a "constituted relation". But, if the research-claim is true, a complex *causal* process involving spatio-temporal sequences is at work. This does *not* mean that the relation is part of (constituted by) either entity. Nor does it mean that certain relations cannot be distinguished from the intrinsic features of the things that stand in those relations and must, therefore, be internal.

To conclude this digression from conventionalism: the fallacy of constitutive (internal) relations emphasises the fact that a relation is not an entity. An entity cannot be constituted by the relations it stands in. (Although the entity is composed of qualities and relations, these relations are not the relations the entity stands in). And, whenever there is a relation, there are at least *two* entities that are related. There cannot be a relation and only one entity.

This fallacy is committed in each of Reichenbach's, Carnap's and Gergen's accounts of science. In Reichenbach's (1920/1965) conventionalism, an object of knowledge is taken to consist in the physical property and the "chosen system of reference" (p. 52 & ff.). That is to say, the object (*b*) is partially constituted by the *a priori* framework (*aR*). The same fallacy appears in Carnap's assertion that the construction and cognition of the object are logically dependent on *a priori* rules.[36] Also, despite the realist tenor of sections of Kuhn's account of science, it is similarly flawed. The work of "normal" science is, in Kuhn's (1970) words, "...to beat nature into line..." (p. 135). And Gergen's account is no different. In claims 7–8, facts (*b*) are supposedly constituted by qualities of the linguistic framework or forestructure (*aR*).

To expand on this: It follows from Gergen's (1994c) characterisation of scientific communities that a community of psychologists is defined by its shared "discursive practices" (e.g., p. 8), and that these practices reflect the interests of the community and the social milieux within which it operates (e.g., p. 53). Claims 5–6 propose that knowledge is the product of these factors. The linguistic framework and interests of the community are said to *construct*, or *bring into being*, what is known. To argue that this involves the fallacy of constitutive (internal) relations is to set aside my earlier claim that constructionists, in their misuse of language, do not mean by the expressions "what is known" and "scientific facts" something ontological, i.e., some aspect of reality. They mean something that is socio-linguistic and conventional. However, the fallacy of constitutive relations comes into play in claims 7–8 because the items constructed are said by Gergen not to have features distinct from the discursive practices, interests and social milieux of the psychology community.

There is another important distinction to be made. Gergen is not simply suggesting that the interests and socio-linguistic forces of a group determine (in the causal sense) what is investigated and what is not. He is not simply claiming (what is surely a fact) that research is not value- or interest-free; that research is a social occurrence subject to cultural, historical, social, and linguistic conditions. If he were, psychology's status as an objective social science would not be at stake. All that Gergen would have proposed is the hypothesis that such conditions are practical (not "in principle") obstacles to objectivity (to finding out what is the case) in that they promote error. This would be to raise an interesting causal question which has nothing to do with the fallacy of constitutive relations. In claims 7–8, Gergen is not doing this. He is denying *logical* independence because all that can be known does not have features separate or distinct from the socio-linguistic conventions.

Causal or material dependence actually presupposes logical *in*dependence. *A* and *b* may, for example, stand in some causal relation—they may causally interact with and affect each other. But, that this can happen, is because of their logical independence. If a causal relation exists between *a* and *b*, whereby one (say *a*) affects the other (*b*), then *b* is logically independent of *a*; *b* is not part of, or contained in, or essentially related to, *a*.

As an example of this distinction (between causal and logical dependence), take the situation where a builder (*a*) constructs a house (*b*). The house is materially dependent for its existence upon the builder (causal determination), but this does not, of course, entail that the house is part of, or is contained in, the builder, or that the house has no features distinct from the builder, or that it can only be described in terms of the features of the builder or of the relation between house and builder. There may be material dependence, but builder and house are logically independent.

Analogously, knowledge-claims are materially dependent for their existence or occurrence upon scientific-communities, and upon the socio-linguistic conventions deployed by those communities. But Gergen's claim is much stronger than material dependence. It is logical dependence which Gergen (1994c) subscribes to when, together with claims 7–8, he says that:

> ... because disquisitions on the nature of things are framed in language, there is no grounding of science or any knowledge-generating enterprise in other than communities of interlocutors (p. ix);

that:

> ... propositional networks are essential constituents of more inclusive forms of action ... (p. 7);

and that:

> To appraise existing forms of discourse is to evaluate patterns of cultural life ... (p. 53).

Knowledge-claims (*b*) can only be described in terms of the discursive practices or conventional framework and the interests and social milieux that characterise the scientific community involved in giving an account of the world (*aR*). That is to say, in Gergen's metatheory, *b* is part of, or essentially related to, *aR*. What the knowledge-claims might be *about* is ignored.

In short, a constitutive notion is sometimes a feature of logical positivism and frequently a feature of social constructionism. The latter fact is confirmed in Danziger's (1997) elucidation of the constructionist critique of expert authority:

> It [language] does not *represent* a previously existing objective world but *constitutes* such a world. Any known world is therefore always a co-constituted world, and the manner of its constitution depends on discursive relationships (p. 406).

I have belaboured these matters concerning the logic of a constitutive theory of relations because constructionists, despite their recognition of the importance of relations in psycho-social life, have ignored the logic of this subject. And, as I suggested earlier, they have also, time and again, been careless in their choice of words and/or negligent in their use of inverted commas. Here are a few more examples from the constructionist literature which reflect these defects:

> In Collins' example it is language itself that provides the tools for constructing a reality beyond words (Edwards et al., 1995, p. 31).

> In effect, [Foucault's metaphor 'regimes of truth'] has brought a new object into the world: a regime of truth. That is, his discourse has produced a new thing, and this thing can be described and discussed (Potter, 1996b, p. 86).

> ... descriptions and accounts *construct the world*, or at least versions of the world (Potter, 1996b, p. 98).

> It [the world] is *constituted* in one way or another as people talk it, write it and argue it (Potter, 1996b, p. 98).

> ... constructionists see objects as produced by representations (Potter, 1996b, p. 220).

> Without the content [of the social representation of madness] the phenomenon would be lost (Potter & Wetherell, 1998, p. 140).

> Social representations construct the nature and value of those [social] worlds (Potter & Edwards, 1999, p. 449).

> ... binary oppositions obscure the mutually constituted relationship of interdependence between the terms (Wetherell & Potter, 1998, p. 362).

> ... if we accept an epistemology/ontology dichotomy, as realism does, we separate the world from our knowledge of it and our talk about it (Burr, 1998, p. 24).

> [Classically minded critics] all simply take it for granted that the "reality" we must investigate in our scientific moments is already a reality existing independently of us (Shotter, 1994, p. 158).

These last two comments suggest that realists take the world to be "over there" whilst they (as knowers) are "here" with a perspective-less view of it all. This, of course, is not the case; the realist notion of independence entails nothing of the sort. More worthy of consideration is the fact that the last quotation, from Shotter, immediately follows his claim that the critics ignore the "... sociohistorical production of what came to be known as 'scientific facts'" (p. 158). Shotter decries our neglect of contexts of production and, in so doing, appears to assert a *causal* dependence thesis. He appears to be making the, quite reasonable, claims that social milieux determines what is investigated, and that realists have ignored this aspect of the scientific process. But this causal dependence thesis, as I said, is immediately followed by the quotation above which, though ambiguous, suggests *logical* dependence—reality (*b*) is constituted by us in the process of investigating (*aR*).

Another example of logical dependence appears in Shotter's reference to the central concepts of the social sciences. He claims that "... their nature is such that disputes about their nature... are an intrinsic part of what they are concepts of..." (1994, p. 150). This may be a reference to the truisms that the central concepts of the social sciences are concepts of social process, and that disputation is itself a social process. But *disputes about* such concepts are not *constituents* of the concepts of social process. The former are not internal to the latter.

In a later paper, Shotter (1998a) maintains that social constructionism involves "... a turn away from rooting claims to knowledge in abstract theory toward basing them in our social practices" (p. 247). Here, like Gergen, he gives the impression that there is no relation between knowledge-claims and what those claims are *about*. The features of the situations talked about are irrelevant. This idea appears again in Shotter's (1998b) claim (quoting Foucault) that "... our disciplinary discourses form the objects of which they speak..." (p. 37), i.e., what the claims are *about* is constituted in discourse.

More recently still, Shotter (2003) has made explicit the idea that a participatory stance toward language entails a rejection of *external* relations. Yet this is contradicted in his proposal that we enter into dynamic, responsive relations with our surroundings and with others. The latter assumes logical independence in that if we enter into some relation with something or somebody, there must be two things and the relation between them is not internal to either.[37] Here, again, is the inescapable central feature of a realist philosophy: a non-constitutive theory of relations.

Returning to the topic of conventionalism, but staying with the theme of self-contradiction, conventionalism actually presupposes its own contradictory, i.e., it presupposes the notion of independence. This is best demonstrated, however, in the following section, where it is made plain that the constitutive notion is coupled with dualism.

5.6.3. CONVENTIONALISM INVOLVES DUALISM

Gergen's reason for the constitutive notion is the belief (held widely among constructionists) that to invoke a distinction between the knowing subject and the object of knowledge is to invoke a form of dualism (e.g., 1988a, p. 32; 1988b, p. 287; 1990c, p. 575; 1994c, p. 69, pp. 120–121; 1995b, p. 18). The constructionist "solution" is to say that what is known is constructed or constituted by scientific communities; *b* is constituted by *aR*, and the problem of dualism is supposedly overcome.

Dualism is the thesis that some things have a distinct type of existence from others, that there are two realms, two different ways of being. Yet, entities in one realm are said to "participate in", "imitate", "share in", or "interact with" entities in the other, and the consequence is that the original distinction cannot be maintained. Time and again in the history of philosophy, distinctions between kinds of entity, such as mind and body, forms and particulars, the non-empirical and the empirical, the super-natural and the natural, have been proposed. None has survived critical analysis. Quine's (1951/1990) and White's (1950/1952) appraisals of the analytic-synthetic distinction are a case in point.

Social constructionism objects specifically to a dualism between mind and world. Gergen refers to this as "... a separation of mind from world, subject from object ..." (1988b, p. 287; see also Shotter & Lannamann, 2002, p. 581). Shotter (2003) speaks of a "disembodied mind" which produces "inner representations" of the "isolated, neutral objects around us" (p. 445). Their objection is, in large part, an objection to current mainstream psychology (see, for example, Danziger, 1997; Jones, 2002).[38] The discipline is, constructionists claim, committed to a du-alistic metaphysics. Psychology is part of the "tradition of Western individualism" and "individual knowledge". Cognition, the emotions, rational thought, memory, intentions, etc., are presumed to be internal (psychological) processes, and not, as constructionists believe, derivatives of social interchange or "historically contin-gent constructions of culture" (Gergen, 1994c, p. 70). In their opinion, "... there is no mental world to be considered (Gergen, 1988a, p. 32). So, psychology's understanding of "subject" in the subject-object relation is "deeply problematic" (Gergen, 1995b, p. 17). There is, according to constructionists, no individual know-ing subject.

Let us, for the moment, grant Gergen and others this much and replace the in-dividual subject with a social group (e.g., a particular scientific community). Still, they will not grant the *logical* independence of a social group and world or object. Their metatheory is not merely a macroscopic "reduction" of psychology to the social; an attempt to "socialise" psychology. Recall Gergen's claim that "... the very idea of an 'independent world' may itself be an outgrowth of rhetorical de-mands" (1991a, p. 23). The function of such demands, he claims, is to maintain the illusion of objectivity; to imply distance between the object and the observer (1994c, pp. 173–175). Although Gergen does not deny reality, reference to the world is, for him, fatuous. In short, he believes that the Western academic concep-tualisation of both terms in the subject-object relation is problematic.

Social constructionism is, in large part, an attempt to collapse the subject-object distinction, because that distinction is said to involve dualism. The alter-native to this "dualism", they say, is one where knowledge-claims are *essentially* related to the discursive practices, linguistic forestructures, etc., of the social group in some kind of closed system of language, one in which the "referents" are not grounded in reality. The result is, however, a constitutive notion of relations (5.6.2).

Before I develop the realist response to this line of thought, I should comment briefly on Heidegger's rebuttal of the subject-object distinction. I am far from appreciating the complexities of *Sein und Zeit* (1927), but a crucial difference between Heidegger and realism is that the former maintains that "... language is the house of Being" (Kusch, 1989, p. 218); language *is* the universal medium. Realism, on the other hand, takes the universal medium to be space-time, i.e., temporal existence or occurrence. To maintain that *language* is the house of being denies the "aboutness" which characterises language (Collier, 1998). (This was the subject matter of Ch. 3.) A further response to Heidegger's objection to the distinction is that there is nothing in realist philosophy which entails a transcendent object. The "object" is simply a complex situation or state of affairs which exists on the same level of reality as everything else that exists or occurs. We cannot step outside of this, we have no God's eye view. Moreover, as I argued in 5.6.2, realism rejects the notion of disinterested inquiry. My point is that Heidegger's target, the subject-object distinction, is one at odds with realism's conceptualisation of same.

Now social constructionists are wrong in their belief that this distinction involves dualism. It does not. It involves two independent entities which exist on the same level of reality as everything else, and which may or may not be related. Constructionists are also wrong in maintaining that the distinction involves the existence of a Godly, perspective-less knower. It does not. As I intimated above, there can be no such thing. We (as knowers) cannot transcend *all* perspectives; we are all situated beings, as are the things known. But this does not entail that we cannot shift from one perspective to another. Nor does it entail that we cannot see and describe things as they are. The fact that we are frequently wrong about things does not entail that we can never be right. To repeat my earlier point: what is meant by the *logical* independence of the subject or knower and object or thing known is that each is distinct from the other. Each is situated and each can be described without reference to whatever it may be related to. Constructionists (correctly) wish to avoid dualism, but because they fail to distinguish between dependency relations which do not preclude logical independence and those which do, they attempt, mistakenly, to collapse the subject-object distinction.

In fact, Gergen re-establishes the dualism of the logical positivists, although this is not, of course, immediately obvious. The *raison d'être* of social constructionism is, after all, to avoid such conceptual mistakes.[39] Nevertheless, the dualism reappears under a slightly different guise. It cannot be avoided when there is a commitment to conventionalism. Consider, first, the dualism of the logical positivists.

The division of propositions into those which are analytic and *a priori* (nonempirical), and those which are synthetic and empirical, was a hallmark of logical positivism. This division Gergen rejects. That the division cannot be consistently maintained is implied in 5.6.1, but it is manifest in Poincaré's and Schlick's extension of conventionalism to scientific theories. Both argue for the distinction between analytic and synthetic propositions, both also assert identity between them. Poincaré (1902/1952) clearly intends that a convention or definition in disguise somehow has properties in common with an empirical proposition when he proposes that a principle can ". . . predict correctly new phenomena" (pp. 166–167), and that we are justified in constructing a convention when we are certain that no experiment will contradict it (p. 136). This, of course, raises the (unanswerable) question how a principle can predict correctly new phenomena, or be disconfirmed by experimental evidence, and yet not be empirical. The same anomaly appears in Poincaré's claim that when the convention is correctly predicting new phenomena, it is "applicable" (p. 166). The question of what Poincaré means by a convention's "applicability" is crucial. If a principle has applicability, then the state of affairs expressed in the principle obtains in at least one situation or context; this is what is *meant* by something's being applicable. In that case, such a principle has empirical content, and is true. Similarly, Schlick (1925/1974, p. 70) says that an uninterpreted system of judgements may "coincide fully", or correspond exactly, with a network of empirical judgements. In Schlick's account, this assertion of identity between the two kinds of proposition involves not just identity in form, but identity in content. This, of course, contradicts the original distinction.

Moreover, the logical positivist distinction between non-empirical and empirical propositions entails a dualistic theory of truth; the truth of a non-empirical proposition is given by convention, the truth of an empirical proposition is given by the way the world is. This, too, is not a feature of Gergen's metatheory. Gergen is more consistent than the logical positivists if only because, in his metatheory, all propositions are of one kind, viz., non-empirical, and because he is, in general, nihilistic about truth. Interestingly, though, in one of his infrequent uses of the word "true", Gergen relies on the logical positivists' notion of conventional truth. This is evident in claim 4 (5.5.1), but it is worth presenting a little more of what Gergen (1988a) has to say on this matter:

> It is my present contention that propositions relating the mental and the physical world are essentially analytic. That is they represent the extension of a system of linguistic equivalencies. Their truth value is neither derived from nor dependent upon observation. Rather it is dependent on and derived from linguistic systems of definition (p. 37).

If, as Gergen thinks, "psychological discoveries" are better called language-based "inventions" or "constructions", this suggests truths which we stipulate or determine by fiat, viz. truths by convention. Still, nihilism with regard to truth dominates Gergen's metatheory and it would be a distortion to suggest that he mirrors the logical positivists in proposing two kinds of truth.

The kind of dualism which Gergen embraces in his commitment to conventionalism involves a disjunction between language and the world.[40] There are "systems of conventions", or "linguistic forestructures", which have no semantic links to their apparent referents. They are "semantically free-floating" (5.5.1); there is no external reference. This disjunction is not at odds with Gergen's contingency thesis (that language acquires meaning through its use in socio-linguistic practices). The conventional system or forestructure is said to emerge from, or to be a product of, socio-linguistic practices while at the same time being *disconnected* from the world that it refers to.

Gergen cannot avoid inconsistency. Despite his expressed commitment to non-empirical propositions, his account of theoretical development rests on the unproblematic nature of *empirical* propositions. Gergen's thesis is that it is in the interests of the community of psychologists to be concerned with the process of liberation. He says that if psychology is to develop discursively, liberation from the constraints which a theoretical system imposes is essential. The "... potentially debilitating consequences of existing conventions and constraints" must be exposed (Gergen, 1994c, p. 14), and for this process of liberation to be achieved, the psychological community must, Gergen (1992b) says, engage in a process of "critical self-reflection" (p. 24). In fact, "critical self-reflection" is said to mark the paradigm shift from that of critique to a "... transformational stage in discursive development" (Gergen, 1994c, p. 48). Chapter 1 outlines some of the constraints which Gergen believes psychology to be not only hampered by, but actively perpetuating: the correspondence theory of truth, external reference and individualism. Gergen's position, then, is this: the importance of this process of liberation through self-reflection would be recognised by psychology if psychologists fully appreciated proposition A2 (1.5). If A2 were accepted, psychology would be ontologically mute; it would cease to talk about what "exists or occurs", and would start to talk about "talk about what exists or occurs". This would reveal the socio-linguistic conventions, the interests of the community, and the social milieux within which it operates, all of which combine to enable the *a priori* constitution of psychological "facts".

There is, however, a vicious infinite regress entailed in Gergen's proposal. If we cannot talk about "what exists or occurs" but can only talk about "talk about what exists or occurs" then, because talk itself is something which exists or occurs, we cannot talk about it, we can talk only about "talk about talk about what exists or occurs"... and the regress is under way. Gergen would no doubt want to halt the regress by claiming privilege for "talk about what exists or occurs". Yet, if he is to be consistent, the regress cannot be stopped. Given his wholesale rejection of objectivity, we are never in a position to utter statements that (truly) describe *any* states of affairs, irrespective of whether these statements are about psycho-social phenomena or about our discourse about psycho-social phenomena. Thus, a claim of privilege for talk about "talk about what exists or occurs" cannot be sustained.

The regress brings out the fact that the intelligibility Gergen is seeking cannot be found by moving further down the path on which he has begun. Moreover, in treating psycho-social phenomena, and talk about them, as if both were fundamentally unclear, whilst at the same time implying that talk about talk is transparent, Gergen (unwittingly) sets up his own dualism. In effect, he presupposes an *a priori-a posteriori* distinction. The process of self-reflection is said to yield *a posteriori* knowledge—empirical propositions which express the unfavourable consequences of the "received view" and the interests (and ideologies) of the psychological community. At the same time his conventionalism is such that knowledge—all knowledge—is constituted by linguistic forestructures, and is, therefore, conventional, analytic, *a priori*.

Gergen is, then, a dualist. He implies a division between types of existence. There is talk about talk about psycho-social phenomena, as an object of knowledge, and this has a different status from that of talk about psycho-social phenomena. The former (he believes) unproblematic; why else should he say that it is this to which we must turn our attention? The latter, of course, is (he believes) exceedingly troublesome.

If the regress could be stopped at the point where Gergen wishes it to be, where psychologists are merely talking about their psychological discourse, then realism (specifically a *non*-constitutive theory of relations) is presupposed in that Gergen recognises the absence of logical dependence. If we cannot study the facts that are talked about but can study the fact that they are talked about in certain ways, then talk about psychological discourse is not *essentially related* to the features of the psychological community; that such talk can be accurately described and is, therefore, uncontaminated or unmodified by the community's particular characteristics. Gergen presupposes (both in stating his own view, and in his belief in the importance of critical self-reflection) that the entity (b) to be modified by aR is initially unmodified and can be accurately described. As we saw with Shotter in the previous section, this is to allow that relations are external to their terms; that an entity is what it is, although related to other entities. Gergen admits implicitly what he denies explicitly: that there are objective facts to be discovered, and that the process of discovery will involve psychologists asserting what is the case.

The same difficulty befalls Rouse (2002). He rejects the "deeply entrenched" conception that situated communities of investigators and phenomena of interest interact, because this presupposes their independence from one another. Our conception should instead be of ". . . a complex field of material-discursive practice" (pp. 77–78). According to Rouse, we should attend to ". . . the phenomena most central to empirical work in recent science studies . . . : the embodiment of scientific understanding in laboratories and material practice, in non-verbal images and models, and in the textual materiality of language" (p. 68). But this recommendation, presupposes that the phenomena are what they are, and that investigators may come to be related to them, in that they may come to know them. Yet again, the *unavoidability* of some kind of realist philosophy is revealed, specifically a non-constitutive theory of relations. The *logic* of the knowing relation will not disappear.

5.6.4. Linguistic Conventions Are No Substitute for Logic

If logical principles expressed only linguistic conventions about the use of "not" and its cognates, the conventions could be wilfully changed, the outcome

being a different set of logical principles. Logical positivism and social constructionism fail to demonstrate the conventionality of logic. This can be seen by examining Schlick's interpretation of, and Gergen's attack on, the bivalent logical
system.

Schlick's view, as stated previously, is that the principles of excluded middle
and non-contradiction are, like arithmetical rules, tautologies and conventions
which assert nothing about reality. He would concede that a statement such as
"My friend will either meet me tonight, or not" speaks of reality, because it speaks
of my friend and a possible meeting, but he insists that it asserts nothing about my
friend and our meeting. Disregarding possible elliptical features of this statement,
and the fact that it is in the future tense, Schlick (1932/1979c) maintains that it
expresses a state of affairs about which we can be absolutely certain.[41] This is the
basis for Schlick's claim that such a statement is uninformative. Here he assumes
that what is certain has no information content.

However, a statement that expresses no specific information or no new information is not prevented from expressing a fact. The example concerning my
friend conveys no more information about the world than any other statement of
the same form (e.g., "Either it is raining here or it is not"). But this is not to say that
all statements of the same form do not convey exactly the same information *about*
the general, formal structure of the world, viz. the world cannot, at any given time,
contain a situation and its contradictory. Schlick does not demonstrate that, even
when expressed in symbolic form (either p or not-p), the principle of excluded
middle does not convey general information about everything and is, therefore,
empirical (in the sense of conveying something general about the world we experience). This may not be informative; the information is neither specific nor (to
you and me) new, but it is still a fact. If either p or not-p were simply a linguistic
convention, the world might be different from this, in which case bivalent logic
would be useless. The fact of its usefulness should have alerted Schlick and others to the possibility that a conventional account of logic was mistaken. In short,
Schlick has not ruled out the possibility that the bivalent logical system conveys
something of the nature of reality, and he holds to a narrow conception of what it
is for a proposition to be informative.

Gergen's (1994c) fruitless attempt to re-present the bivalent logical system
as conventions of negation only demonstrates the fundamental significance of
bivalence.[42] He proposes that there are three conventions of negation which function rhetorically. They serve as "...effective counters to any given nucleus of
intelligibility" (p. 11), and their employment is said to mark the critical phase of
a paradigm shift. The three conventions are not clearly identified, and his account
at this point is generally obscure (see pp. 9–11). Probably (the reader has to resort
to conjecture) the conventions are: (i) binary opposition, (ii) absence, and (iii)
contrast. Using examples provided by Gergen, binary opposition involves casting things *empiricist* in opposition to *rationalist*. Absence involves the casting of

empiricist against all things *nonempiricist*. And contrast involves the collapsing of "empiricist" and "rationalist" into *Western philosophy* and contrasting this with *Eastern philosophy*. Gergen's claim is that, because the conventions of negation can be divided into three, we are misguided in focusing on "...the single binary basis of meaning (object and opposition)..." (p. 9).

When one theoretical or philosophical system is contrasted with another, features or qualities of each are identified and differences noted. This process depends on intension, i.e., on the set of characteristics which a term connotes. In Gergen's example, it depends on the intension of "Western philosophy" and on the intension of "Eastern philosophy". From this it is clear that Gergen engages, again, in an acceptance (illicit, for him) of *objective description*. Furthermore, contrasting one thing with another involves pointing out qualities of the one which are present (or absent) in the other. There is no third possibility—a quality is present, or it is not. Thus, in his *objection* to bivalence, Gergen *presupposes* bivalence. The bivalent logical system involves the universal fact that there is no alternative to either "being" or "not-being" (Anderson, 1927/1962, p. 5). The claim that the principles of non-contradiction and excluded middle refer to everything (have universal reference) does not entail that they are not about two universal facts. The world cannot, at any given time, contain a situation and its contradictory, and it must contain one or the other.

Schlick and Gergen, then, in their arguments against what the propositions of logic are, employ the very notion they are trying to refute—the principles of identity, non-contradiction and excluded middle reflect a reality that is not of our making. If non-contradiction and excluded middle were merely conventions about our use of the word "not", if they had no empirical content, then altering them would make no difference. But altering them does make a difference. If "either p or not-p" (excluded middle) is rejected as a statement with empirical content, then from "all x is y", no other statement is ruled out from being true. In particular, the statement "some x are not y" could be true. From this, anything goes—nothing is ruled out. Describing anything has been rendered impossible. It is a necessary condition of description, and of discourse, that these logical principles are *not* conventions.

Gergen would object to an emphasis on the importance of the bivalent logical system, on the grounds that this is a typical realist exercise in "foundationalism". He rejects Margolis' (1991) arguments that the bivalent logical system should, under certain conditions, be replaced by a many-valued system, for the same reason. Despite finding the spirit of Margolis' analysis well-suited to the social constructionist position, in Gergen's (1994c) words, Margolis' account "...suffers from its attempt to replace one form of foundationalism with another (albeit a less restrictive one)" (p. 297, n. 18).

Although conversational activity is surely a "foundational principle" for social constructionism, as is the conventionality of language-use, Gergen's objections to foundationalism are unambiguous. They are also frequently *ad hominem*.[43] A foundationalist thesis is, he suggests, characterised by its defenders' reliance on perceived certainties or "first principles" such as the *cogito* (Gergen, 1994c, p. viii) or, for example, old familiar concepts, such as "power" (p. 73) and "objective truth" (p. 78). Foundationalists, Gergen maintains, attempt to establish as superior and incorrigible a particular view, and in so doing they "...restrict the range of proper tellings" (p. 79). More worthy of consideration are Gergen's assertions that foundationalist positions generally are: (i) unable to justify their own "grounding ontology" and "valuational investments" (p. 75), and (ii) unable to supply a rationale for:

(a) how the underlying structures could ever be identified;
(b) how the relationship between particular structures and particular outcomes could be determined, and
(c) how the superiority of one structural account over another could be justified.

These are, in his opinion, in principle inabilities. It is impossible, Gergen believes, ever to establish as superior one set of foundational claims over another "...outside its own peculiar language commitments..." (p. 76).

Firstly, Gergen's rejection of foundationalism cannot be used to distance his own metatheory from logical positivism. As this chapter demonstrates, the conventionalism of Schlick, Reichenbach and Carnap is such that the meanings of terms and concepts are contextual; they are relative to the system in which they are employed. They are not fixed or immutable, but shift under the pressure of pragmatic demands. And it is a feature of logical positivism, as it is of social constructionism, that issues of meaning come to take priority over epistemological and ontological matters. Taken together, these features do not support the received view of logical positivism as foundationalist (foundationalist in the sense that they took some pieces of supposed scientific knowledge to be known with certainty). This conclusion echoes Friedman's (1999), Uebel's (1996) and Richardson's (1998) claims that logical positivism was anti-foundationalist.[44]

Secondly, it is, of course, a truism that the principles of logic cannot be established (through argument or discourse), and it is also a truism that nothing can be said about anything without using language. But *denying* the principles of logic is self-refuting. Anyone, in the act of denying the principle of non-contradiction, assumes it (see Hibberd, 2002, p. 690).

In addition, Gergen's observation that foundationalist positions fail because they are unable to justify their own assumptions mistakenly presupposes that an inability to justify a group of statements implies that that they cannot *be* true. (This, of course, fuels Gergen's truth nihilism). However, this assumes a verificationist notion of truth, i.e., that a statement is not true until it has been established as true (Hibberd, 1995). This is to take for granted precisely what is in dispute between a realist and non-realist account of truth. A verificationist notion of truth begs the question that truth is independent of proof. This mistake is a further remnant of logical positivist philosophy.

5.7. CONCLUSION

The insidious spread of conventionalism from the axioms of geometry to generalisations in the physical sciences (by Poincaré) and to the propositions of logic, mathematics and scientific theory (by the logical positivists) has not been halted by the advent of Gergen's social constructionism. In fact, by way of Kuhn's philosophy, and with no analytic-synthetic distinction to restrict conventionalism to certain components of a theory, Gergen's metatheory takes conventionalism to an absurd extreme.

Conventionalism is not a doctrine which can be consistently maintained. It denies the objective truth (or falsity) of statements because it rests on the condition of internal reference, i.e., an "internal" view of relations. Referential relations are conceptualised as internal to axiom-structures, systems, or linguistic frameworks.[45] Yet, unfolding the implications of conventionalism, and examining the conventionalist's defence of his own position, one is repeatedly confronted with empirical claims, i.e., claims that something is the case, claims which are about the world we experience and which can be tested only by experience, by empirical investigation. This presupposes a *non*-constitutive notion of relations; that relations are external to the terms which stand in those relations, and that what is the case is, in principle, knowable and describable.

Whilst the conventionalism of the logical positivists was intended to defend empiricism against Kant's claim that some knowledge was *a priori*, paradoxically, it is empiricism which has been compromised in the process. The logical positivists and Gergen have propagated the view that systems or frameworks are *a priori* in the sense of being "before knowledge", because what counts as knowledge is said to be determined by whatever we stipulate the referents of terms to be. This view is a direct consequence of two further convictions. The first involves a substantial overestimation of the extent to which definitions are stipulative, as opposed to reportive. Usually, stating what we mean by a term involves reporting some regularity of usage, which is to report or describe an original (and now widely accepted) stipulation of what the term refers to. This is not the same as introducing a novel stipulation by stating what meaning *we* are going to give to a term. The second conviction appears to be that the arbitrariness of signification precludes external reference. Yet, even if we granted such arbitrariness—that terms could mean whatever we stipulate—external reference would not be undermined. In Gergen's case, an indication as to why he believes that it is appears in 1.7.1. His reasoning is: if language "mirrored" or "pictured" things, then our use of language to signify would be constrained by what things were like. But the "picture" theory is mistaken. There are no such constraints. Hence, there is the arbitrariness of signification and the absence of external reference. This reasoning not only reveals the self-refuting character of internal reference, it also (incorrectly) assumes the necessity of the "picture" theory to external reference, as if *m* can only refer to *s* if *m* has some natural relationship with *s*, such as "features in common".

The exhibiting of conventionalist similarities between logical positivism and social constructionism highlights other features of constructionist metatheory which support my argument that it is not radically dissimilar from his positivist predecessors. The constructionist commitment to a constitutive theory of relations is sometimes present in logical positivist philosophy; Gergen's metatheory does not escape the dualism of logical positivism with respect to non-empirical and empirical statements; Gergen and Schlick both endorse, but inevitably fail to demonstrate, the conventionality of logic. Finally, what is presupposed in Gergen's rationale for anti-foundationalism is a verificationist notion of truth. This residue of logical positivist thinking introduces the topic of the next chapter—the relationship between Schlick's verifiability principle, the doctrine of operationism, and the better known *a posteriori* aspect of social constructionism—that language acquires its meaning through its use in socio-linguistic practices.

NOTES

[1] Conventionalism, then, entails non-factualism (Ch. 3). If a proposition is true by convention, it is not saying anything about the world.

[2] Hacking (1999) observes that the metaphor of "construction" has its origins in Kant's philosophy and that, such is Kant's influence, the metaphor is present in Russell's logicism, Brouwer's intuitionism, Carnap's phenomenalism, empirical psychology, Goodman's "world-making", and Foucault's notion of morality.

[3] Frege (1903/1971) raised many objections to Hilbert's formalism. The following are particularly pertinent: (i) Hilbert's failure to distinguish between axioms and definitions (p. 7ff), (ii) his assumption that, in constructing a system of axioms, nothing was known (p. 8ff), and (iii) his insistence that the absence of contradiction amongst a set of axioms is the criterion of their truth (p. 12).

[4] A related point is that Hilbert's axiomatic system has certain features in common with the "hermeneutic circle". Individual features are intelligible only in terms of the entire context and the entire context is only intelligible through the individual features. In order to understand the axiomatic system, a constant movement from part to whole and back again is necessary.

[5] Gergen's ambivalence may be due to the fact that this position involves bivalent logic. If a set of propositions is internally consistent, no one proposition contradicts any other; no one proposition affirms what another proposition denies. Constructionists' objections to logic and to bivalence are addressed in 5.5.2 and 5.6.4 respectively.

[6] Again, this raises the question, "What is meant by 'consistency'?"

[7] Le Roy suggested that, from a constant stream of occurrences and experiences, the observer extracts certain features and builds them up into convenient, though not true (in any realist sense) thought

structures. These structures become the constituents of scientific theories and enable science to maintain its appearance of certainty, but *they are nothing more than useful fictions constructed with a purpose in mind*—to facilitate effective action as we pursue our needs; to help us deal with an unstructured and complex world (Smith, 1967).

Before 1900, conventionalism of this kind had been anticipated in the work of the German physicist, Heinrich R. Hertz (a pupil of von Helmholtz) in *The Principles of Mechanics Presented in a New Form* (1894, English translation 1899), and was evident in chemistry in G. Milhaud's (1898) *Le Rationnel* (Passmore, 1966). Mach's *Popular Scientific Lectures* (1898) also contained features of this conventionalist thesis. He referred to the "pictorial" parts of a theory.

8   Past summations of the conventionalist thesis have not done it justice. Agassi (1966), for example, neglects to mention, firstly, that, in some versions, experience has a limited role in the construction of a convention and, secondly, that, in Poincaré's version at least, it is not the whole theory which is conventional. Similarly, Popper (1935/1968) overstates Poincaré's thesis when he claims that the conventionalist holds that "... the 'laws of nature' are ... our own free creations; our inventions; our arbitrary decisions" (p. 79). Reichenbach (1920/1965) does likewise (5.3.2).

9   All subsequent references to Poincaré's work are to his *Science and Hypothesis* (1902).

10 The idea that logical positivism embraces conventionalism is not original. For example, Baker (1988), Earman (1993), Richardson (1998), Friedman (1991; 1999) and Irzik Grünberg (1995) have provided accounts of the conventionalist theses of Schlick, Reichenbach and Carnap.

11 Wittgenstein's earlier views on conventionalism are similar to those of the logical positivists. His later views suggest a change of emphasis to the more holistic notion of language game (Ben-Menahem, 1998).

12 In the following chapter it is shown that, under the influence of Wittgenstein during the post-*Tractatus* period, Schlick replaces this ontological emphasis with an emphasis on rules of grammar.

13 Influenced by Russell and Whitehead's *Principia Mathematica*, the logical positivists accepted that the basic propositions of mathematics were deduced entirely from the propositions of logic.

14 Schlick's emphasis on how propositions are understood reflects the influence of Wittgenstein's *Tractatus*. Wittgenstein (1921/1974) attended to what is necessary in order to understand a proposition (e.g., 4.024), because he believed that the problems of philosophy arise from misunderstanding the logic of language (p. 3).

15 Similar views can also be found in Hahn (1959, p. 152ff.) and Ayer (1946, pp. 78–79).

16 Ayer (1946) also conflates the two (see p. 84).

17 The excerpt also reveals one of many similarities between Carnap's and Kuhn's views of science. Like Carnap's postulations, aspects of Kuhn's paradigms are also deployed with a less than conscious knowledge of their features (e.g., Kuhn, 1970, p. 44).

18 Slife & Williams (1995), for example, maintain that positivism is a more moderate position than realism (p. 176).

19 Duhem's (1914/1962) and Quine's (1951/1990) *confirmation holism* functions similarly. All hypotheses are linked to the rest of the theory. Therefore, the theory as a whole is subject to experimental refutation and, in Quine's words, "... it becomes folly to seek a boundary between synthetic statements, which hold contingently on experience, and analytic statements, which hold come what may" (p. 211).

It is evident in Duhem's account that meaning holism is presupposed in his argument for confirmation holism. Hypotheses do not exist in isolation just because their meanings depend on the theoretical system in which they are deployed (Duhem, 1914/1962, pp. 185–187). Not surprisingly, therefore, meaning holism is seen as an argument for confirmation holism and for rejecting the analytic-synthetic distinction, as in Kuhn's account of science.

20 For example, Slife & Williams (1995) mistakenly take Kuhn's account to be "... a direct challenge to positivism" (p. 178).

[21] Gergen underemphasizes the linguistic properties of a Kuhnian paradigm (e.g., Kuhn, 1970, pp. 183–184).

[22] In most places I have, for brevity, paraphrased Gergen.

[23] Unfortunately, this custom also appears in the writings of those who are not constructionists of the Gergen-Potter-Shotter kind. Danziger (1990), for example, is happy to use inverted commas around words such as "variables", "natural kinds" and "solved", presumably to convey his scepticism about the things and practices to which these words purportedly refer. Yet the word "knowledge" is always without quotation-marks. Success is thereby implied, despite it being contrary to the thesis of his book, and despite his recognition of the distinction between knowledge and *what is identified* as knowledge or *what is to count as* knowledge.

[24] The synonyms which Gergen uses to refer either to a system of conventions or to the products of that system are, not surprisingly, different from those of the logical positivists. In claim (6), Gergen makes reference to a "linguistic forestructure", whereas in *Realities and Relationships*, the expressions "intelligibility nucleus" (p. 6), "system of intelligibility" (p. 9), "knowledge structure" (p. 10) and "discursive paradigm" (p. 12) are used.

[25] Note 7 conveys the turn-of-the-century view that conventions were thought to be the mentalistic products of the individual scientist. Even later, Hans Vaihinger's (1935) *Philosophy of "As if"* exemplified this form of conventionalism. Vaihinger distinguished between hypotheses and "scientific Fictions", the latter being artificial thought-constructs, never verifiable but employed because of their utility (p. xlvii).

[26] I examine the reasons for this jointly held assumption in Ch. 7.

[27] This commonality is explored in Ch. 8.

[28] I have not included Popper (1935/1968) here. His criticisms of conventionalism are of a doctrine that is not the conventionalism of Schlick, Reichenbach and Carnap (see ftn. 8).

[29] This does not rule out Held's (2002) "indirect knowing" (p. 657). By this she means using a theory which, if true, enables knowledge of phenomena which are not directly accessible.

[30] On the very same page, Liebrucks proposes that knowledge is that which is acquired, perhaps suggesting (contradictorily) that it is something discovered. He does, mistakenly, think that the "knowledge is produced" thesis is consistent with all moderate forms of realism. Hacking (1999) is also unclear. "Facts, truths, knowledge, and reality are not in the world like protozoa … " (p. 80), but statements do not become facts. "Statements state facts, and scientific facts do not come into being" (p. 81).

[31] Kusch's (2002) claim that the existence of knowledge is dependent upon our recognising it as such (p. 168) is wrong. *a* knowing *x* does not entail that *a* recognises that (i.e., knows that) s/he knows *x*.

[32] The word "entity" here refers to an object, or to its qualities, or to a state of affairs. It does not refer to some atomistic particular to which complex situations can be reduced.

[33] Hence I reject essentialism—the thesis that a thing has properties some of which are necessary (essential) to its being the thing it is. I say more about this in 6.5.3.

[34] Armstrong's (1997) commitment to internal relations is on the understanding that such relations are not ontological (p. 12). But, if not ontological, what are they?

[35] Given that relations are not properties and properties are not relations, the philosophical notion "relational properties" is illogical.

[36] Richardson (1998) notes that Carnap oscillates between the view that objects are constituted and the view that concepts are constituted because Carnap judges these two views to be nothing more than "… two interpretive modes of speech" (p. 6). But this negation of the distinction between what is there and how we conceptualise or talk about what is there, is precisely the issue.

[37] This criticism does not imply that I disagree with Shotter's (2003) central thesis that expressive-responsive bodily activity pre-dates other forms of discourse. However, his claims in this paper express a contemporary version of late 19th and early 20th century idealism, where the world is

conceived of as "an indivisible living unity" (see p. 462). Shotter's denial of (external) relations entails the monism of idealists such as F. H. Bradley, who maintained that there is only one thing, and that "distinctions" within this one thing are not real. I return to this in Chapters 7 & 8.

[38] Realists, in particular, have been taken to task by social constructionists for persisting in the dualisms purportedly inherent in Cartesian philosophy (see Rouse, 2002; Shotter & Lannamann, 2002). This is not the case. A thoroughgoing version of realism will endorse the constructionist objection to *any* form of dualism.

[39] The constructionists' desire to avoid dualism, and their opposition to foundationalism, may have contributed to the view that they are radically different from logical positivism. It is, after all, the received view that the logical positivists were dualists and foundationalists (see Ch. 3, Table 4.1).

[40] Danziger (1997) correctly judges the dualism in Shotter's work to be that between the dialogical (conversational activity) and the monological (written text).

[41] Schlick makes no reference to possible ellipticity and permits statements about future facts to be true (see 1932/1979b, p. 345).

[42] See also Gergen (1998b, p. 52), where he attempts to deny the principle of identity.

[43] Potter's criticisms of "realists' rhetorical moves" are sometimes similar in tenor (e.g., Edwards et al., 1995), as are Shotter's judgements about those who engage in academic debates (e.g., 1998a; 2002).

[44] Friedman (1999) is particularly critical of Rorty's (1979) portrayal of modern philosophy as that which is based on foundationalist epistemology, because that portrayal includes logical positivism.

[45] This is akin to mental representationism where the representation's referential relation is said to be internal to the representation.

CHAPTER 6

MEANING AS USE

6.1. INTRODUCTION

The previous chapter noted that the notion of *a priori* tacitly used by Gergen (and Shotter, on occasion) is that of the logical positivists. For them, as for Gergen, *a priori* means "before knowledge", but not "for all time" and not "independent of experience", and they use this notion because they reject a thoroughgoing empiricism whilst claiming to avoid a defining characteristic of idealism—rationalism.

The present chapter examines the *a posteriori* aspects of their conventionalism. In logical positivism it pertains to the development of verificationism, while in social constructionism it involves the claim that language acquires meaning through its use in socio-linguistic practices.

This claim results from the influence on constructionist thinking of Wittgenstein's post-*Tractatus* view that the meaning of a word is its use. Evidence of this influence and a short account of Wittgenstein's thesis were given in 1.7.3, but further elaboration is now required. Again, some philosophical scene-setting is necessary. My aims are: firstly, to demonstrate that because of Wittgenstein's influence both on social constructionism and on Schlick, constructionism has features in common with Schlick's verificationism and the doctrine of operationism; secondly, to reveal further inadequacies in constructionist metatheory as a result of these commonalities.

6.2. WITTGENSTEIN'S IDENTIFICATION
OF MEANING WITH USE

The identification of meaning with the kind of use a word (phrase, etc.) has, involves a behaviourist notion of meaning. Such a notion is evident, for example, in

John Dewey's writings. Meaning, Dewey (1929) asserts, "... is primarily a property of behavior ... " (p. 179). The particular property of behaviour that meaning might be is the use. So, if the semanticist is to study the meanings of words, he or she must study their use.

This view of meaning is central in Wittgenstein's *Philosophical Investigations*, where Wittgenstein explicitly identifies the meaning of a word with its use.[1,2] The constituents of an expression's meaning are the rules for the use of that expression (Hacker, 2003). However, throughout Wittgenstein's post-*Tractatus* period, he is not altogether consistent in his statements about the meaning-as-use thesis. For example, he declares that the meaning of a word is constituted by its place in grammar (PG, p. 59), and by its use in a language game (PG, p. 60; §43), but he also states that not every use is a meaning (1982, p. 40e, §289), and he leaves open the possibility that meaning might *not* be use when he says "... if the meaning is the *use* we make of the word, ... " (§138). Such pronouncements are at odds with his declaration that use *determines* meaning (§139), and leave Wittgenstein's meaning-as-use thesis in need of interpretation. It may be that in identifying the meaning of a word with its use, "identification" is not to be understood in its strict sense. That is, Wittgenstein is not proposing "the meaning of a word is its use" *and* "the use of a word is its meaning", but suggesting instead that although every difference in meaning is a difference in use, sameness in meaning does not imply sameness in use; sameness in meaning can co-exist with differences in use. The meaning of a word, in that case, would not identify the context in which the word is used, but the latter would identify the word's meaning. It is not my intention, however, to determine whether this interpretation, or any other, is correct, but simply to point out that Wittgenstein's position on this issue is not clear.

Wittgenstein's identification of meaning with use arises from his rejection of what he calls "Augustine's theory of language", a theory which had been foundational to Wittgenstein's *Tractatus Logico-Philosophicus*. Augustine's theory is that words are names whose meanings are the objects named, and that this relation is established by ostensive definition, which in turn establishes a mental association between word and object. A corollary of this position is that sentences are combinations of names which function as descriptions of states of affairs. This corollary and the theory itself are, of course, antithetical to the condition of internal reference.

Wittgenstein's indictment of this theory consists, in part, of the following: Augustine's theory, in its preoccupation with description, ignores differences between the functions of words; these differences lie in their uses or applications; to know what a word means is insufficient to settle its use, whereas to know how to use a word renders redundant any enquiry into what it means.

Wittgenstein is also concerned to point out that the meaning of an expression is not a mental accompaniment (an image or idea) of that expression. It does not follow from this that a theory of meaning is not, in part, a psychological theory, but this is the inference which Wittgenstein appears to draw when he gives pre-eminence to how words are used. In *Philosophical Investigations*, then, Wittgenstein asks the reader what the words of a language signify "... if not the kind of use they have?" (§10) and, in §43, he proposes that:

> For a *large* class of cases—though not for all—in which we employ the word "meaning" it can be defined thus: the meaning of a word is its use in the language.

This section contains Wittgenstein's famous aphorism—the meaning of a word is its use in the language. Importantly, his qualification "For a *large* class of cases—though not for all" is not intended to suggest exceptions to his dictum. Rather, he is alluding to the fact that other things can be meant by "meaning" (Baker & Hacker, 1983, p. 99), such as the meaning of a ritual or gesture, nimbus clouds mean (signal) rain, meaning (intending) to wash the car, etc.

In giving priority to use, Wittgenstein frequently refers to the "function" (§§5, 11, 17, 274, 340, 556, 559), "aim", "goal", or "purpose" (§§5, 6, 8, 88, 566) and "role" or "employment" (§§30, 156, 182, 421) of words. This might be taken to signify that Wittgenstein's notion of use has affinities with the pragmatism of Dewey, Peirce and William James, in which the meaning of a word consists in the practical effects that would follow from its use. This is not what Wittgenstein intends. For him, "use" means "circumstances of application" or "circumstances in which the expression functions" and these, according to Wittgenstein, are the expression's conventional or grammatical role. The meaning of a word is the function it has as a matter of linguistic convention. That is, the place of a word in grammar is its meaning, and grammar consists of conventions (PG p. 59, p. 190).

Wittgenstein's notion of "grammar" is idiosyncratic. He does not appear to distinguish between conventions and rules, leaving the reader to assume that he takes them to be equivalent. In some respects language and games are similar (§§65–67). Grammatical rules (conventions) are like the rules of a game, and the constitutive rules of a language-game are rules of grammar. These determine the roles which words have in the language-game, or the use to which the words are put (Glock, 1996. p. 193). They distinguish sense from nonsense (Hacker, 2003).

The concept of meaning for Wittgenstein is connected not only with "use" but also with "explanation". To find out what the rules of grammar are, we must ask the speaker (the participant in the language-game) to *explain* the meaning of the words. In Wittgenstein's opinion, the speaker's knowledge of the rule is expressed in the explanation she or he gives of the rule (§75–80). The speaker's explanation of the meaning provides the rules for the correct use of the word. She or he will express the "use" to which the words or sentences are put, and what is expressed is the grammatical rule. The word's meaning is the rule for the use of the expression.

Not only are these rules said to be revealed by explanations of the meanings of words, their substance or existence is said to be evident in the speaker's behaviour or practices (Baker & Hacker, 1983, p. 113). Nor do they apply to any language; they are relative to some one particular language (Hacker, 1986, p. 181). To try to clarify what is meant by a rule, Hacker (1986) gives the following examples: (i) ostensive definitions of the kind "That $\rightarrow$ is V" (pointing at a sample); (ii) propositions such as "Magenta is a colour" or "Pain is a sensation"; (iii) propositions of arithmetic (as rules of the grammar of number words), and (iv) propositions of geometry (as rules of the grammar of spatial concepts) (pp. 182–183). Although ostensive definition by indication of an instance, as in "That $\rightarrow$ is V", has the form of an assertion, very often its role is to explain meaning in that a rule for the correct use of "V" is given. In Wittgenstein's theory, such an explanation does not consist of an empirical proposition. It is a rule or convention (PG, p. 68, p. 190).

Wittgenstein's liberal notion of "grammar" is, in part, the outcome of a change in the analogy he employs to describe the phenomenon of language. Initially (1929–1933), he likened the activity of speaking a language to operating a formal calculus of rigid rules. Later, he likened it to the *practices* involved in playing a particular game. Post-1933, the notion of "grammatical" remains, but it is conceptualised broadly as conventions or practices involved in the playing of a game.

To summarise: In contrast both to Augustine's theory of language and to the claims in the *Tractatus*, Wittgenstein's position is that the meaning of a word consists of the grammatical rules for the use of the word. To believe that the meaning of a word is given by the object which that word denotes, is to suppose that the *only* language-game is that of naming objects. The diversity of linguistic activity, however, reveals the "...countless different kinds of use of what we call 'symbols', 'words', 'sentences'" (§23).

A final (historical) point is of significance. Wittgenstein's identification of meaning with use does not appear only in his later work, that is, only in work close to, or after, the publication of *Philosophical Investigations*. The same identification appears in *Philosophical Remarks*. The foreword to this book was written in 1930, and there is much in it which continues the themes of the *Tractatus*. However, in Chapter 2, Wittgenstein (1975) says that a rod is only a lever when it is being used as such and, similarly, the complexity of a gearbox is given by its use (or even its intended use). Language, he claims, is no different:

> ...I would like to say in the case of language: What's the point of all these preparations; they only have any meaning if they find a use.

> You might say: The sense of a proposition is its purpose. (Or, of a word 'Its meaning is its purpose'.) (p. 59).

By 1930, then, Wittgenstein is clearly of the opinion that use is a necessary condition for meaning and that the meaning of a word is somehow related to its use. Only when a rod is used to lever, is it proper to refer to it as a "lever". He is also prepared to equate the terms "purpose" and "use". Evidently, the seeds of his meaning-as-use position had begun to germinate by 1929–30, the period of his discussions with Schlick and Waismann, in Vienna. Baker & Hacker (1983) note too that *Philosophical Investigations* is the culmination of Wittgenstein's work over a sixteen year period, that is, from 1929 to 1945.

6.3. SCHLICK'S ADOPTION OF WITTGENSTEIN'S CRITERION

Schlick's post-1931 statements on the verifiability principle reflect Wittgenstein's influence on him. Schlick does not explicitly adopt Wittgenstein's concept of "language-game", although Wittgenstein introduced it into his account of language in 1932. However, Wittgenstein's identification of meaning with use, his broad conceptualisation of a grammatical rule, and his belief that the identity of such a rule is revealed by the speaker's behaviour or practices, are evident in Schlick's *later* attempts to identify meaning with verifiability. Social constructionism has been influenced by exactly the same Wittgensteinian views. As a consequence, there are definite similarities in theoretical content between logical positivism and social constructionism.

An outline of the development of Schlick's statements on the verifiability principle shows that his earlier statements on the principle by no means represent his final position. Arguably, Schlick's views on meaning mirror the transition which Wittgenstein makes from the Augustinian theory of language in the *Tractatus* to the post-*Tractatus* theory of meaning-as-use.

6.3.1. THE PRINCIPLE OF VERIFICATION: EARLY POSITION — MEANING IS LINKED TO STATES OF AFFAIRS

Schlick's lecture *The Future of Philosophy* (delivered in 1931), is not his first statement on the principle of verification, but it is a useful starting-point because it articulates his early position. In arguing that philosophy must be distinguished from the sciences, because the latter is concerned to discover truth while the former is concerned to discover meaning, Schlick (1931/1979) suggests that:

> We know the meaning of a proposition when we are able to indicate exactly the circumstances under which it would be true (or, what amounts to the same, the circumstances which would make it false) (p. 217).

Furthermore:

> ... meaning and truth are linked together by the process of verification; but the first is found by mere reflection about possible circumstances in the world, while the second is decided by really discovering the existence or nonexistence of those circumstances (p. 218).

There is no doubt that in these passages, Schlick, when referring to "circumstances", means "states of affairs". Meaning is linked to possible states of affairs. Schlick is not, at this point, referring to any actual or possible procedure which may be employed to determine whether some state of affairs obtains. One has only to imagine what would be the case if the proposition were true. The meaning of a proposition involves external reference—reference to some state of affairs.

Schlick's position here is consistent with an important aspect of the Augustinian theory of language. Correlating declarative sentences with states of affairs is the key to this concept of meaning, which is the view of language exemplified in Wittgenstein's *Tractatus*, and is, of course, consistent with logical positivism's expressed commitment to empiricism.

6.3.2. The Principle of Verification: Middle Position—Meaning Is Sometimes Identified with Use

In *Form and Content* (the title of three lectures delivered in 1932), Schlick's articulation of the principle of verification is ambiguous, but frequently different from his earlier association of meaning with states of affairs. He now says that the meaning of a statement:

(1) ... can be given only by indicating the way in which the truth of the statement is tested (Schlick, 1932/1979b, p. 309),

and

(2) ... consists in defining the use of the symbols which occur in the sentence (p. 310).

This requires us to:

(3) ... indicate the rules for how it shall be used, in other words: we must describe the facts which will make the proposition 'true', and we must be able to distinguish them from the facts which will make it 'false'. In still other words: The Meaning of a Proposition is the Method of its Verification (pp. 310–311, inverted commas in the original).

Furthermore:

(4) ... we call a proposition verifiable if we are able to *describe* a way of verifying it, no matter whether the verification can actually be carried out or not. It suffices if we are able to *say* what must be done, even if nobody will ever be in a position to do it (p. 312).

That is to say, the meaning of a proposition is now given by:

A. the rules concerning how the proposition is to be used (excerpts 2 and 3), and
B. a description of the experimental conditions, procedure or method employed to test for the truth of the proposition (even though, as before, practical possibility is not a necessary condition for verifiability) (excerpts 1 and 4).

Conditions A and B appear to be distinct. But Schlick makes no mention of this and, so, attempts no reconciliation of the two. Secondly, it is possible that Schlick's earlier (1931/1979) linking of meaning with states of affairs is to be found in excerpt (3); that when Schlick states "we must describe the facts which will make the proposition 'true'... " he is repeating the proposal that the meaning of a proposition is given by some possible state of affairs.

There is, however, another possibility. In the third excerpt, Schlick is clearly endorsing Wittgenstein's meaning-as-use thesis, which rejects the notion that the meaning of a word (sentence) is a state of affairs which that word (sentence) purportedly refers to. Schlick states that the only way to convey the meaning of a sentence is to indicate the rules for using the sentence. Also, Schlick's expression "in other words" indicates that what follows in the excerpt is synonymous with the preceding sentence. What follows is Schlick's belief that showing someone how to use a sentence (as in, say, pointing to a sample of cloth and saying "The colour of this cloth is magenta") involves describing facts which will make the sentence true. Yet Schlick's use of inverted commas for the words "true" and "false", at this point in his paper, is odd. He does not use them on other occasions. Inverted commas are typically used to indicate a sense different from the usual, and given that Schlick has in mind Wittgenstein's meaning-as-use theme in this passage, it is possible that he is here invoking Wittgenstein's notion "grammatical truth". This is that the "grammatical truth" of a proposition consists in accurately expressing a rule, not in stating how things are (Glock, 1996, p. 151).[3] If this is the case, then "describing the facts which will make the proposition 'true'" should not be understood as "stating how things must be if the proposition is true", but as "accurately expressing the use to which the statement is put".[4]

This possibility is speculative, especially since, in the same sentence, Schlick refers to "facts". However, it is notable that Wittgenstein, in his post-*Tractatus* period, does not see facts as spatio-temporal entities to which propositions correspond, but as linguistic items of a particular kind. They are descriptions; things that are stated, as in "statements of fact", not states of affairs (Glock, 1996, pp. 119–120). Whether this shift has found its way into segments of Schlick's thought is not clear, but in any case it is apparent that, by 1932, the seeds of Wittgenstein's thesis were emerging in Schlick's attempts to explicate the verifiability principle. Verifiability is, in places, not associated with stating how things are, or might be. Possibly Schlick links verifiability to grammatical truth and, therefore, meaning, although, if so, this is expressed inchoately.

6.3.3. THE PRINCIPLE OF VERIFICATION: LATE POSITION — MEANING IS IDENTIFIED WITH USE

In one of his last papers, *Meaning and Verification* (1936/1979), Schlick provides a lengthy "clarification" of the verifiability principle as a criterion of meaning. He states that:

> ... whenever we ask about a sentence, 'What does it mean?', what we expect is instruction as to the circumstances in which the sentence is to be used; we want a description of the conditions under which the sentence will form a *true* proposition,

and of those which will make it *false*. The meaning of a word or a combination of words is, in this way, determined by a set of rules which regulate their use and which, following Wittgenstein, we may call the rules of their *grammar*, taking this word in its widest sense. . . . [5]

Stating the meaning of a sentence amounts to stating the rules according to which the sentence is to be used, and this is the same as stating the way in which it can be verified (or falsified). The meaning of a proposition is the method of its verification.

The 'grammatical' rules will partly consist of ordinary definitions, i.e., explanations of words by means of other words, partly of what are called 'ostensive' definitions, i.e., explanations by means of a procedure which puts the words to actual use. . . . in most cases the ostensive definition is of a more complicated form; . . . In these cases we require the presence of certain complex situations, and the meaning of the words is defined by the way we use them in these different situations (pp. 457–458).

This "clarification" expands on conditions A and B (6.3.2), and in it Wittgenstein's influence is explicit. Schlick's earlier (1931), and better known, view that giving meaning to a sentence involves "indicating the circumstances under which a proposition would be true" is repeated in this excerpt. But it is encircled by the other view which is that giving meaning involves "instruction as to the circumstances in which the sentence is to be used".

On the page following the above excerpt, Schlick suggests that the logical positivists' criterion of meaning is derived from common sense and from scientific procedure. He links the criterion to the operationism of Bridgman and Einstein, noting that operationism was an independent attempt by Bridgman to formulate a criterion (for all the concepts of physics) which was consistent with Einstein's response to the problem of specifying the meaning of "distant simultaneity". Schlick (1936/1979, p. 459) recounts that Einstein's answer to the question "What do we mean when we speak of two events at distant places happening simultaneously?" is to describe an experimental method which results in establishing the simultaneity of such events. Einstein stipulates *what must be done* in order to verify the simultaneous occurrence of the events. In this way, the proposition "Two events at distant places can occur simultaneously" is rendered meaningful, as opposed to metaphysical nonsense.

Within a few more pages, Schlick (1936/1979) has identified verification with logical (not empirical) possibility, the latter involving nothing more than the rules of grammar:

(i) "Possibility of verification", not "verifiability", is the criterion of meaning (p. 464).
(i) "Possibility of verification" means logical possibility of verification, not empirical possibility (pp. 464–465).
(ii) Logical possibility is determined by the rules of grammar we have stipulated for our language (pp. 464–465).

Although Schlick then speaks of logical impossibility as a discrepancy between the definitions of our terms and the way in which we use them, this, he
says, means "... that the rules of our language have not provided any use for such
combinations; ... " (p. 465). Hence, although there is the suggestion that logical
impossibility might be, in part, ontologically determined, i.e., given by the way
the world is, this is undermined in Schlick's elucidation where recourse is to the
rules of language only. Schlick (1936/1979) then concludes:

> The result of our considerations is this: Verifiability, which is the sufficient and
> necessary condition of meaning, is a possibility of the logical order; it is created by
> constructing the sentence in accordance with the rules by which its terms are defined.
> The only case in which verification is (logically) impossible is the case where you
> have *made* it impossible by not setting any rules for its verification. Grammatical
> rules are not found anywhere in nature, but are made by man and are, in principle,
> arbitrary; so you cannot give meaning to a sentence by *discovering* a method of
> verifying it, but only by *stipulating* how it *shall* be done. Thus logical possibility or
> impossibility of verification is always *self-imposed*. If we utter a sentence without
> meaning it is always *our own fault* (pp. 349–350).

For instance, take Schlick's (1936/1979) proposal that a sentence such as "My
friend died the day after tomorrow" does not obey the rules of grammar and is,
therefore, logically impossible (p. 465). This sentence is (he thinks) meaningless
not because "died" refers to a past event, whereas "the day after tomorrow" is
a future time. The sentence is said to be meaningless not because it is logically
impossible *in an ontological sense*, for this would suggest an association with
Augustine's theory of language. It is said to be meaningless because it is logically
impossible *in a grammatical sense*. It violates a rule of grammar.

In following Wittgenstein, Schlick also obscures the distinction between *rules
of grammar* and *rules of use*. Schlick does not make explicit which grammatical
rule is violated in the sentence "My friend died the day after tomorrow". If we
assume that it is just the narrow rule that the verb is past tense whilst the adverbial
complement is future, this implies that any grammatically correct sentence is
logically possible and, therefore, meaningful. But Chomsky's (1965) sentence
"Colourless green ideas sleep furiously" is a sentence that the logical positivists
would identify as nonsense and, so, logically impossible. More than a violation
of a narrow rule is, it seems, necessary for logical impossibility. Hence Schlick's
broadening out of rules of grammar into rules of use. To reiterate: the sentence,
Schlick (1936/1979, p. 465) says, is logically impossible because the rules of
grammar have not provided any use for such a combination of words.

Recall Wittgenstein's liberal notion of grammatical rules (6.2). They are the
conventions or practices embodied in the behaviour of language-users as they
"play" a particular language-game. The Chomskyan would wish to maintain that
the sentence "Colourless green ideas sleep furiously" is semantically anomalous but syntactically correct and that, therefore, rules of use are not the same

as grammatical rules; Wittgenstein denies this. He maintains that "it cannot be the case that an expression is excluded and yet not quite excluded—excluded because it stands for the impossible, and not quite excluded because in excluding it we have to think the impossible." (cited in Glock, 1996, p. 263). Sentences such as "My friend died the day after tomorrow" and "Colourless green ideas sleep furiously" are logically impossible because it is believed that, in both cases, there is the absence of an established use. Rules of grammar are taken to be the same as rules of use, rules for the sentence's application.

Schlick's account depends on this argument, and this explains his failure to reconcile condition A with condition B (6.3.2). If we extrapolate from Schlick's conclusion (the last passage cited) to his interpretation of Einstein's response to the problem of specifying the meaning of "distant simultaneity", then, in Schlick's opinion, Einstein has articulated the rules for the use of the phrase by stipulating what must be done in order to verify a sentence containing the phrase. That is, Einstein has created certain grammatical rules by stipulating the methodological *practices* involved in determining the simultaneity of two distinct events, and it is this rule that makes the proposition "Two events at distant places can occur simultaneously" meaningful. It is not surprising, then, that Schlick is not alert to possible distinctions between conditions A and B. He regards rules for use as grammatical rules, and maintains that grammatical rules involve "stipulating how it shall be done" or setting out "the rules for verification". Logical possibility, according to Schlick, is determined *only* by rules of grammar, but these are not to be understood in a narrow sense.

In summary, elements of Wittgenstein's thesis are evident in Schlick's middle and later expositions of the principle of verification, though this is not to say that Schlick does not distort some of Wittgenstein's ideas. However, Schlick does equate meaning with use, and relies on Wittgenstein's liberal notion of rules of grammar. When verification is impossible, this is because of the man-made rules of grammar which stipulate how sentences are to be used. The meaning of a sentence or a term is given by how it is to be used; by stipulating a use for it. Such a stipulation is a grammatical rule which makes verification logically possible, and it is this possibility which distinguishes sense from metaphysical nonsense.

In Schlick's attempts to refine the verifiability principle as a criterion of meaning, there is a gradual movement away from the Augustinian theory of language (in which the meaning of a word or sentence is correlated with some thing or situation) to a theory which correlates the meaning of a word with rules or practices concerning the word's use.

Despite this, the verifiability principle was regarded by Schlick as an *empiricist* criterion of meaning, on the grounds that reference to ostensive definition (a grammatical rule) is reference to experience (Schlick, 1936/1979, p. 458). This is consistent with what is typically understood by an empiricist criterion—that the meanings given to words result from the experience of states of affairs (involving red items, aggression, etc.). But Schlick (no doubt unwittingly) misleads the reader. The distinction between the experience of red items and aggression and the experience of the rules or practices concerning the use of the words "red" and "aggressive" becomes blurred, despite Schlick's claim that experience of the latter involves experience of the former. This claim assumes experience of circumstances in which the word is *correctly* used. If I experience (i.e., hear, see and understand) the rules or practices concerning the correct use of the word "red", then I must at some time have experienced something that is red, and not another colour. But this is at odds with Schlick's claim that grammatical rules are, in principle, arbitrary. In this case, the referent of the experience is said to be of no consequence, and verifiability is not an *empiricist* but a *man-made* criterion of meaning.

6.3.4. THE CONNECTION WITH OPERATIONISM

It was observed in 6.3.3 that Schlick links his final formulation of the verifiability principle to the views of Einstein and Bridgman. There is an important similarity between Schlick's verificationism and Bridgman's operationism. Both equate meaning with use.

Bridgman's (1927) position is that the meaning of a term is given by a set of operations: "... the true meaning of a term is to be found by observing what a man does with it, not by what he says about it" (p. 7). His critical assertion is: "In general we mean by any concept nothing more than a set of operations; *the concept is synonymous with the corresponding set of operations*" (p. 5). The meanings of terms are operations, and these operations are physical acts or procedures.[6] Influenced by positivism and American pragmatism, Bridgman frequently used the phrase "rules of operation" and, from 1922, identified these rules with the meanings of concepts (Moyer, 1991).

In displaying the similarities between Bridgman's operationism and verificationism, it is helpful to consider the distinctions which have been drawn between them. There are, typically, two. First, verificationism links meaning to *sentences*; sentences are meaningful if in principle they are capable of being verified by observational test. It is a *sentence* which can be either confirmed or disconfirmed. By contrast, operationism links meaning to *concepts* or to the *terms* representing those concepts, if the concepts or terms are indeed capable of operational definition. Also, verificationism is associated with truth, operationism is not. A concept cannot have a truth value, but an assertoric sentence may. The second distinction is that Bridgman's operationism refers to physically realisable procedures, whereas what is meant by "method of verification" is the logical possibility of verification (e.g., Ashby, 1967, p. 240).

In Schlick's later account of verificationism, these two distinctions are obscured. For one thing, in explicating verificationism as a criterion of meaning,

Schlick sometimes vacillates between discussing the meaning of *propositions* and discussing the meaning of *words* (e.g., Schlick, 1936/1979, p. 458).[7] The basis for the first distinction between verificationism and operationism is blurred *ab initio*.

Secondly, Schlick's verificationism associates "logical possibility" with "rules of grammar", not with states of affairs (6.3.3), and these are to be understood as "rules for the use of the words". If grammatical rules always involve a "stipulation of how it shall be done" or an "explanation by means of a procedure which puts the words to actual use", and if this is what Schlick means by "logical possibility" (as it seems it is), then the second basis for the distinction between verificationism and operationism is also unclear. Verificationism is not distinct from "physically realisable procedures". Ostensibly, the difference is that Schlick is concerned with the *logical possibility* of verification, whilst Bridgman is concerned with the *actual* operations involved in the use of the term. However, in describing Einstein's procedure for measuring the length of bodies in motion, Bridgman (1927, p. 12) admits the possibility of defining certain concepts by *non-actual* operations, such as mathematical convention. This echoes Wittgenstein's view that the grammar of spatial concepts consists of rules or conventions (6.2). A definition of "force" is similarly given by non-actual operations ". . . involving . . . hypothetical experiments in laboratories situated far out in empty space" (Bridgman, 1927, p. 106). What Schlick's verificationism and Bridgman's operationism do have in common is that in neither case is meaning associated with the objects or attributes that a term stands for, and, in both cases, meaning is identified with use—either stipulation of the practices that will put the term to use (Schlick) or the set of operations involved in the use of the term (Bridgman).

6.3.5. CONCLUDING REMARKS

It is evident that, from at least the 1920s, the identification of meaning with use was a feature of a general philosophical outlook. Despite subtle differences in what "use" is taken to be, the thesis is a dominant feature of Wittgenstein's post-*Tractatus* account of language, it characterises Bridgman's operationism, and it forms the basis of Schlick's attempts to develop verificationism as an empiricist criterion of meaning.

In the following section, it is shown that this situation has not changed. Constructionists, and others subscribing to the received view (Ch. 4), have not realised that, in its account of meaning, social constructionism reiterates notions already common in early 20th century philosophy of science. Specifically, the adoption of Wittgenstein's meaning-as-use criterion unites social constructionist metatheory with Schlick's "old-fashioned" verificationism. The adoption of the same criterion also unites constructionism with "old-fashioned" operationism.

6.4. THE CONSTRUCTIONISTS' ADOPTION
OF WITTGENSTEIN'S CRITERION

6.4.1. THE CONTEXTUAL DEPENDENCY OF MEANING

Social constructionism's endorsement of the post-*Tractatus* Wittgenstein has always been unequivocal and uncritical (e.g., Gergen & Gergen, 2003; Potter, 2000; Shotter, 2003). Potter's explicit support is moderate, but Gergen's and Shotter's enthusiasm for Wittgenstein's deliberations appears unlimited. Constructionism justifies its notion of the contextual dependency of meaning by recourse to the meaning-as-use criterion (1.7.3). Gergen's interpretation of Wittgenstein is that words acquire their meaning through the ways they are used in social practices (1994b, p. 413; 1999, pp. 34–35); by their function within a set of circumscribed rules (1994c, p. 53). "Rules", here, is interpreted liberally. "Rules", for Gergen, are the rules of the "language-games"; the context; the socio-linguistic conventions, and the patterns of social interchange. These are said to be the sole determinants of meaning.

Whether this interpretation of Wittgenstein is correct is not relevant to the material in this book. However, it is not at all clear that Gergen understands "identification" (of meaning with use) in the weaker sense set out in 6.2. He claims that:

> ... any scientific term derives its meaning from its context of usage, which can also include the syntactic conventions governing its use. To illustrate, in the case of psychology, a term like "aggression" derives its meaning from the many contexts in which it is employed. There are also many different contexts of usage, thus giving the term a far different meaning depending on whether one is speaking about soldiers at war, tennis players, investment policies, woodchopping, or weed growth in the spring (1986a, p. 139).

If a different context of usage does give the term "aggression" "a far different meaning", then it seems that the meaning of a word is its use and the use of a word is its meaning; i.e., Gergen understands the meaning-as-use thesis in the strict sense. Sameness in meaning cannot (he thinks) co-exist with differences in use.

Shotter intends something more sophisticated. He uses Wittgenstein's meaning-as-use thesis to underpin his call for an awareness of a dialogical, relationally responsive form of discourse which is to be distinguished from monological, representational-referential forms (e.g., Shotter, 2003). Recall from 1.4 that his aim is to understand the complex effects of words *in their speaking*. Yet what Shotter *says* suggests a position similar to Gergen's. The meaning of a word, he declares, "... is a matter of circumstances, a matter of its *special* usage in the *particular* context of its occurrence. ... In other words, meaning is not a property of words or deeds, but of the situations or contexts in which they are used" (Shotter, 1994, p. 151); citing Volosinov, Shotter & Lannamann (2002) state that "... our

words have their meaning only in terms of their 'position between speakers ... '"
(p. 581). The local, the particular, the context, is, then, crucial in determining
the meaning of a word, and this, apparently, is the case regardless of the form of
discourse—dialogical or monological.

It is helpful to consider Gergen's claims about the contextual dependency of
meaning by reference to some familiar psychological concept. Take, for example,
the term "regression". It has at least four different meanings: astronomical; geolog-
ical; statistical and psychological. Following Gergen's adoption of Wittgenstein's
thesis, deciding what the term "regression" means is a question of determining
how the word "regression" is used. The question really is how propositions employing the word "regression" are used. Given Gergen's assimilation of Austin's
concept of the purely performative utterance (3.5), how each proposition is used
depends on: (i) what illocutionary force the utterance has (is the speaker judging,
describing, promising, warning, etc.); (ii) when the term "regression" is used (is the
speaker addressing psychoanalysts or statisticians?) and, (iii) how the audience responds to the utterance (do they nod their heads in agreement, appear puzzled, roar
with laughter, or leave the lecture theatre in droves?). These factors (among many
others) constitute the "context", the conditions under which the term is employed.
It is, according to Gergen (1994c), the context which supplements the speaker's
action, and "creates" and "constrains" meaning and gives the action "... a function
within the relationship" (p. 265). It is context which must be determined in order
to answer the question "How is the word "regression" used?", which is equivalent
to the question "What does the word "regression" mean?"

It is important to be clear about what Gergen does not mean by "contextual
dependency". He does not mean that context provides an epistemic service by
removing ambiguity when a term, such as "regression", can stand for different
kinds of things, and, therefore has, as we might say, a multiplicity of meanings.[8]
In his view terms do *not* stand for *kinds* of things. There is not, he believes, some
feature common to certain situations that the term "regression" refers to. For a
realist, the importance of context is unquestioned; in Gergen's metatheory it is the
only factor. The meaning of "regression" is given *solely* by the context in which
the term is used. Hence the variation in the term's meanings. Meanings *cannot* be
fixed because contexts vary (Gergen, 1994c, p. 267).

Of course, neither Gergen nor Shotter deny the existence of relatively stable systems of meanings. Gergen claims that "context" may refer to a particular
community of psychologists constituted through the various rhetorical features
of a particular linguistic framework (1994c, p. 8). These features include often
"... long-standing patterns of interchange ... " (p. 306, n. 11/3) that serve, to some
extent, to constrain the meanings generated, preventing a situation whereby anything goes. Similarly, Shotter (1993a) states that "[u]tterances have their meaning
within a *genre*, that is within a *way* of speaking associated with a form of social life ... " (p. 180).[9] This raises more questions than it answers. For example,

what is it that determines the "proper" level of generality of a context-as-meaning-determiner, and how do the participants get to know about this?

Despite this mention of stability in meaning, variation in meaning is taken by constructionism to be the stronger socio-linguistic phenomenon. The absurd implication of this is that since every occasion (context) is different from every other, no term ever has the same meaning twice. This was precisely the criticism originally made of Bridgman's operationism (see Russell, 1928).

6.4.2. The Similarities with Schlick's Appropriation

The contextual dependency thesis of social constructionism has a modern flavour, and bears (it might be thought) little resemblance to Schlick's later explications of the principle of verification. Yet when certain extracts of Schlick's claims are re-presented, similarities between the two are immediately obvious. Recall:

> The meaning of a word or a combination of words is, in this way, determined by a set of rules which regulate their use and which, following Wittgenstein, we may call the rules of their *grammar*, taking this word in its widest sense (Schlick, 1936/1979, pp. 457–458).

> ... we require the presence of certain complex situations, and the meaning of the words is defined by the way we use them in these different situations (p. 458).

Although social constructionism, unlike Schlick, makes use of the term "language-game" and does not employ the adjective "grammatical", the resemblance between the two interpretations of Wittgenstein is striking. Both rely on the meaning-as-use criterion, both make use of the notion of "rules" as determining use (and, therefore, meaning), both interpret "rules" broadly, and both require a social context in which meaning is given.

Moreover, Schlick's use of inverted commas for the words "true" and "false" is a practice not only (sometimes) employed by Gergen (e.g., 1985a, p. 271–272) but possibly one employed for the same reason. If my suggestion in 6.3.2 has merit, in neither case is "true" intended to be associated with stating how things are, i.e., with truth. In 3.5.1, it was made clear that Gergen's "true" does not mean true, but rather Austin's notion of felicitous. We may *say* of a certain utterance that it is true, but this is not to say that it refers to some state of affairs. It is just to say that a sentence (more accurately, a performative utterance) fits appropriately or congenially into a procedure or social convention. Schlick, of course, does not reject truth. However, it was suggested that by his use of inverted commas around the word "true", Schlick means "grammatical truth". That is, a sentence is "true" when it accurately expresses the use to which the statement is put. Together with Schlick's statement on what logical impossibility involves, this can also be taken to mean "the absence of any discrepancy between the words in the sentence and the circumstances of their use". It is a short step from this to Gergen's notion of a fit between the (performative) utterance and the context in which the utterance is used.

Gergen is simply wrong, then, to claim that social constructionism is antithetical to logical positivism. His error arises from a superficial appreciation of (i) the verifiability principle in general, and (ii) Schlick's interpretations of it in particular. In *Realities and Relationships*, Gergen (1994c) reports that:

> the "verifiability principle of meaning" ... held that the meaning of a proposition rests on its capacity for verification through observation; propositions not open to corroboration or emendation through observation are unworthy of further dispute (p. 32).

Gergen is quite right to read logical positivism as intent upon establishing "... a close relationship between language and observation" (p. 32). However, a philosophical movement's expressed intentions are logically distinct from the content of their assertions, which are, in turn, logically distinct from the expressed intentions of their subsequent interpreters; what the logical positivists asserted was, at times, different from their intentions. In the positivist literature, it is repeatedly declared that a proposition is meaningless only when it is not *theoretically* possible to verify the proposition (e.g., Blumberg & Feigl, 1931). (Schlick's own comment about the *possibility* of verification was noted in 6.3.3, notwithstanding his obscureness on this matter). The logical positivists' expressed empiricist *intention* to establish a close relationship between language and observation is compromised in their recognition of the fact that to restrict verifiability (as the sufficient and necessary condition of meaning) to propositions that could *actually* be verified was absurd.

Evidently, Gergen does not assess logical positivism in terms of the content of its assertions, i.e., in terms of what is actually asserted by logical positivists in accounts of the verifiability principle. Perhaps he interprets the principle in the light of expressed wishes of logical positivist interpreters (within, say, psychology), notes the failure of the principle ever to be coherently articulated, and concludes that such wishes just can't be fulfilled. Social constructionism, he implies, has learnt from logical positivism's failure, it knows better than to have the wishes or intentions which the logical positivists had, and so it *is* radically different from the positivist movement. Gergen's error is one of selective *in*attention to the content of logical positivist assertions.

The same kind of inaccuracy appears in Gergen's reporting of Schlick's notion of ostensive definition. Gergen (1994c) tells the reader that, in attempting to account for the relation between propositions and things observed, Schlick "... proposed that the meaning of single words within propositions must be established through ostensive ('pointing to') means (p. 32).

However, Gergen fails to say that Schlick takes the ostensive definition to be *a constituent of the grammatical rules concerning the use of the sentence.* Ostensive definitions are, in Schlick's (1936/1979) words "... explanations by means of a procedure which puts the words to actual use" (p. 458) which, typically, is of a sufficiently complicated form to "... require the presence of certain complex situations, and the meaning of the words is defined by the way we use them in these different situations" (p. 458). Moreover, Schlick's notion of ostensive definition is consistent with Wittgenstein's (as articulated in *Philosophical Investigations*, §28–30), and is one which Gergen need not object to.

Clearly, Schlick's and constructionism's views are not identical, but the latter has adopted ideas which were present in Schlick's later defence of the verifiability principle. In summary, these are: (i) rejection of the Augustinian theory of language; (ii) Wittgenstein's meaning-as-use criterion (or, at least, one interpretation of it); (iii) the notion of "rules" as the determinant of use and, therefore, of meaning; (iv) a broad interpretation of "rules"; (v) the importance of social context to language-use, and (vi) (perhaps) a replacement for truth which involves the notion of "fit given the social context". These commonalities between Schlick and social constructionism arise from their mutual dependence on Wittgenstein. They are joint heirs of Wittgenstein's legacy.

6.4.3. SOCIAL CONSTRUCTIONISM AND OPERATIONISM

An account of the similarities between social constructionism and operationism is tangential to this part of the book, which is concerned with the relationship between social constructionism and logical positivism; operationism emerged relatively independently of logical positivism. Still, a small digression is justified because Bridgman's operationism and Schlick's verificationism are conceptually connected (6.3.4). Also, some facts about operationism in psychology today and the initial exposure of psychology to operationism and logical positivism in the 1930s combine to lend a certain irony to the accepted view of the relationship between social constructionism and logical positivism.

In psychology today, operationism is manifest in, for instance, textbooks on research design and methodology, many of which continue to recommend operationism as a methodological practice (e.g., Babbie, 2004; Bordens & Abbott, 1991; Dunn, 2001; Kerlinger, 1986; Mitchell & Jolley, 1996; Pittenger, 2002; Schweigert, 1994).[10] Kerlinger's *Foundations of Behavioral Research* is a case in point. Schooled in the tradition of logical positivism, Kerlinger acknowledges that his understanding of operationism relies heavily on a chapter from the book *The Nature of Physical Reality* (1950) written by the philosopher Henry Margenau. Margenau's (1950) text is logical positivist philosophy *par excellence.* In one chapter, "The Role of Definitions in Science", Margenau builds on contributions made by Bridgman and Carnap. Kerlinger does not refer to the operationism of S. S. Stevens, although he is perhaps aware of it because he quotes Stevens' definition of measurement.

Despite caveats to his reader that there is a looseness about his discussion of operational definitions (Kerlinger, 1986, p. 28) and that operational definitions yield only limited meanings of constructs (p. 29), Kerlinger states that an operational definition defines or gives meaning to a variable by spelling out "... the activities of the researcher in measuring a variable or manipulating it" (p. 28). For example:

   i. the meaning of "self-concept" is given by spelling out that what was done to measure it was to obtain responses on a figure-drawing test;
  ii. the meaning of "guilt" is given by spelling out that what the investigators did was to induce their subjects to lie.

That is, concepts are to be defined in terms of how they are measured, or defined in terms of what is done to induce the phenomenon for which the concept stands. Guilt is *defined* in terms of what is done to induce guilt. This is a (muddled) notion not to be confused with the empirical hypothesis that when certain things are done, guilt will result.

In social constructionism's interpretation of Wittgenstein's meaning-as-use criterion, the meanings of terms are said to be given by the context in which the terms are employed. For example, the meaning of the term "regression" is said to consist in what the language-users are doing, who they are relating to, and where they are at the time (the practices of the psychology community using the term), just as the meaning of "guilt" consists solely in what is done to bring guilt about. It follows that, in both operationism and social constructionism, each different context of usage or operation gives a different meaning to a term. Sameness in meaning cannot co-exist with such differences.

Although social constructionism and operationism both identify the meanings of terms with their use, there are obvious differences. Most importantly, operationism does not reject the relation of external reference; words are said to denote (correspond to) the operations involved in their use. Gergen, of course, explicitly rejects such a relation. Also, in Gergen's metatheory, the rules of a language-game are not *identical* to the actual procedures or operations involved in the use of a term. Nonetheless, both maintain that it is not any hypothesised features of the phenomenon under investigation which contribute to a term's meaning, only the context of its use.

The initial presentation of operationism to psychologists occurred in the 1930s when a series of papers, unfolding the implications of operationism for psychology, appeared in psychological and philosophical journals (e.g., Brunswik, 1937; McGeoch, 1935, 1937; McGregor, 1935; Seashore & Katz, 1937; Stevens, 1935a, 1935b, 1936, 1939; Tolman, 1936; Waters & Pennington, 1938). Prominent amongst these papers was S. S. Stevens' explanation of what he considered to be the implications of operationism and logical positivism for psychological research. Stevens urged that psychologists should attend to these recent developments in the philosophy of science because of the similarities between them and behaviouristic psychology.

Paradoxically, the direction in which Gergen has taken social constructionism, partly as a result of his interpretation of Wittgenstein's thesis, was anticipated by Stevens in his attempt to extend the ideas of Bridgman and Carnap to psychology. However, because logical positivism and operationism were presented as philosophies of science which had coalesced into a new version of scientific empiricism (one which resulted from the development of the theories of relativity), the radicalism of Stevens' message was overlooked. Yet, in Gergen's claims about psychology's observations, psychological theory and psychological phenomena (1.6), the resemblance to Stevens' philosophy of psychological science is apparent. The unfolding of proposition A1 (1.6.1) resonates with Stevens' (1936, pp. 99–100) rejection of the attempts by Margenau and Feigl to distinguish between the "language of constructs" and the "language of data". For Stevens, the language of data has to do with immediately given experience. But such experience is, he believes, always defined operationally in terms of some behaviour such as pointing or, more fundamentally, a discriminatory response. As Stevens (1936) says, "... the discriminatory reaction is the only objective, verifiable thing denoted" (p. 95).

Again, there are differences in detail here between Stevens and Gergen, but these should not obscure the points of general agreement. First, Gergen, too, rejects the notion of uncontaminated, raw sense-data and, like Stevens, maintains that certain contextual factors determine psychologists' descriptions, making a nonsense of the theory-observation distinction. In both accounts, these factors include the immediate conditions under which an utterance or concept is employed, localising the determinants of meaning to particular situations; the meanings of words do not transcend the operations (context) which determine them. Neither permits a phenomenon under study to be a "thing denoted". Ontological neglect, then, is as much a feature of Stevens' operationism as it is of Gergen's social constructionism.

Second, the alleged relativity of space and time leads Stevens (1936) to the position that the phenomenon under investigation "... is conditioned in part upon the nature of the human experimenter" (p. 94). This indeterminacy thesis is consistent with Bridgman's (1927) view that "... it is meaningless to attempt to separate 'nature' from 'knowledge of nature'" (p. 62), and accords with Gergen's belief (proposition A3) that what we refer to as "psychological phenomena" are not discourse-independent; that what is "known" is determined by characteristics of the psychology community, especially its shared discursive practices.

Third, Stevens and Gergen agree about the significance of certain social processes to the research enterprise. Gergen's account of knowledge as socio-linguistic echoes Stevens' emphasis on the social aspect of knowledge. In a footnote to his first non-experimental publication in psychology, Stevens (1935a) states that:

> Not only is science a social convention, but, as Carnap and others have shown, language itself, including the rules for its use, is a convention based upon social sanction. From the social usage of words, there is no appeal (p. 327, ftn. 4).

This echoes a claim of Gergen's (1994c) previously cited: that "... because disquisitions on the nature of things are framed in language, there is no grounding of science or any knowledge-generating enterprise in other than communities of interlocutors" (p. ix).

Furthermore, in Gergen's and Stevens' emphasis on the (banal) fact that social processes determine conventions of language, the view that knowledge is a *pre*-sociolinguistic cognitive relation between the knower and the known, is implicitly dismissed out of hand. Moreover, Gergen's conflation of knowledge with the printed assertions found in textbooks, journals, etc., (1.6.2) parallels Stevens' (1935a) insistence that science is a body of knowledge, not knowledge-*claims* (p. 327). And although Stevens (1936, p. 97), unlike Gergen, does not relinquish all notions of truth, he does make consensus between scientists a sufficient condition for truth. This, he happily admits, means that "Truth is no more absolute than space or time ... for what is true to-day was not true yesterday and may not be true to-morrow" (p. 97). Despite their dissimilarities then, Gergen's and Stevens' views are unfoldings of anti-realism, and, caught up in the conventionalism of the logical positivists, Stevens was, it would seem, as little concerned with self-criticism as is psychology's contemporary post-modernist.

6.4.4. RECONSIDERATION OF THE RECEIVED VIEW

In contrast to the received view (Ch. 4), Schlick's verificationism and the operationism of Bridgman and Stevens have features in common with social constructionism. Importantly, they all incorporate variants of the meaning-as-use thesis. One consequence of this is a preoccupation with the usage of words, of *what it means to say "x"* rather than *what it means to be x*. This was an early twentieth century philosophical characteristic which continues to this day; social constructionism has simply carried on the tradition. Verificationism, operationism and social constructionism all require that attention be drawn to the context of usage, i.e., to what is being done and to what is being said. Whether the context is experimental or not does not matter. "Use" is interpreted liberally by Schlick to mean not only an experimental method, but also the conventions or practices involved in any situations in which the words are used (6.3.3). Gergen and Shotter have adopted this interpretation without realising that the same criterion of meaning characterises Schlick's verificationism. Meaning is given by the conventions or practices involved in a particular context. An investigator's description of an experimental method is one example of this; how and when a word such as "regression" is used, is another.

On the evidence presented in this and the previous chapter, psychology's judgements about positivism's *denial of the subject, decontextualised ideals, empiricism* and *foundationalism* (4.4) need to be re-considered. Further, Schlick's and Bridgman's claims resulted, in part, from Einstein's account of certain methodological practices. Thus, in this respect, they believed they were describing scientific practice, not prescribing a philosophy of science. In a similar vein, because Stevens (1936, p. 92–93) adheres to the notions of relativity, conventionalism and operationism, he explicitly rejects the possibility of *prediction*, yet prediction is judged to be a *sine qua non* of positivist philosophy. And it is a further anomaly of the received view that the very conditions said to be ignored by positivism, *reflexivity*, *indeterminacy* and *contestability*, are clearly recognised in the epistemology of Bridgman's and Stevens' operationism.

6.5. CRITICAL COMMENTS

6.5.1. THE INCOMPLETE CHARACTERISATION OF MEANING

The identification of meaning with use involves the kind of fallacy discussed in 5.6.2. In the present context, however, meaning is confined to activity (the *a posteriori* aspects of conventionalism), and the recurrent fallacy (of constitutive relations) involves a slightly different schema. It concerns an incomplete characterisation of meaning.

Meaning is relational. A word such as "dog", in and of itself, has no meaning. If it is used to refer to furry animals which bark, this involves a relation: j is used by a to refer to z.[11] j's meaning can then be said to be z, and use is a necessary condition for meaning; j's meaning does indeed derive from its use. Here we have a 3-term relation ($R[a, j, z]$) of the kind discussed in 3.2. The error of identifying meaning with use is that the relation of a using j (in the manner described) is not a complete characterisation of ($R[a, j, z]$). Furthermore, when it is said that z (the kind of thing referred to) is completely defined by a using j, the logical independence of z is denied, as is the relation of "referring to". It is not clear, given the ambiguities in Wittgenstein's identification of meaning with use, that he commits this logical error (6.2). However, much scholarship has been devoted to redressing Wittgenstein's expressed rejection of traditional philosophical theories and assumptions and to restoring a robust (as opposed to deflationary) philosophical conception of meaning, one that recognises not only the role of agreement in our shared linguistic practices, but what makes such agreement possible—the objects, events, states of affairs (z) that we want to speak of (e.g., Gamble, 2002; Verheggen, 2003).

Verificationism, operationism and social constructionism, each in their own way, confuse the thing referred to, or a term's meaning, with *what is being done* in using the term.[12] This confusion involves, again, the constitutive notion of relations (5.6.2). In Schlick's account, the meaning of "distant simultaneity" is supposedly given by describing an experimental procedure. Operationism maintains that the meaning of "guilt" is given by spelling out what some investigators did (get their subjects to lie). In Gergen's "aggression" example: what is meant by "aggression" consists in factors concerning the context of the speaker's use of the term. In Shotter's case, word meaning is produced in the unfolding relations between particular people in a specific context. In each case Rz is ignored, and this is to ignore what the term is being used to refer to. To put it another way, *what is referred to* is confused with *our use of language to refer*. What is referred to is ignored in a manner akin to Berkeley's (1710/1945) ignoring of reality in his judgement that reality is constituted by our perception of it (§23). Replacing an inquiry into the features of z with an inquiry into the features of aRj is symptomatic of this.

This logical blunder has an important corollary. If the meaning of a term is identified only with the rules for its use, the practices involved in the use of the term, or the context in which the term is used, then, logically, these factors cannot be the *cause* of the meanings of the terms. Cause and effect are logically distinct. If guilt, for example, is *identified* with inducing subjects to lie, then, logically, inducing subjects to lie cannot *cause* guilt. Cause and effect must be distinct existences.

Disregard for logical independence often means that this corollary is ignored (5.6.2). For example, despite Kerlinger's (1986) caveat to the reader that "... there is no need to use the touchy word "cause" and "related words" (p. 32), he tells her that "Freedman, Wallington, and Bless operationally defined 'guilt' by inducing their subjects to lie. Telling lies was presumed to engender guilt. (Apparently it did.)" (p. 29). Kerlinger's "engender" is, of course, just a synonym of "cause", and he is advocating an absurdity: that inducing subjects to lie is a definition of, and (at the same time) a possible cause of, guilt.

Gergen commits the same error time and again in his repeated claim that the meanings of psychological terms are given, and also caused, by contextual factors. For example: "... language *acquires its meaning* not through a referential base but through its use in social practices (Gergen, 1994b, p. 413, my italics); that it is "... social processes [that are] *responsible for* establishing and negotiating reference ... " (Gergen, 1994c, p. 50, my italics); and that: "... samples of language ... [are] not maps or mirrors of other domains—referential worlds or interior impulses—but *outgrowths* of specific modes of life, rituals of exchange, relations of control and domination, and so on" (p. 53, my italics).

However, if y "acquires its meaning through" x, or if x is "responsible for establishing" y, or if y is an "outgrowth" of x, then what is meant is that x is at least a partial cause of y in some context. This implies the temporal priority of x, which in turn implies the distinctiveness and independence of x and y. It follows that x cannot be identified with y.[13] (Here, for the sake of brevity, I have avoided the symbols a, j, z and R, but my point still stands. For example, if j acquires its meaning through the context in which a uses j, these contexts are the *cause* of j's meaning and cannot *be* j's meaning).

6.5.2. WITTGENSTEIN'S EXAMINATION OF THE CONCEPT "GAME"

It is likely that some critics of the arguments in the preceding section would think that my claims rest on the untenable assumption that phenomena, such as guilt, aggression, etc., *can* be defined; that is, that the *general* features or qualities of some situation can be set out. They may say that it is just because this cannot be done that they turn their attention to context. From Wittgenstein's assertion (not proof) that there is nothing common to all games, that there is just a set of "family resemblances" (§§66–67), they may conclude that this demonstrates the impossibility of specifying the meaning of *any* term. There is no general or common meaning to *any* term, because amongst *any* class of objects (such as games) there is no one thing common to the members of that class. Games have no essence. Certainly Gergen is of this creed, and whilst Harré is not, he does accept without question Wittgenstein's assertion, hence his criticism of Gergen (2.6). Harré & Krausz (1996) point out that Gergen has forgotten Wittgenstein's lesson. Gergen takes the various socio-linguistic practices to have something in common, to have an essence—that of being non-referential—and, in so doing, he commits the "family resemblance fallacy".

About this, Harré & Krausz may be correct. But their claim, and the belief that there is no general or common meaning to *any* term, is based on an uncritical acceptance of Wittgenstein's thesis that the class of language-games (and hence of language) share nothing more than family resemblance. Wittgenstein did *not* demonstrate that this was the case. Consider sections 65–67 of *Philosophical Investigations*. In response to an imaginary interlocutor who objects because Wittgenstein fails to say what the essence of language is, Wittgenstein responds:

And this is true.—Instead of producing something common to all that we call language, I am saying that these phenomena have no one thing in common which makes us use the same word for all,—but that they are *related* to one another in many different ways. And it is because of this relationship, or these relationships, that we call them all 'language'. . . . (§65).

Consider for example the proceedings that we call 'games'. I mean board-games, card-games, ball-games, Olympic games, and so on. What is common to them all?— Don't say: 'There *must* be something common, or they would not be called 'games''— but *look and see* whether there is anything common to all.—For if you look at them you will not see something that is common to *all*, but similarities, relationships, and a whole series of them at that. To repeat: don't think, but look! . . .

> And the result of this examination is: we see a complicated network of sim-
> ilarities overlapping and criss-crossing: sometimes overall similarities, sometimes
> similarities of detail (§66).

> I can think of no better expression to characterize these similarities than 'family
> resemblances'; for the various resemblances between members of a family: ... And
> I shall say: 'games' form a family (§67).

Here, using the example of a game, Wittgenstein says that he finds no property common to all games and, similarly, no property common to all language-
games and, hence, to language. The class of language-games is, arguably, polythetic as opposed to monothetic, i.e., there is no single feature common to all its
members.

But this "argument" does not establish that there is no such property or feature,
nor, *a fortiori*, that *no* class has such a property. Games *may* be a class with
particularly unclear boundaries, as Wittgenstein believes (§71), but consider the
class *inhabitants of Australia*, for example. What is true of games may not be
true of other classes. What Wittgenstein provided is an hypothesis which requires
further investigation.

In his proposal of the notion of "family resemblances", Wittgenstein appears
to reject the Socratic theory of definition with respect to language.[14] The Socratic
theory rests on a distinction between *definition* and *division*, a distinction which
mirrors the *intension-extension* distinction. To provide a definition is to refer to
some quality that certain objects, acts, events, etc. have in common. A definition of "kangaroo", for example, sets out the characteristics which an object must
have to be included in the class *kangaroos*. The *intension* of the term "kangaroo" is these characteristics. Division, on the other hand, provides instances of
such objects; those instances, the kangaroos, are the term's *extension*. Division
involves identifying creatures which have the required characteristics. This is not
definition, because identifying instances of a set does not indicate what the requirements of set membership are. According to Wittgenstein, then, there *is* no
intension for the term "language"; language cannot be defined in the Socratic
sense.

This claim Wittgenstein justifies on at least two grounds. Firstly, he believes
that, in philosophy, it is fruitless to seek a rigorous definition of terms generally
and of the term "language" in particular. Philosophy is, he believes, a grammatical
study. It is quite different from science. It does not advance hypotheses from
which deductions can be made, and it does not explain anything. It involves only
attention to how words are used (§109). Secondly, if the family of language-games
(i.e., languages) have no condition in common, trying to find such a condition is
futile. Wittgenstein makes no attempt, then, to identify the conditions necessary
and sufficient for membership of the class "language"—he believes there to be
none (§65).

As an alternative, he provides examples of specific language-games (§23), and says that various resemblances exist between them. To reiterate: Wittgenstein's listing of various language-games is not understood by him to be because the examples share characteristics which are necessary and sufficient for class membership. It is said to be on the basis of a "network of similarities" (§66). Members of the genus "language" have nothing more than family resemblance. Wittgenstein identifies specific language-games and notes the relations they enter into, viz. relations of similarity.

But what does this mean? It means that there are similarities between some language-games, but not between others, with respect to some attribute, say y. "Similarity" means "identity in at least one respect". Therefore, those language-games which have y will be members of a class; y is necessary for membership of that (sub)class. So, even if the "phenomena [of language] have no one thing in common", a (sub)class would still exist with respect to attribute y, and y is the intension of the term which refers to this attribute (Sutcliffe, 1993). The difficulties involved in specifying such attributes are neither proof that such attributes do not exist, nor proof that such attributes are not known.[15]

Not all classes are disjunctive "families". If they were, no account could ever be given of anything. For example, assume "language" to be a disjunctive class, consisting of either x or y or z. To unfold what is meant by x or y or z, either the necessary and sufficient conditions for each must be specified or x, y, and z must themselves be taken to be disjunctive (each may consist of a conjunction of attributes). But the regress cannot go on forever. At some stage it must be stopped by specifying the (non-disjunctive) conditions of class membership; by stating the conditions necessary and sufficient for something to be x, something to be y, and so on. You have to speak about the monothetic (sub)class in order to say what you mean by the polythetic class. The latter is ultimately a disjunction of monothetic classes. The point is that Wittgenstein's "argument" does not avoid the Socratic theory of definition. Identifying specific language-games and noting relations they enter into (division) is *not* an exclusive alternative to definition.

This defence of the Socratic theory is contrary to the orientation of contemporary research into the psychology of classification. This orientation is reproduced in Harré's (2002a) examination of the topic; it is polythetic in spirit. Harré says that Wittgenstein's notion of "family resemblance" *is* an alternative to the Aristotelian system of necessary and sufficient conditions (see pp. 262–263). But in providing "evidence" for an abandonment of the classical system, Harré confuses what people do in the act of classifying with the features of a system of classification. The fact remains that if there is no property or attribute common to a class or sub-class, there are no "kinds of thing". If there are no "kinds of thing", there can be no "different kinds of thing". If there are no "different kinds of thing", no categorical distinction can ever be made—no distinction can be made between one class, polythetic or otherwise, and any other (Sutcliffe, 1996). Polythetic classification, which Wittgenstein, Harré, and others rely on, would be impossible. Yet Wittgenstein implicitly demarcates between language-games and other aggregations which are not language-games, and Harré (2002a) distinguishes between oarsmen, birds, and so on.

In short: it may be the case that all language-games have no common property, but Wittgenstein certainly did not demonstrate this; and, notwithstanding Wittgenstein's apparent repudiation of definition, definition *cannot* be avoided.

6.5.3. A DISREGARD FOR THE GENERAL

It has been said that "... Wittgenstein shows no interest in articulating generalizations about human thought and language ..." (Friedman, 1998, p. 253). If Wittgenstein does have a propensity for the particular, this is something shared with operationism, verificationism and social constructionism. Bridgman's operational definitions were an attempt to replace the Socratic theory of definition. If, as Bridgman says, "the concept is synonymous with the corresponding set of operations", then each different set of operations is (corresponds to) a different concept. There would be, for example, at least as many different kinds of "guilt" as there are sets of activities of researchers who investigate it. But the fact is that the researcher (tacitly) recognises certain general features of all instances of guilt. This recognition is necessary for, and prior to, any decision about a particular experimental procedure intended to manipulate guilt.

Similarly, underlying Schlick's claim that what is necessary for logical impossibility is a discrepancy between the definitions of our terms and the way in which we use them (6.3.3) is a tacit recognition of the general—that the terms "died", "day", "after" and "tomorrow" have meanings which preclude *any* use for such a combination of words, and therefore, precede use. Although Schlick *says* that the rules of grammar have not provided any use for such a combination, he has not at all demonstrated that the sentence "My friend died the day after tomorrow" is meaningless because "died" refers to the past, and "the day after tomorrow" refers to the future.

Gergen, too, in his aggression example, illustrates (unwittingly) that because there are features common to "aggression", the term can be used to refer to weed growth, playing tennis, etc. He does not, for example, and for obvious reasons, refer to hats or books as aggressive. Labouring the point, nor does the "regression" example preclude the tacit recognition that "regression" has a general meaning. The example does, of course, illustrate the triviality that the term does not mean the same thing to a statistician as it does to a psychoanalyst. But it is only because the word has a general meaning in the first place, that the statistician and the analyst can each mean different, specific things by the term. Only because the term "regression" means generally *to return or to revert to a former place or condition* can the analyst use the term to refer to *the adoption of behaviour by an adult or adolescent that is more typical of a child*, and the statistician use the term to refer to *a regressing from the Y variable back to the X variable—accounting for Y in terms of X*, or *a regression towards the mean*, as in back towards some average value. If, as Gergen's account implies, asserting "I suggest that x is an example of regressive behaviour" is performing a certain kind of illocutionary act, this is a consequence of the fact that "regressive" means what it does; it is not an *explication* of that meaning. The general meaning of the term "regression" (its intension) is necessarily prior to specific meanings. In this case, meaning *precedes* use, and cannot, therefore, be *equated* with it. Significantly, the tacit recognition of the *general* meaning of terms is not consistent with the identification of meaning with use.

At this point, it may be apposite to say a little more about the doctrine of essentialism and the widely held view that all realists are essentialists. I have maintained that there are *kinds* of things (e.g., oarsmen, birds) and *kinds* of situations (e.g., those involving guilt, cognition, the use of language). This may fuel the belief that if we accept that there are such general kinds, we are committed to essentialism. Realists, so it is said, accept the former and are, therefore, committed to the latter. This inference is invalid for the following reason.

Essentialism is the doctrine that a thing has properties some of which are necessary (essential) to its being the thing it is. If those essential properties are lost, the thing ceases to exist as that kind of thing; it becomes a thing of a different kind. Typically, essentialists wish to distinguish between a thing's essential properties and its accidental properties (e.g., Bunge, 1996). An accidental property of a thing is said to be one which is not essential to that thing, in that it makes no difference to that thing's essential properties. An oft-repeated example is that 'being musical' is accidental to Socrates, whereas 'being rational' or 'being an animal' is not.

The essential/accidental distinction is not easy to defend, but realism is not committed to this doctrine. It *is* committed to the view that things and situations consist, in part, of properties, but these properties are not essences (and thereby distinct from a thing's accidental properties). Just what the properties are is a *factual* matter. It is not one of necessity, because to define something in terms of certain properties entails a number of proposals, each of which is open to investigation.

I repeat the point made earlier: we constantly refer to kinds of things and to kinds of situations. We do this because we recognise in any particular instance certain *general* features. This does not involve "carving up" the world, but sometimes some general features are cognised (Heil, 2003). Whether they are so depends on our qualities and interests at that time. Social constructionism frequently maintains that universality resides only in the language we use, but such nominalism results, in part, from disregarding the realist claim that particulars and universals are *not* two exclusive classes of entities (contra Russell, 1912/1959), that any situation exhibits *both* particularity and generality; that in the particular there is the general.[16]

6.6. CONCLUSION

The primary aim in this chapter has been to set out the way in which social constructionism perpetuates the logical positivist thesis that the meaning of a term is given by the conditions under which that term is used.

The constructionist thesis that meaning is contextually dependent is influenced by the Wittgensteinian views which influenced Schlick's final statements on the verifiability principle. Wittgenstein's impact on 20th century philosophy of science has been to cause a movement away from the Augustinian picture of language, and a broadening of what is meant by "grammatical rules" to encompass socio-linguistic conventions. These conceptual shifts did not begin during the emergence of post-positivist philosophy in the 1950s; they were present in 1932 in Schlick's development of the verifiability principle.

Social constructionism's adoption of the meaning-as-use thesis means that it can also be likened to the operationism of Bridgman and Stevens. Neither constructionism nor operationism gives precedence to the object of study. Ontology is devalued, because both are committed to the dictates of other factors, such as language, procedures, or practices. And because neither embrace an objectivist epistemology, knowledge is conflated with knowledge-claims.

The commonalities between social constructionism and Schlick's verificationism and operationism falsify the received view. In particular, similarities between social constructionism and operationism bring closer to home the irony of the received view, not just because of the influence which operationism has had upon psychology, but also because that influence is concurrent with the influence of social constructionism. Gergen's metatheory shows that aspects of positivism do remain in psychology, camouflaged as post-modernist theory.

The identification of meaning with use involves an incomplete characterisation of meaning, and is not consistently maintained by its proponents. It treats Wittgenstein's game analogy as though he had demonstrated a truth, and not merely put forward an hypothesis. Moreover, Wittgenstein's propensity for the particular does not escape the Socratic theory of definition. This can also be said of verificationism, operationism and social constructionism.

Gergen's preference for the particular might, indeed, have contributed to his failure to detect the similarities between his metatheory and logical positivism and operationism. His lack of scholarly attention to the actual content of Schlick's verificationism and operationism suggests a preoccupation with difference, with revolution (in the Kuhnian sense), to the neglect of themes that can be seen to continue across "revolutions".

NOTES

[1] The meaning-as-use theme received attention in Wittgenstein's earlier *Philosophical Grammar*, which was completed in 1933–4 and which is noticeably similar in tenor to *Philosophical Investigations*. In many respects, *Philosophical Grammar* is a less difficult book than *Philosophical Investigations* and, for this reason, reference to it will be made on those occasions where *Philosophical Investigations* is judged not to be clear on some matter.

[2] All references to *Philosophical Investigations* are to sections; references to *Philosophical Grammar* (PG) are to page numbers (e.g., PG, p. 190).

[3] Post-*Tractatus*, Wittgenstein rejects the correspondence theory of truth as metaphysical nonsense concerning the relations of language and reality. However, he does not reject the notion that the proposition *p* is true if things in fact are as it says they are. He simply wishes to reject the metaphysical baggage that once accompanied this notion—namely that language when reduced to its elements (names) is connected with metaphysical simples and that these simples give the names their meaning (Baker & Hacker, 1984b, p. 32).

[4] How accurately expressing the use to which the statement is put could be done in the case of, for example, "The book is on the table", without indicating that what is required is for a book to be on a table, is a puzzle.

[5] Schlick's substantial acknowledgement of Wittgenstein's influence occurs immediately after this paragraph. The acknowledgement was judged by Wittgenstein to be inadequate and, as he also did of Carnap, Wittgenstein accused Schlick of plagiarism (Malcolm, 1958, pp. 58–59).

[6] Bridgman's operationism must be distinguished from the view that operationism is simply the specification of operations necessary to produce the phenomenon for which the concept stands. There is nothing erroneous about this view. It involves only the recognition that a certain set of operations causes a particular phenomenon. Bridgman's operationism, on the other hand, involves a logical error, the nature and significance of which is discussed in 6.5.1. Only Bridgman's kind of operationism is of concern at this point.

[7] This is also characteristic of Gergen (1994c, Ch. 3), despite the fact that he is aware of objections concerning this fluctuation (e.g., p. 32).

[8] Nor, in Gergen's opinion, has its meaning originated within individual minds.

[9] In a later paper, however, this appears to be denied. Shotter (1994) claims that the "... meaning a word has for us does not arise out of it having a place *within an already existing system*, but that its meaning is a matter of circumstances, a matter of its *special* usage in the *particular* context of its occurrence (p. 151).

[10] Although these texts do not always mean quite the same thing by the term "operationism", the operationist precept is common to all—operations define concepts.

[11] Lest there be some confusion, given my example, this relational account of meaning does not depend on *z* being a simple object (like "dog") for which *j* stands. For instance, *z* could be "a number divisible only by 1 and by itself". Nor does this account depend on a picture theory of representation.

[12] Just why they do this is examined in the following section and in the next chapter.

[13] Gergen would not, of course, accept my interpretation of his thesis as one which involves causation—a fact notable in itself, for it adds substance to my argument that there are similarities between his philosophy and logical positivism. Both Schlick and Gergen reject causation as an ontological category. Schlick (1932/1979a) replaces it with "functional interdependence" (pp. 240–247) and Gergen (1994c) with "interdependence" (p. 192). Schlick reduces the concept of causation to an epistemological category linked to scientific practice. Gergen reduces it to a semantic category embodied in the conventions of everyday life and various scientific and philosophical groups.

[14] I refer to this theory of definition as "Socratic" and not "Aristotelian", because Socrates began the development of this theory; Aristotle's contributions were extensions to it (Guthrie, 1969, pp. 425–437).

[15] As is evident from 6.2, it is a feature of Wittgensteinian theories explaining meaning (e.g., Baker & Hacker, 1984a; Dummett, 1973) that if a speaker knows a rule, he can say what that rule is. But, this is a *non sequitur*. As I maintained in 5.6.2, knowing is a relational situation: a cognises some state of affairs (s). This does not imply that a can articulate s. His knowledge may be tacit. This point of logic also applies to our discernment of different kinds when we engage in classificatory practices. Not being able to *say* what distinguishes x from y does not imply that we don't *know* that x is different from y.

[16] This is endorsed by Harré (2002b, p. 616).

Chapter 7

PHENOMENALISM AND ITS ANALOGUE

7.1. INTRODUCTION

The similarities between social constructionism and logical positivism, and the former's ignorance of these, are not confined to semantic matters. In this chapter, some epistemological likenesses are identified. In fact, the semantic connections between logical positivism and social constructionism have their roots in a shared epistemological assumption. The epistemic base of logical positivism (in its re-construction of scientific knowledge) incorporates an ill-conceived anti-realism, a component of the Kantian philosophy which it struggled to relinquish. The failure of social constructionist metatheory involves a similar anti-realist path. It draws conclusions with which, shorn of their modern-day flavour, Kant would not have disagreed.

7.2. THE PHENOMENAL "GIVEN" IN LOGICAL POSITIVISM

Except for some of Schlick's early papers, Continental logical positivists did not engage in traditional epistemology. They were not concerned with the kinds of issues pursued by Ayer, for example, issues such as "perception", "memory" and "other minds". In this respect they differed from some of their predecessors with positivist tendencies (e.g., Hume) who attempted to substitute epistemology for metaphysics (Passmore, 1948, p. 1).

However, Schlick and Carnap did assume, in the construction of scientific knowledge, a *phenomenalist* epistemology.[1,2] But it does not follow from this that they were foundationalists, taking some aspects of supposed scientific knowledge to be known with certainty (see 5.6.4). To appreciate this, it is essential to understand how they conceptualised the relationship between phenomenalism, conventionalism, and scientific knowledge. It was *not* a case of the phenomenalistic base infecting scientific knowledge with its supposed certainty and other epistemic values, through some kind of "trickle up" process (Friedman, 1999; Richardson, 1998).

In Schlick's (1932/1979d) account, what is immediately perceived is "the given" and this is ". . . a term for what is simplest and no longer open to question" (p. 261). A similar position is taken by Carnap, both in the *Aufbau* and in *The Unity of Science* (1934). In the *Aufbau*, the central thesis is that it is, in principle, possible to reduce all concepts to the immediately given, which is an unbroken stream of elementary experience (Carnap, 1928/1967, pp. 107–109).

It has been suggested that Carnap's phenomenalist base in the *Aufbau* is *merely* a matter of convention, one chosen by him to elucidate the construction of scientific knowledge (Tennant, 1994; Uebel, 1996). There is little support for this *unqualified* suggestion. It is at odds with the remarks of commentators contemporary with Carnap, such as Weinberg (1936, pp. 211–212) and Werkmeister (1937, p. 286). In Passmore's (1943) opinion, ". . . Carnap is still assuming in *The Unity of Science* that protocol statements do refer to the given" (p. 81). Ayer (1946, p. 32), too, is in no doubt that Carnap (and Schlick) endorsed phenomenalism. More recently, Goodman's (1977) exposition of the *Aufbau* also assumes its phenomenalistic basis, and Quine (1994) has explicitly discounted the "conventionalist" suggestion:

> I picture Carnap as having been a single-minded phenomenalist when he devised the constructions that went into the *Aufbau*. When the book was about ready for printing, I picture Neurath pressing the claims of physicalism. I then picture Carnap writing and inserting those paragraphs of disavowal by way of reconciling the book with his changing views. Significantly, he took the physicalist line in his subsequent writings, and refused permission to translate the *Aufbau* for more than thirty years (p. 345).

More recently still, the view that the *Aufbau* is a clear defence of phenomenalistic empiricism has been staunchly defended (Friedman, 1999). Thus, the suggestion that, during the 1928–1934 period, Carnap's phenomenalism was not a conviction but a tactical choice made by an already thoroughgoing conventionalist, takes the "logical positivists as conventionalists" thesis too far. There is no doubt that Carnap moved towards confining discussion to language alone (in taking up radical physicalism) and there is no doubt, too, that the *Aufbau* frequently relies on conventions in its reconstruction of concepts (5.3.3). But there is little evidence for the claim that, during this period, phenomenalism was not at the heart of Carnap's system of knowledge. A more accurate portrayal of Schlick's and Carnap's position at that time locates their epistemological thesis in the context of language and meaning, rather than construing their accounts as *purely* conventionalist.

This interweaving of epistemology with language is manifest in one of Schlick's (1934/1979) final papers, where he suggests that an "affirmation" is the linguistic expression of the given. Affirmations, he claims, are not protocol propositions, because they are not hypotheses. They are of the form "... 'Here now so-and-so', e.g., 'Here now two black spots coincide' ... " (p. 385) and, as utterances about what is immediately perceived, they are, Schlick believes, certain.[3] Schlick does not make clear the precise relationship between the uncertain protocol or observation statements of science and the certain affirmation utterances which express "the given". He does, however, say that the former are "framed by", "occasioned by" or "created by" the latter (p. 412).[4] My point is that no sooner is Schlick's phenomenalism presented to the reader, than it is embedded in linguistic matters. Similarly, in Carnap's (1934, p. 44) account, the directly given experiences are reported or described by the subject, and such reports are said to belong to the "protocol language" or to the "phenomenal language". Again these are supposed to be indubitable, because the referents are immediate, involving no inferential leap. Setting aside social constructionism's justifiable repudiation of "certainty", this interweaving of epistemology and language is, of course, a feature of their metatheory, albeit with a present-day flavour.

In both cases, talk of material things (e.g., "Sodium has a double line in the yellow region of the spectrum" (Schlick, 1935/1979, p. 409)) is grounded in a phenomenal language (e.g. "Two yellow lines here now") about which there can be no doubt. The phenomenal language is said to refer to the given. This matches Mackie's (1969) depiction of the doctrine of *linguistic phenomenalism*. Statements about things, events, processes, etc. can be translated into, or reduced to, statements about such mind-dependent items as "the given" or "sense-data".

If what is known directly is "the given" or "sense-data", material things are not known directly. Thus the argument for linguistic phenomenalism can be set out:

(A) Contrary to direct realism, we are not immediately aware of material objects or states of affairs.

(B) What people perceive directly are mind-dependent entities, "sense data" or "the given", and from these they infer the existence of objects and states of affairs.

(C) Consequently, statements about things, events, processes, etc. can be either translated into or reduced to statements about such mind-dependent items as sense-data. Therefore, what we're actually referring to when we say "There is a book on the table" is not that there is a book on the table, but that there are various sense-data such as roundness, brownness, etc.

This blend of epistemology with language was the basis from which Schlick's and Carnap's account of the construction of scientific knowledge was to proceed. I return to this at the end of the section but, first, what of phenomenalism?

Phenomenalism is an implausible account of knowledge (e.g., Anderson, 1927/1962; Armstrong, 1961; Hirst, 1959; Sosa, 1995) and linguistic phenomenalism fares no better. Firstly, the equivalence between material object statements and sense-datum statements does not obtain. The truth-conditions of the former are not the truth-conditions of reports about complexes of experiences (Mackie, 1969). For example, lap-top computer-like sensa may occur, but the item on the desk may not be a lap-top computer, just something which looks and feels like one. Also, it is unlikely that there could ever be sense-datum statements that are not parasitic on material object statements, making the "reduction" of the latter to the former circular (Mackie, 1969). In considering the lap-top computer, "Rectangular, grey here now" would not differentiate the lap-top from, say, a box of photographs, and so the temptation is to say "Rectangular, grey, lap-top computer-like sensa here now". Generating an extensive list of sense-datum statements for just one material object statement does not solve this problem.

Secondly, and crucially, linguistic phenomenalism rests on phenomenalism's central thesis—that the immediate objects of knowledge are mind-dependent entities (premise B)—a thesis which incurs the logical error that has been a recurring theme of previous chapters—the fallacy of constitutive relations (5.6.2; 6.5.1). "The given", "elementary experiences" and "sense-data" have only a relative existence, in that they are only ever spoken of as present *in the act of knowing*. They are somehow constituted by their being sensed, i.e., they depend for their existence on the experiencing subject. Schlick's account appears to be a case in point. Schlick (1917/1979, pp. 282–287) speaks as though "the given" has independent existence—it stands, he says, for that which we immediately experience—but nowhere does he suggest that "the given" *may* or *may not* be perceived. Thus, he implies that what is experienced is constituted by the relation of being aware. To invoke the relational schema, *aRb*: *b* ("the given") is constituted by *R* (the relation). If "the given" has no ontological independence, Schlick's linguistic phenomenalism rests on a constitutive doctrine.

It is also important to make clear the insurmountable difficulty of Carnap's linguistic phenomenalism, and Carnap's "solution" to this difficulty, because the latter resembles strategies employed by both Schlick and social constructionism. Carnap's radical physicalism was the thesis that protocol statements stand in a relation of equivalence to statements about things or "the language of physics". (It is expressed in conclusion C in the argument above). In presenting an analysis of language, Carnap (1934) says that there are two modes of speech, one the material mode, the other the formal mode. In the material or "usual" mode of speech, reference is to objects, states of affairs, and the meanings of words (p. 38). In the formal or "correct" mode of speech, reference is to the formal linguistic properties of protocol statements (pp. 38–41). So, if the formal mode is adopted, the issue of reference (to material things) is replaced with reference to linguistic forms. Applying this to a discussion about protocol statements: in the material mode reference is to "the given", in the formal mode reference is to the syntactical properties of protocol statements.

Carnap (1934) recognised that protocol language in the "material mode", could "... *be applied only solipsistically*; [that] *there would be no intersubjective protocol language*" (p. 80). If a protocol statement refers to the experience of a certain person, it cannot also refer to the experience of a different person (p. 78). Therefore, it could not be known by anyone except the person reporting the directly given experience. This, he suggested, led to the impossibility of specifying the inferential connection between the protocol statements and physical statements (pp. 81–82). He concluded that protocol statements, when described in the "material mode", could not sensibly function as the bases of a system of knowledge. In Carnap's opinion, "... the use of the material mode leads us to questions whose discussion ends in contradiction and insoluble difficulties" (p. 82).

Carnap's (1934) "solution" was to "... avoid the use of the material mode entirely ..." (p. 83) and adopt the formal mode. The issue of (external) reference to material things was replaced with reference to linguistic forms (intra-linguistic reference). This, of course, is illogical. On the one hand protocol statements in the "material mode" are the "ultimate verifiers"; they refer to "the given"; they were essential to logical positivism in its opposition to metaphysics and its commitment to empiricism. On the other hand, protocol statements can only sensibly function as propositions basic to a system of knowledge if we forget that they refer to "the given" and treat them as statements in the "formal mode". Three points are worthy of note.

First, as Passmore (1943) points out, Carnap, in recognising the contradiction and insoluble difficulties of protocol statements in the "material mode", sought not to question the claim that what is immediately known is the "private experience of the given", but instead resolved not to speak of it. *Premise B of the argument for linguistic phenomenalism was not challenged.*

Second, Carnap's "solution" retained some of the earlier themes of the *Aufbau*. In this earlier work, the philosophical motivation was neo-Kantian. "The given" were recognised as subjective, and the whole point of proceeding from "the given" to scientific knowledge via a constructional system was to place the sense data into that system, because the latter was deemed to be objective. In the traditional empiricist tradition, "... *certainty* flows ... from the bottom up ...", but in the neo-Kantian tradition, "... *objectivity* flows from the top down" (Friedman, 1999, p. 129).

Third, Carnap's "solution" is similar to the "solution" which Schlick had employed earlier, albeit with a less logistical emphasis. In *Allgemeine Erkenntnislehre*, a concrete definition is said to involve pointing to something real, and the features of the thing pointed to "... can be ascertained only by intuition; for whatever is given, is given us ultimately through intuition" (Schlick, 1925/1974, p. 28). However, Schlick reasons, what if all intuition is blurred because what is intuited is a Heraclitean flux of experiences? Schlick resolves not to address this issue (p. 31) and turns instead to conventionalism in order to "...sav[e] the certainty and rigour of knowledge ..." (p. 30). We must appeal, he thinks, to the kinds of implicit definitions illustrated in Hilbert's conceptualisation of geometry (pp. 31–39). Implicit definitions, unlike concrete definitions, are detached from the given in intuition and, thus, will form the certain and intersubjective starting-point for a system of knowledge that concrete definitions cannot.[5] Again, *premise B is left unchallenged*. Carnap's avoidance of protocol statements in the material mode, and Schlick's turning away from the issues that he raises in his question about the "flux" of experience, ignore epistemology and undermine the *experiential* meaning of concepts.

A major factor in Schlick's and Carnap's failure to question premise B was that neither had, at this point, completely detached himself from Kantian idealism. Although they claimed to reject the Kantian proposition that objects or things in themselves are unknown to us (see Schlick, 1925/1974, pp. 269–270), they *did* in fact assume that we cannot know things as they are in themselves, because we cannot know them *directly* (premise A). Schlick (1925/1974), for example, says that:

> Seeing an object proves to me that it exists only in so far as I can infer this from the given visual sensations; and to make this inference I need a series of premises about the constitution of the sense organs, about the nature of the processes through which these sensations are aroused, and much more (p. 218).

Knowledge of things in themselves, then, is detached from intuition or experience. Such knowledge requires an inductive inference from the phenomenal or sensible qualities of "the given". Schlick's understanding of this "distinction" between immediate and mediate knowledge is made clear in an earlier paper:

> Through the conceptual system of the sciences we actually know the *essence* of extramental reality. It is not *unknowable*, as phenomenalism has continued to maintain since the days of Kant; it is merely in*experienceable*, not a possible object of acquaintance, and that is quite a different matter (Schlick, 1917/1979, p. 285).

Thus, immediate knowledge is arrived at through experience, mediate knowledge of things in themselves is not. The latter "...always involves subsumption under concepts and...always goes beyond the immediately given" (Friedman, 1999, p. 19). There is, at this point in Schlick's philosophy, a clear-cut distinction between knowing things in themselves and immediate experience.[6] As is the current inclination (5.6.2), knowledge in general and scientific knowledge in particular is *detached from experience*.

Given this epistemological "picture", Schlick and Carnap cannot be firmly located on the Kantian (idealist) side of the epistemological divide. However, to suggest, as Schlick does, that the inexperienceable is knowable is not only to abandon the empiricism which logical positivism was so concerned to defend, it is also to accept the proposition that we cannot know things as they are in themselves, where "know" is taken to mean "direct knowledge of". This is a proposition which Kant would not have disputed.

7.3. SOCIAL CONSTRUCTIONISM'S CONTINUATION OF "KNOWLEDGE AS MEDIATED", AND THE LINK TO KANT

The logical positivist substitution of metaphysics and interweaving of epistemology with issues about language, is reproduced in social constructionist metatheory. This occurs because, like logical positivism, social constructionism also retains a crucial link to Kant (Hacking, 1999).

As always, there is more to draw on in Gergen's writings than those of Potter and Shotter. So, first, Gergen's repudiation of ontological issues: it is based upon the premise that such issues cannot, in principle, be attended to. This was broached in 1.6.3, and is at the heart of Gergen's defence against the charge of ontological relativism (2.5). To repeat the passage quoted in 2.5, social constructionism:

> ... makes no denial concerning explosions, poverty, death, or 'the world out there' more generally. Neither does it make any affirmation. As I have noted, constructionism is ontologically mute. Whatever is, simply is. There is no foundational description to be made about an 'out there' as opposed to an 'in here,' about experience or material. Once we attempt to articulate 'what there is,' however, we enter the world of discourse (Gergen, 1994c, p. 72).

Social constructionism is, then, silent about what exists and what occurs because the language-game of "description" is said to be thoroughly constrained by the systems of language in which we live.

As Chapters 3, 5 and 6 have made clear, there is no reason to interpret Gergen charitably in this passage. Although the phrase "we enter the world of discourse" could be taken to mean "we enter a world of which discourse is about", that cannot be what Gergen means, because such an interpretation cannot accommodate social constructionism's most distinctive thesis—that discourse is not *about* (does not refer to) states of affairs. Gergen's phrase "we enter the world of discourse" must be interpreted in the context of his commitment to internal reference. To "enter the world of discourse" is to be embedded in a closed system of language, one which precludes the "referents" from being grounded in anything external to that system (5.6). Nor should one be hoodwinked by the truism in this passage—that we cannot say anything about the world, or anything about the relationship between language and the world, or anything about anything, without using language. Such self-reference (i.e., using language to refer to language) is commonplace and unproblematic.

Of course, despite Gergen's pretensions to "ontological muteness", the passage contains a series of ontological (empirical) claims, claims which purport to convey facts about the world. Gergen's insistence that social constructionism doesn't do this is noteworthy for its affinity with Carnap's insistence that the adoption of a particular linguistic system does not license any ontological conclusions (5.3.3). Gergen frequently, but not consistently, makes use of inverted commas in order to convey the absence of any ontological commitment on his part. Phrases and terms, such as: "the thing in itself" (1994c, p. 70); "fact", "envy", "flirting", "anger" (1985a, p. 268); "command", "obedience", "events" (1986a, p. 147; 1987b, p. 8); all that "can be known" (1987c, p. 121); "experience" (1994c, p. 71); "the truth" (1985a, p. 271–2); "the prolonging of life" (1989b, p. 473); "brute facts" (1990c, p. 291), "aggression" (1986a, p. 149); "object of description" (1994c, p. 37); "the external world" (1994c, p. 70) are deemed to require the use of inverted commas in order to give them some extraordinary but unspecified sense which Gergen's "ontological muteness" demands. This practice is analogous to the logical positivists' reduction of material object statements to phenomenal language. Both strategies are based upon the belief that we are mistaken about the referents of material object statements (Schlick and Carnap) or descriptives in general (Gergen).

This belief is a consequence of the conviction that modification (of some kind) is necessarily involved in what is known; that we can never know reality as unmodified things-in-themselves. Gergen's "solution" is that of Schlick and Carnap. It is simply to turn away from epistemological issues. Just as Schlick and Carnap failed to confront the epistemological issues involved in premise B of the argument for linguistic phenomenalism, Gergen maintains, as does constructionism generally, that questions about "experience", "self-knowledge", and "other minds", etc., are the wrong questions (e.g., 1994c, pp. 70–71), and he turns instead to language and its social consequences.

Beneath Gergen's smokescreen of "social constructionism doesn't comment on matters ontological", there exist two ideas from Kant.[7] The first is Kant's notion of the known, phenomenal world as one created through the imposition of concepts (5.2.1). The basis of Gergen's rejection of this particular charge of Kantianism would, presumably, be the same as for his dissociation from Kuhn's account of science. He would maintain that terms such as "concepts" and "cognition" presuppose individualism, and he would repeat his claim that ". . . it is *description* not *cognition* that constructs the factual world" (Gergen, 1994c, p. 37).

But Gergen's distinction between description and cognition is of no consequence when weighed against the fact that if Kant's term "concepts" is substituted for Gergen's phrase "linguistic forms", the two claims are identical. Kant's belief that "the known, phenomenal world is one created through the imposition of concepts" is transformed into "the known, phenomenal world is one created through the imposition of linguistic forms", which is Gergen's position, as 5.5.1 demonstrates. Gergen's implicit epistemology simply replaces Kant's categories of the understanding with linguistic forms in the form of socio-linguistic conventions.[8]

The second Kantian idea presupposed by Gergen, is the notion of a noumenal world independent of enquirers, a world which is inaccessible and unknowable. Gergen replaces ontological issues with issues about language because of the constructionist belief that *there is no direct, referential access to a language-independent world*. Premise A of the argument for linguistic phenomenalism is as much a feature of Gergen's metatheory as it is of logical positivist epistemology. To say, as Gergen does, that "Whatever is, simply is", in conjunction with claims 5–8, in 5.5.1, is to imply that what exists and occurs cannot be known. In Gergen's epistemology, psychological communities are enveloped by socio-linguistic conventions and these preclude direct knowledge of things as they are.

This is equivalent to Kant's "unknowability of things-in-themselves" or his idea of the "transcendental object". Gergen's belief is consistent with Kant's interpretation of the *noumenon* as something that cannot be known in the sense of knowing its characteristics. Kant recognises that he is not entitled to assert the existence of noumena, but he maintains that the idea of a noumenal world is one which must, *of necessity*, accompany the idea of a phenomenal world (Caygill, 1995, pp. 301–303). Gergen's neglect of ontology is caused by this Kantian belief that the constituents of reality are not accessible, and that what is not accessible is unknowable and cannot be commented upon.

In claiming that both logical positivism and social constructionism accept premise A because of their links to Kant, two points of clarification must be made. First, the fact that logical positivism explicitly rejected the Kantian notion of an unknowable noumenal world should be reiterated. Second, neither constructionism in general, nor Gergen's metatheory in particular, is phenomenalist. Gergen does not accept the view that knowledge of the world is mediated by sense-data, or any other kind of mentalistic "given".

This having been said, the epistemological similarities between logical positivism and Gergen's constructionism are obvious. Both incorporate the view that we can never know things as they are in themselves; that we can only know things as they present themselves *after* the "conceptual system of the sciences" (Schlick and Carnap) or the "linguistic forestructure" (Gergen) has *mediated* between the enquirer and the object of knowledge, or *imposed* itself on the object of knowledge. Crucially, both detach knowledge of things or events from experience. Whilst neither denies that things are experienced, they hold to the view that the source of this "knowledge" lies in conceptual or linguistic systems that are conventional in nature. They have organised their semantic theses around an anti-realist epistemology.

And what of Potter and Shotter? Unlike Gergen, neither suggests a silence about ontology but, like Gergen and like logical positivism, they also substitute traditional epistemology with issues about language, albeit language as a *practice*.

Potter, we know, thinks that theories generally, and the traditional concepts of epistemology in particular, are non-situated, decontextualised, abstractions. Debates about epistemology function only as situated rhetorical practice (Edwards et al., 1995; Edwards & Potter, 1992; Potter & Edwards, 1999), and such practices are to be treated as primary (Potter, 2000). This is what the linguistic turn of logical positivism has evolved into.

Shotter's (somewhat different) turn to language is also seen as a replacement for traditional epistemology and theories generally. Shotter's view of theories as abstractions far removed from "...the buzzing confusion of social action ..." (2002, p. 593) calls to mind Schlick's belief that systems of truths generated from implicit definitions "float freely" (1925/1974, p. 37). Both believe that parts of a theory, at least, fail to designate anything real. But Shotter emphasizes the "precarious", "vague", and "unstable" nature of our social world. He provides no argument for this—merely citing Wittgenstein is deemed sufficient to render its veracity obvious. There is, Shotter thinks, a "flow of continuous communicative activity", a flow which is not orderly; the world is conceived as an "indivisible living unity"; events are without structure (e.g., Shotter, 1993a, pp. 179–181; 1994, p. 166; 1996, p. 293; 2003, p. 462). Such suggestions are evocative of Schlick's (Heraclitean) flux of experiences. Recall that the latter were the reason for his turning to conventionalism (7.2). Schlick's faith in implicit definitions to provide a certain and objective starting-point for scientific knowledge is not, of course, shared by constructionists. Nevertheless, Shotter does think that the words used to describe events "lend" them the structure they're lacking, a view not unrelated to Schlick's belief that the world is rendered knowable only when we impose systems of implicit definitions on the flux of experiences.

There is a final point to be made about Gergen, Potter and Shotter.

7.3.1. THE WORST ARGUMENT IN THE WORLD: SOCIAL CONSTRUCTIONISM'S "GEM"

Social constructionism, like logical positivism, maintains that we cannot know things as they are in themselves (where "know" is taken to mean "have direct knowledge of"). The constructionist position is that knowledge, in particular scientific knowledge, is mediated by and contaminated by language. This proposition is the conclusion to an argument now known as "the Gem".

The Gem's history is this: in 1985, the philosopher David Stove held a competition to determine the worst argument in the world. The criteria were: (a) the intrinsic awfulness of the argument; (b) its degree of acceptance among philosophers, and (c) the degree to which it has escaped criticism (Stove, 1995, p. 66). The winner was the argument that he himself (Stove) had submitted, which he later referred to as "the Gem" (Stove, 1991).[9] The Gem, he said, is "... an argument so bad ... that it is hard to imagine anyone ever being swayed by it" (p. 147). The Gem appears in different guises but its general nature is:

(A) We cannot X things unless condition C, which is necessary for X-ing things, is satisfied,

So,

(B) We cannot X things as they are in themselves.

Substitutes for X include "know", "talk of", "interact with", and "refer to". Once the substitute for X is known, the substitute for C can usually be determined. For example, if X is replaced with "describe", C might then be "within, or subject to the limitations imposed by, or through, forms of language". The premise of the Gem is a tautology, but the conclusion is not, so the argument is invalid because a non-tautological conclusion cannot be deduced from a tautological premise. The conclusion is the Kantian one discussed in the previous sections.

Stove may have erred in not finding a version of the Gem in logical positivist philosophy. However, in social constructionism, the Gem is ubiquitous. It appears in various forms but, with regard to knowledge, it materialises as:

(A) We can know things only through:

- daily interactions between people
- different forms of negotiated understandings
- socio-linguistic conventions
- fact construction

So,

(B) We cannot know things as they exist or occur in themselves.

The premise is tautological. Each of the conditions deemed necessary for knowledge, i.e., social interaction, forms of understandings, and so on, involves knowing. So, the premise repeats elements previously stated—we can know things only through knowing things. The conclusion is as before. It involves the internalism that exemplifies Kantian, neo-Kantian, and logical positivist philosophy.[10] Although idealism depends on the Gem, the Gem does not depend on idealism. However, the transition from the Gem to idealism is psychologically easy: once it is accepted that our knowing a particular psycho-social process (Z) through language somehow contaminates it or turns it into something else, why bother with the noumenal world and processes-as-they-are-in-themselves?

Of course, social constructionism has repeatedly rejected charges of idealism (e.g., Gergen, 1994c; Potter, 2003b), and constructionists *do* bother with social processes-as-they-are-in-themselves. Still, with respect to *metatheory*, the Gem *is* a feature of Gergen's account (see 5.5.1), he does turn his back on things-as-they-are-in-themselves (in his desire for ontological muteness), and his links to Kant were made clear in the previous section. From the textual material provided in this and previous chapters, the Gem is also evident in Shotter's research. Recall, the internalism and implicit idealism that characterises his constructionism (5.6.2). And even if we treat Potter's careless use of language as just that, and not as an unwitting endorsement of idealism (about this, I am in two minds), the Gem is still to be found in his work: he tells us that constructionists consider phenomena not in-themselves, but in terms of people's descriptions (e.g., Potter, 2003b, p. 787).

In short, a thesis central to social constructionism invokes the winner of a worst-argument-in-the-world competition. The constructionist denial of unmediated knowledge of the world is on tautological grounds. All there is to their argument is: our use of language (to know) is our use of language, so we cannot step outside of this (in order to know things as they are in themselves).

7.4. CONCLUSION

Although there was a gradual emancipation from Kantian epistemology, much of the content of the logical positivists' philosophical writings remained suffused with what Maria Reichenbach (1965) referred to as "transitional points of view" (p. xiv). They did not accept that the constituents of reality are directly knowable. The bounds of the phenomenal or "the given" could not be crossed.

Despite differences between their epistemology and that of social constructionism, and despite the latter's desire to overturn "old ways of thinking", this same view has been propagated by constructionists. Both interweave epistemology and language; both maintain that knowing involves a modification of some kind; both keep alive Kant's "unknowability of things-in-themselves". In fact, social constructionism continues the general tradition of anti-realist epistemology, succeeding not only Kant and the logical positivists, but Locke, Berkeley, Hume, J. S. Mill, Russell, Moore, H. H. Price, and Ayer as well. These philosophers were "mind-bound", social constructionism is "language-bound", but they unite in their conviction that the constituents of reality are not directly knowable.

NOTES

[1] This was not a position accepted by Reichenbach, despite the fact that in his early work he was, of the three, the most committed Kantian. Reichenbach (1938) proposed that what was observed were objects, and that an inference was made from these observations to the existence of impressions.

[2] Bergmann's (1954, p. 11) rejection of the claim that the logical positivists were phenomenalists involves the straw-man fallacy. He incorrectly takes the first premise of phenomenalism to be: "All there is are sense data", then correctly states that this is a proposition the logical positivists do not

accept. If the first premise of phenomenalism were "All there is are sense data", "phenomenalism" would just be a synonym for "idealism".

3 Schlick (1934/1979, p. 411) qualified this in his claim that all that could be doubted about an affirmation is the speaker's rules of use for terms such as "black", "spot", "coincide". But this doubt, he believed, is about use, not about the affirmation itself.

4 There is, however, some ambiguity in Schlick's account concerning the temporal location of affirmations in the scientific process (see Schlick, 1934/1979; 1935/1979).

5 This is at odds with the logical positivist claim that the concepts which have an *a priori* conventional status are not independent of experience (5.3).

6 As we saw from the previous chapter, Schlick later attempted to defend a position closer to traditional empiricism than to neo-Kantianism in his verifiability theory of meaning.

7 The critic should not be dissuaded from observing this link, by Gergen's repudiation of a connection between his metatheory and Kantian philosophy (see Gergen, 1994c, p. 94, p. 99, p. 124).

8 This is not to suggest that, with respect to the origin of the categories, Gergen's account bears any resemblance to Kant's nativism. Chapters 5 and 6 make clear that this is not the case.

9 I doubt that Stove's book *The Plato Cult and Other Philosophical Follies* will have been read by many (if any) social constructionists. It is far too pungent for their present-day sensitivities; they would abhor most of its characteristics. But the book is teeming with common-sense and logic. It is also frequently hilarious.

10 Given Poincaré's influence on logical positivism (5.2.4), it is worth noting Stove's (1991) observation of a version of the Gem in Poincaré's *The Value of Science*. The Gem is also found in Schopenhauer's *The World as Will and Representation*, a text which influenced the early Wittgenstein (Monk, 1990).

CHAPTER 8

CONCLUSIONS AND SPECULATIONS

The aim in this book has been to examine certain "meta-issues" which have become prominent in the social sciences following the advent of social constructionism. I have argued that the charges levelled at constructionism, of non-trivial (episte-mological) relativism and (absolute) self-refutation, do not have the force which some assume them to have. Both charges depend on concepts and assumptions which constructionism has rejected. If questions are not begged in favour of these concepts and assumptions, Gergen's metatheory exemplifies a trivial form of rel-ativism and is not necessarily false, but *operationally* self-refuting. He cannot succeed in providing an internalist account of language-use, but the truth of such an account is a contingent matter. If true, it could never be said. Gergen's attempt to provide such an account rests on constructionism's piecemeal (mis)appropriation of Austin's concept of performative utterances. Gergen *must* demonstrate that all indicatives operate as pure performatives, but he does not succeed in this. His example of "a local game of description" does not exclude matters of fact being conveyed by discourse. Nor does it exclude the possibility that all speech-acts have components which are fact-stating.

My second contention is that the received wisdom in theoretical psychology, and in the social sciences generally, is wrong. Social constructionist metatheory is not antithetical to positivist philosophy of science, if by "antithetical" is meant that the two share nothing which is central to each.

A major deficiency of logical positivism was its development of convention-alism. Conventionalism, the positivists thought, would provide the perfect blend of rationalism and empiricism without compromising the latter. Certain concepts in scientific theories and the "necessary truths" of logic and mathematics were

177

said to have an *a priori* conventional status, where *a priori* was taken to mean not "independent of experience", and not "for all time", but "before knowledge".

Gergen has unwittingly appropriated this notion of *a priori* and the conventionalism of the logical positivists in general. But conventionalism cannot be consistently maintained. It rests on the condition of internal reference, a condition which cannot be defended without recourse to empirical realism. The philosophical errors of logical positivism are, because of their joint commitment to conventionalism, the same errors of Gergen's social constructionism. In addition, aspects of Gergen's metatheory: (i) echo the implications of Hilbert's research on the status of geometrical axioms, and (ii) are, in certain respects, consistent with Poincaré's conventionalism. Not only that, Potter, Shotter and Gergen frequently confuse relations with properties and qualities, display (at times) an ambivalence towards ontology, disregard traditional logic, perpetuate the notion of construction, and misuse the word "knowledge". In these respects, they continue the tradition and the errors of logical positivist philosophy.

Social constructionism's perpetuation of philosophical error is also apparent when its *a posteriori* thesis, that language acquires its meaning through use, is compared with Schlick's later developments of verificationism. Wittgenstein's influence on Schlick and constructionism is such that both rely on the meaning-as-use criterion, both make use of the notion of "rules" as determining use (and therefore meaning), both interpret "rules" broadly, and both require a social context in which meaning is given. In addition, Gergen's use of Austin's doctrine of felicity is perhaps related to Schlick's notion of logical impossibility.

Schlick's verificationism and social constructionism are also, despite some differences, conceptually related to Bridgman's and S. S. Stevens' operationism. Operationism, too, requires that attention be drawn to context of usage as a determinant of meaning. Moreover, there are important epistemological similarities between Stevens' and Gergen's accounts of the scientific process. The concern expressed by some psychologists—that methodological aspects of positivism remain in social and psychological science—takes on an unintended twist. Aspects remain, not only because operationism is still a recommended methodological practice in psychology, but also because, in some respects, social constructionism maintains the tenets of operationism.

The identification of meaning with use gives an incomplete characterisation of meaning. Possible objections to this claim may be based upon an uncritical acceptance of Wittgenstein's thesis that there is nothing common to all games. It might be believed that the Socratic theory of definition has been supplanted. This is not the case: polythetic classes are simply a disjunction of monothetic classes. Furthermore, in employing the meaning-as-use thesis, Schlick's verificationism, operationism and social constructionism share a propensity for the particular, but in all cases certain general features of things are implied. The fact that we recognise in any particular instance certain *general* features of things does not commit con-structionists, realists, or anyone else to the doctrine of essentialism.

Finally, there is an epistemological connection between Gergen's metatheory and logical positivism. Gergen's pretension to "ontological muteness" is comparable with Schlick's and Carnap's reduction of material object statements to phenomenal language. This occurs because both retain a link to Kant. Both take it for granted that the source of knowledge lies in the imposition of concepts or linguistic forms; that we cannot know things as they are in themselves. Both continue the tradition of anti-realist epistemology. Like their positivist forebears, Potter, Shotter and Gergen substitute traditional epistemology with issues about language and they detach what is meant by "knowledge" from that which is discovered.

Many commentators might take social constructionism to be a fine example of the anti-scientific movement which is the target of Sokal & Bricmont's *Intellectual Impostures* (1998) or Gross & Levitt's (1996) *Higher Superstition*. The latter claims that in the last two or three decades the "academic left" has displayed an "... open hostility toward the actual content of scientific knowledge ..." (p. 2), and that the scholarly quality of their research ranges from "... seriously flawed to hopelessly flawed" (p. 41). I hope to have demonstrated that constructionism's scepticism toward the scientific enterprise is grounded in certain intellectual traditions embraced by those who, unlike some of their successors, *did* undertake their work with a rigorous scientific attitude. Social constructionism has preserved aspects of logical positivism—albeit some of its inconsistent, non-realist aspects. The former is an extension of the latter's original identification of linguistic analysis with philosophy; logical positivism and social constructionism both replace a study of situations with a study of language and the circumstances of language-use. Both judge a non-factualist stance to be an essential corrective to the unwarranted metaphysical or ontological emphasis which the "naïve" philosopher or psychologist is so reluctant to relinquish.

If the claims and arguments of Chapter 5 are correct, then one aspect of the history of thought about the status of scientific theories in the past 150 years can be characterised as a decreasing emphasis on empiricism together with an increasing emphasis on conventionalism. In Chapter 7, I suggested that the intellectual motive for conventionalism was the Kantian anti-realist thesis that we cannot know things as they are in themselves.

Why has this epistemic scepticism advanced in certain areas of psycho-social science? In attempting to answer this question, I remind the reader that (i) I am concerned only with social constructionism as a metatheory, not with constructionist theories of emotion, the self, etc., and (ii) the contributors to the metatheory are by no means united in their views, though there are important points of agreement. Moreover, my answer to this question is speculative, embryonic, and incomplete; what follows must be understood as such.

The first few pages of Bridgman's *The Logic of Modern Physics* (1927) are a forceful reminder of the extreme turmoil caused by the displacement of Newtonian physics by Einstein's theories of relativity. When this displacement occurred, in the early part of the 20th century, the resultant dogma was "Trust not even the most established of scientific theories, viz. those of physics". Such scepticism intensified throughout that century, it did not diminish. Stove's (1998) observation, that the philosophies of Popper, Kuhn, Lakatos and Feyerabend embody this scepticism, can be extended to current metatheories, such as social constructionism. What Stove identifies as scepticism about the *un*observable (e.g., electrons or space-curvature) among the Popper-Kuhn generation has now expanded to include scepticism about *describing the observable*. Social constructionist metatheory frequently (though not consistently) exemplifies the latter. No part of any theory, even a "low-level" hypothesis, can be understood as describing, for this (the constructionists believe) would involve the scientific community's belief in those claims, something to be avoided at all costs if the mistake of being fully committed to a false theory, and the turmoil which that mistake once brought about, is not to be repeated. This antipathy to believing that *p* is true lies at the heart of constructionist objections to realism, a philosophy which constructionism (falsely) assumes to be committed to the certainty of foundational claims (5.6.4).

What does conventionalism offer as an alternative? First, it deflects interest from what was once, and could be again, an object of disappointment—a theory which purportedly describes certain aspects of the world. Attention is turned to the language used in the theory. Second, conventionalism decrees that "knowledge" changes in accord with a change of convention, and it proposes that a change of convention is a social practice which cannot involve the notion of "error" or "mistake". "Knowledge" change is in the hands of individuals or groups who negotiate the use of terms and introduce new definitions ostensibly for pragmatic reasons only. They are relieved of the burden and of the obligation to discover things as they are. No longer need they experience the helplessness and frustration associated with not knowing or with being mistaken, because they exercise control over what is "known". Perhaps, then, the rise in conventionalism is driven by an increasing need to defend against being mistaken, and so to defend against disappointment. And perhaps these defences are associated with the rise in hostility, in certain quarters, toward the scientific enterprise (Gross & Levitt, 1996).

Much of mainstream empirical psychology has, slowly but surely, diverted its attention from general wide-ranging theories to insubstantial detail. There appears an inability and an unwillingness to tackle the conceptual difficulties that seem to overwhelm it. Perhaps a diversion of a similar kind has occurred in some areas of philosophical and theoretical psychology? It is conceivable that social constructionism exemplifies this malaise. There is a despair about understanding why we behave as we do. So demoralised are the proponents of constructionism that they agree that psychology cannot explain psycho-social phenomena.

The "truth game" is renounced in favour of "a search for culturally useful theories" (Gergen, 2001b), exploring "mutually responsive conversation" (Shotter & Lannamann, 2002), and "going beyond critique" (Morss, 2000).[1] If, as Sennett (1998) claims, failure is the great modern taboo, one way of avoiding coming to terms with failure is to treat psychology's theories not as proposals that may or may not say something about the world, but as reflections of the social milieux in which they are constructed. Our theories (as possible explanations) are, then, irrelevant and so psychology's history of its theories (as possible explanations) is rendered irrelevant.

This was their (the constructionists') stance in a recent exchange with realists in the journal *Theory & Psychology* (vol. 11[3]).[2] My attempt, in that issue, to consider the similarities between social constructionism and logical positivism, was politely dismissed as "so obvious as to be insignificant". Gergen went on to protest that he finds robust, vigorous debate to be ". . . lodged within a tradition of argumentation committed to a goal of truth . . . " (2001a, p. 431). He is drawn into these debates in an attempt to "sustain the dialogue", but he no longer considers the tradition "a viable one" (p. 431). In fact, he finds it detrimental to the betterment of psychology. Shotter & Lannamann (2002) subsequently claimed that academic theory-criticism-and–debate is a rhetorical and non-productive ritual which involves a set of Cartesian presuppositions, viz., representationalism, dualism, and abstractionism.[3,4] Potter, as we know, has eschewed such debates for some time.

Psychology's past, and my attempt to link its past with the present, were deemed irrelevant. Of course, social constructionism *is* sensitive to history: it claims to offer an emancipation from the repressive positivist conditions of the past. But it does not, for one minute, want seriously to contemplate the intellectual issues at stake. Perhaps this is a strategy of survival? Like the person who dismisses his past as "irrelevant" in explaining current psycho-social difficulties, or the society that disowns its history of white Australia's relations to Aborigines, social constructionism trivialises my drawing on the past in an attempt to have a serious discussion about a contemporary metatheoretical trend. Yet, one consequence of not genuinely considering the similarities between social constructionism and logical positivism is that our understanding of the ideas common to both continues to be impeded, and any insights to be had from psychology's repetitious engagement with these ideas are out of reach. Psychology is left disconnected from its past with no promise of a future where a better understanding of its philosophical basis might be gained.

The forward-looking attitude of some social constructionists involves the shallow goals of finding "significant cultural meaning", of "creating intelligibilities that may foster worlds to come", of "celebrating diversity", of "showing the conversations that constructionists are engaged in", of "creating conversations with different voices", and so on. Of course, some aspects of psychology's theories may well affect certain individuals/groups to the extent that their beliefs, actions, etc.

can change and, in this sense, "intelligibilities may foster worlds to come". But there is something disconcerting about the social constructionist's disavowal of the nature of the world as a determinant of scientific description and explanation. Not only is this view false, as I have argued, but presenting the world as a relatively inert backcloth inflates the sense of self-importance amongst constructionists; their role and achievements become exaggerated and this, arguably, fuels their omnipotence. The idea that the "rules" of logic are something to be played with if one so chooses is, I suggest, symptomatic of this. The social constructionist wishes to place us (as the constructors of knowledge) at the centre of the universe, and this functions both to wish away the great difficulty we have in understanding psychological systems and to "overcome" that difficulty from a position of omnipotence. It is, after all, better to feel important than to feel inadequate. In this regard, the pragmatism which drives social constructionism is similar to idealism. It reduces what is knowable to something anthropocentric, to whatever the psychological community creates.

I have noted that social constructionism rejects charges of idealism, but that their position is just one psychologically easy step away from that philosophy (7.3.1). Stove's (1991) analysis of idealism leads him to the conviction that the idealist seeks a reassuring, consoling, kindred universe. This, I suggest, is evident in the research of Gergen and Shotter. In its insipid approach to vigorous debate, in its desire for all voices to be heard and none to be "eradicated", in its repetitive call for tolerance, social constructionism apparently yearns for freedom from conflict. The claim that we are enveloped in momentary social realities whose influences we resist "at our peril" (Shotter & Lannamann, 2002, p. 585), and the belief that opposition is "perilous" (Gergen, 2001b, p. 806) bring to mind the "longing for Paradise" phantasy in which there is a yearning for oneness with the primary object; where total harmony and a conflict-free unitary reality reign supreme; where rejection does not occur; where there is no distinction between subject and object. The mother is not yet perceived as a separate, independent entity. She is simply "there", symbiotically woven into the infant's fabric of needs. It may be excessively speculative to propose a connection between this and the denial of logical independence, the internalism, which pervades social constructionist metatheory. Still, I suggest that the metatheory, far from directing psychology into "creating our future", is regressive—regressive because it persists in living by illusion.

NOTES

[1] These conjectures apply less to Potter than to others.

[2] Although it also features in earlier publications (e.g., Gergen, 1996; Morss, 2000; Potter, 1998; Shotter, 1997).

[3] The widely held belief that Descartes was a clear-cut mind-body dualist is false. In the *Passions de l'âme* (1649), Descartes introduces the concept of embodied mind. Earlier, he had attempted to explain the relationship between mind and body through the analogy of a body's weight, i.e., a body's weight is not something distinct from that body (Gaukroger, 1995, pp. 388–394).

[4] Because Shotter & Lannamann's analysis of their realist critics achieves such "...a prodigy of misunderstanding" (Maze, 2003, p. 1), it would be hard to know where to begin in responding to their claims. The straw manning of situational realism, in particular, seems to involve a deliberate attempt on the part of constructionists *not* to comprehend. However, realists of this kind should perhaps accept some responsibility for this. They have not always presented their arguments in sufficient detail, nor with their critics' objections in mind.

REFERENCES

Agassi, J. (1966). Sensationalism. *Mind, 75*, 1–24.

Alliger, G. M. (1992). The theory and structure of industrial/organizational psychology. In K. Kelly (Ed.), *Issues, theory, and research in industrial/organizational psychology* (pp. 3–27). Amsterdam: North-Holland.

Anderson, J. (1927/1962). Empiricism, *Studies in empirical philosophy* (pp. 3–14). Sydney: Angus and Robertson.

Anderson, J. (1927/1962). The knower and the known, *Studies in empirical philosophy* (pp. 27–40). Sydney: Angus and Robertson.

Anderson, J. (1930/1962). Realism and some of its critics, *Studies in empirical philosophy* (pp. 41–59). Sydney: Angus and Robertson.

Anderson, J. (1962). *Studies in empirical philosophy*. Sydney: Angus and Robertson.

Apfelbaum, E. R. (2000). And now what, after such tribulations? Memory and dislocation in the era of uprooting. *American Psychologist, 55*, 1008–1013.

Aristotle. (nd/1966). *Metaphysics* (H. G. Apostle, Trans.). Bloomington: Indiana University Press.

Armstrong, D. M. (1961). *Perception and the physical world*. London: Routledge & Kegan Paul.

Armstrong, D. M. (1997). *A world of states of affairs*. Cambridge: Cambridge University Press.

Ashby, R. W. (1967). Verifiability principle. In P. Edwards (Ed.), *The encyclopedia of philosophy* (Vol. 8, pp. 240–247). New York: Macmillan Publishing & The Free Press.

Attewell, P. (1990). What is skill? *Work & Occupations, 17*, 422–448.

Austin, J. L. (1955/1975). *How to do things with words* (2nd ed.). Oxford: Clarendon Press.

Avis, M. (2003). Do we need methodological theory to do qualitative research? *Qualitative Health Research, 13*(7), 995–1004.

Ayer, A. J. (1946). *Language, truth and logic* (2nd ed.). London: Gollancz.

Babbie, E. (2004). *The practice of social research* (10th ed.). Belmont, CA: Wadsworth/Thomson.

Baker, G. P. (1988). *Wittgenstein, Frege and the Vienna Circle*. Oxford: Basil Blackwell.

Baker, G. P., & Hacker, P. M. S. (1983). *An analytical commentary on Wittgenstein's Philosophical Investigations* (Vol. 1). Oxford: Basil Blackwell.

Baker, G. P., & Hacker, P. M. S. (1984a). *Language, sense and nonsense*. Oxford: Basil Blackwell.

Baker, G. P., & Hacker, P. M. S. (1984b). *Scepticism, rules and language*. Oxford: Basil Blackwell.

Baker, L. R. (1987). *Saving belief: A critique of physicalism*. Princeton: Princeton University Press.

Barnes, B., & Bloor, D. (1982). Relativism, rationalism and the sociology of knowledge. In M. Hollis & S. Lukes (Eds.), *Rationality and relativism* (pp. 21–47). Oxford: Basil Blackwell.

Barthes, R. (1975). *The pleasure of the text*. New York: Hill and Wang.

Ben-Menahem, Y. (1998). Explanation and description: Wittgenstein on convention. *Synthese, 115*, 99–130.

Berger, P., & Luckmann, T. (1966). *The social construction of reality*. London: Penguin.

Bergmann, G. (1954). *The metaphysics of logical positivism*. New York: Longmans, Green and Co.

Berkeley, G. (1710/1945). *A treatise concerning the principles of human knowledge*. London: Thomas Nelson and Sons.

Bernays, P. (1967). Hilbert, David (1862–1943). In P. Edwards (Ed.), *The encyclopedia of philosophy* (Vol. 3, pp. 496–504). New York: Macmillan Publishing & The Free Press.

Bickhard, M. H. (1989). Ethical psychotherapy and psychotherapy as ethics: A response to Perrez. *New Ideas in Psychology, 7*, 159–164.

Bickhard, M. H. (2001). The tragedy of operationalism. *Theory & Psychology, 11*(1), 35–44.

Bickhard, M. H., Cooper, R., & Mace, P. E. (1985). Vestiges of logical positivism: Critiques of stage explanations. *Human Development, 28*, 240–258.

Blumberg, A. E., & Feigl, H. (1931). Logical positivism: A new movement in European philosophy. *The Journal of Philosophy, 28*, 281–296.

Bohman, J. (1991). *New philosophy of social science: Problems of indeterminacy*. Cambridge, MA: MIT Press.

Bordens, K. S., & Abbott, B. B. (1991). *Research design and methods: A process approach*. Mountain View, CA: Mayfield.

Bornstein, R. F. (1999). Objectivity and subjectivity in psychological science: Embracing and transcending psychology's positivist tradition. *Journal of Mind & Behavior, 20*(1), 1–16.

Brand, J. L. (1996). Can we decide between logical positivism and social construction views of reality? *American Psychologist, 51*, 652–653.

Brewster Smith, M. (1994). Postmodern perils and the perils of postmodernism. *American Psychologist, 49*, 405–411.

Bridgman, P. W. (1927). *The logic of modern physics*. New York: Macmillan.

Brunswik, E. (1937). Psychology as a science of objective relations. *Philosophy of Science, 4*, 227–260.

Bunge, M. (1993). Realism and antirealism in social science. *Theory and Decision, 35*, 207–235.

Bunge, M. (1996). *Finding philosophy in social science*. New Haven: Yale University Press.

Burnyeat, M. (1990). *The Theaetetus of Plato* (M. J. Levett, Trans.). Indianapolis: Hackett.

Burr, V. (1995). *Introduction to social constructionism*. London: Routledge.

Burr, V. (1998). Overview: Realism, relativism, social constructionism and discourse. In I. Parker (Ed.), *Social constructionism, discourse and realism* (pp. 13–25). London: Sage.

Camic, P. M., Rhodes, J. E., & Yardley, L. (2003). *Qualitative research in psychology: Expanding perspectives in methodology and design*. Washington, DC: American Psychological Association.

Capaldi, E. J., & Proctor, R. W. (2000). Laudan's normative naturalism: A useful philosophy of science for psychology. *The American Journal of Psychology, 113*(3), 430–454.

Carnap, R. (1934). *The unity of science* (M. Black, Trans.). London: Kegan Paul, Trench, Trubner & Co.

Carnap, R. (1934/1937). *The logical syntax of language*. London: Kegan Paul, Trench, Trubner & Co.

Carnap, R. (1936). Testability and meaning. *Philosophy of Science, 3*, 420–471.

Carnap, R. (1947/1991). Empiricism, semantics, and ontology. In R. Boyd, P. Gasper & J. D. Trout (Eds.), *The philosophy of science* (pp. 85–97). Cambridge, MA: MIT Press.

Carnap, R. (1963). The development of my thinking. In A. P. Schilpp (Ed.), *The philosophy of Rudolph Carnap* (pp. 3–43). La Salle, Illinois: Cambridge University Press.

Carnap, R. A. (1928/1967). *The logical structure of the world: Pseudoproblems in philosophy*. London: Routledge & Kegan Paul.

Caygill, H. (1995). *A Kant dictionary*. Oxford: Blackwell.

Cerullo, J. J. (1992). From epistemological critique to moral discourse: Reflections on the social constructionist movement in social psychology. *Canadian Psychology, 33,* 554–562.

Chomsky, N. (1965). *Aspects of the theory of syntax.* Cambridge, Mass.: MIT Press.

Chow, S. L. (1992). Positivism and cognitive psychology: A second look. In C. W. Tolman (Ed.), *Positivism in Psychology: Historical and contemporary problems* (pp. 119–144). New York: Springer-Verlag.

Chow, S. L. (1995). In defense of experimental data in a relativistic milieu. *New Ideas in Psychology, 13,* 259–279.

Cloeren, H. J. (1975). The neglected analytical heritage. *Journal of the History of Ideas, 36,* 513–529.

Cobb, S. B. (1991). Conflict resolution: A new perspective. *Acta Psiquiatrica y Psicologica de America Latina, 37,* 31–36.

Coffa, J. A. (1991). *The semantic tradition from Kant to Carnap: To the Vienna station.* Cambridge: Cambridge University Press.

Cohen, M., & Nagel, E. (1934/1963). *An introduction to logic.* London: Routledge & Kegan Paul.

Cohen, M. R. (1946). *A preface to logic.* London: Routledge & Sons.

Cole, P., & Morgan, J. L. (Eds.). (1975). *Syntax and semantics: Speech acts* (Vol. 3). New York: Academic Press.

Collier, A. (1998). Language, practice and realism. In I. Parker (Ed.), *Social constructionism, discourse and realism* (pp. 47–58). London: Sage.

Copi, I. M. (1954). *Symbolic logic.* New York: Macmillan.

Cromby, J., & Nightingale, D. J. (1999). What's wrong with social constructionism? In D. J. Nightingale & J. Cromby (Eds.), *Social constructionist psychology: A critical analysis of theory and practice* (pp. 1–19). Buckingham: Open University Press.

D'Agostino, F. (1992). Social sciences, epistemology of. In J. Dancy & E. Sosa (Eds.), *A companion to epistemology* (pp. 479–483). Cambridge, MA: Blackwell.

Daniels, T. D., & Frandsen, K. D. (1984). Conventional social science inquiry in human communication: Theory and practice. *Quarterly Journal of Speech, 70,* 223–240.

Danziger, K. (1990). *Constructing the subject: Historical origins of psychological research.* Cambridge: Cambridge University Press.

Danziger, K. (1997). The varieties of social construction. *Theory & Psychology, 7,* 399–416.

Davidson, D. (1984). *Inquiries into truth and interpretation.* Oxford: Clarendon Press.

Denzin, N. K. (1982). On time and mind. *Studies in Symbolic Interaction, 4,* 35–43.

DePierris, G. (2003). Quine's historical argument for epistemology naturalized. In F. Stadler (Ed.), *The Vienna Circle and logical empiricism: Re-evaluation and future perspectives* (pp. 189–201). Dordrecht: Kluwer Academic.

Derrida, J. (1976). *Of grammatology* (G. C. Spivak, Trans.). Baltimore: John Hopkins University Press.

Dewey, J. (1929). *Experience and nature.* London: George Allen & Unwin.

Domenjo, B. A. (2000). Thoughts on the influences of Brentano and Comte on Freud's work. *Psycho-analysis & History, 2*(1), 110–118.

Duhem, P. (1914/1962). *The aim and structure of physical theory* (P. P. Wiener, Trans.). New York: Athenum.

Dummett, M. (1973). *Frege: Philosophy of language.* London: Duckworth.

Dunn, D. S. (2001). *Statistics and data analysis for the behavioral sciences.* Boston: McGraw-Hill.

Earman, J. (1993). Carnap, Kuhn, and the philosophy of scientific methodology. In P. Horwich (Ed.), *World changes: Thomas Kuhn and the nature of science* (pp. 9–36). Cambridge, MA: MIT Press.

Edwards, D., Ashmore, M., & Potter, J. (1995). Death and furniture: the rhetoric, politics and theology of bottom-line arguments against relativism. *History of the Human Sciences, 8*(2), 25–49.

Edwards, D., & Potter, J. (1992). *Discursive psychology.* London: Sage.

Edwards, S. D. (1990). *Relativism, conceptual schemes and categorial frameworks.* Aldershot: Avebury.

Falconer, J. E., & Williams, R. N. (1985). Temporality in human action: An alternative to positivism and historicism. *American Psychologist, 40*, 1179–1188.

Feigl, H. (1969). The origin and spirit of logical positivism. In P. Achinstein & S. F. Barker (Eds.), *The legacy of logical positivism* (pp. 3–24). Baltimore: John Hopkins Press.

Feyerabend, P. (1987). *Farewell to reason*. London: Verso.

Fishman, D. B. (1988). Pragmatic behaviorism: Saving and nuturing the baby. In D. B. Fishman, F. Rotgers & C. M. Franks (Eds.), *Paradigms in behavior therapy: Present and promise* (pp. 254–293). New York: Springer Publishing.

Foster, J. (1987). An appeal for objectivism in psychological metatheory. In H. J. Stam, T. B. Rogers & K. J. Gergen (Eds.), *The analysis of psychological theory: Metapsychological perspectives* (pp. 93–111). New York: Hemisphere Publishing.

Frege, G. (1903/1971). *On the foundations of geometry and formal theories of arithmetic*. New Haven: Yale University Press.

Frege, G. (1919/1967). The thought: A logical inquiry. In P. F. Strawson (Ed.), *Philosophical logic* (pp. 17–38). London: Oxford University Press.

Freud, S. (1909). *Analysis of a phobia in a five-year-old boy* (Vol. 10). London: The Hogarth Press.

Friedman, M. (1991). The re-evaluation of logical positivism. *The Journal of Philosophy, 88*, 505–519.

Friedman, M. (1998). On the sociology of scientific knowledge and its philosophical agenda. *Studies in History & Philosophy of Science, 29*, 239–271.

Friedman, M. (1999). *Reconsidering logical positivism*. Cambridge: Cambridge University Press.

Friedman, M. (2002). Kant, Kuhn, and the rationality of science. In M. Heidelberger & F. Stadler (Eds.), *History of philosophy of science. New trends and perspectives* (pp. 25–41). Dordrect: Kluwer.

Fuller, S. (1989). *Philosophy of science and its discontents*. Boulder: Westview.

Gadamer, H.-G. (1960/1975). *Truth and method* (W. Glen-Doepel, Trans.). London: Sheed and Ward.

Gamble, D. (2002). Defending semantic realism. *Language & Communication, 22*, 243–258.

Gardner, H. (1985). *The mind's new science*. New York: Basic Books Inc.

Gaukroger, S. (1995). *Descartes. An intellectual biography*. Oxford: Clarendon Press.

Gergen, K. J. (1973). Social psychology as history. *Journal of Personality and Social Psychology, 26*, 309–320.

Gergen, K. J. (1982). *Toward transformation in social knowledge*. New York: Springer-Verlag.

Gergen, K. J. (1985a). The social constructionist movement in modern psychology. *American Psychologist, 40*, 266–275.

Gergen, K. J. (1985b). Social pragmatics and the origins of psychological discourse. In K. J. Gergen & K. E. Davis (Eds.), *The social construction of the person* (pp. 111–127). New York: Springer-Verlag.

Gergen, K. J. (1986a). Correspondence versus autonomy in the language of understanding human action. In D. W. Fiske & R. A. Shweder (Eds.), *Metatheory in social science* (pp. 136–162). Chicago: The University of Chicago Press.

Gergen, K. J. (1986b). Elaborating the constructionist thesis. *American Psychologist, 41*, 481–482.

Gergen, K. J. (1986c). Interpreting the texts of nature and culture: A reply to Jahoda. *European Journal of Social Psychology, 16*, 31–37.

Gergen, K. J. (1987a). The concept of progress in psychological theory. In W. J. Baker, L. P. Mos, H. V. Rappard & H. J. Stam (Eds.), *Current issues in theoretical psychology* (pp. 1–14). Amsterdam: Elsevier Science Pub. Co.

Gergen, K. J. (1987b). Introduction: Toward metapsychology. In H. J. Stam, T. B. Rogers & K. J. Gergen (Eds.), *The analysis of psychological theory: Metapsychological perspectives* (pp. 1–21). New York: Hemisphere Publishing.

Gergen, K. J. (1987c). The language of psychological understanding. In H. J. Stam, T. B. Rogers & K. J. Gergen (Eds.), *The analysis of psychological theory: Metapsychological perspectives* (pp. 115–129). New York: Hemisphere Publishing.

Gergen, K. J. (1987d). Warranting the new paradigm: A response to Harré. *New Ideas in Psychology*, 5, 19–24.

Gergen, K. J. (1988a). Knowledge and social process. In D. Bar-Tal & A. W. Kruglanski (Eds.), *The social psychology of knowledge* (pp. 30–47). Cambridge: Cambridge University Press.

Gergen, K. J. (1988b). The rhetoric of basic research and the future of transactional analysis. *Social Behaviour*, 3, 281–289.

Gergen, K. J. (1989a). The possibility of psychological knowledge: A hermeneutic inquiry. In M. J. Packer & R. B. Addison (Eds.), *Entering the circle: Hermeneutic investigation in psychology* (pp. 239–258). Albany: State University of New York Press.

Gergen, K. J. (1989b). Social psychology and the wrong revolution. *European Journal of Social Psychology*, 19, 463–484.

Gergen, K. J. (1989c). Warranting voice and the elaboration of the self. In J. Shotter & K. J. Gergen (Eds.), *Texts of identity* (pp. 70–81). London: Sage.

Gergen, K. J. (1990a). Metaphor, metatheory, and the social world. In D. E. Leary (Ed.), *Metaphors in the history of psychology* (pp. 267–299). Cambridge: Cambridge University Press.

Gergen, K. J. (1990b). Proverbs, pragmatics, and prediction. *Canadian Psychology*, 31, 212–214.

Gergen, K. J. (1990c). Social understanding and the inscription of self. In J. W. Stigler, R. A. Shweder & G. Herdt (Eds.), *Cultural psychology: Essays on comparative human development* (pp. 569–606). Cambridge: Cambridge University Press.

Gergen, K. J. (1991a). Emerging challenges for theory and psychology. *Theory & Psychology*, 1, 13–35.

Gergen, K. J. (1991b). *The saturated self: Dilemmas of identity in contemporary life*. New York: Basic Books.

Gergen, K. J. (1992a). Social construction and moral action. In D. N. Robinson (Ed.), *Social discourse and moral judgment* (pp. 9–27). San Diego: Academic Press.

Gergen, K. J. (1992b). Toward a postmodern psychology. In S. Kvale (Ed.), *Psychology and postmodernism* (pp. 17–30). London: Sage.

Gergen, K. J. (1994a). The communal creation of meaning. In W. Overton & D. S. Palermo (Eds.), *The nature and ontogenesis of meaning* (pp. 19–39). Hillsdale, N.J.: Lawrence Erlbaum.

Gergen, K. J. (1994b). Exploring the postmodern: Perils or potentials? *American Psychologist*, 49, 412–416.

Gergen, K. J. (1994c). *Realities and relationships: Soundings in social construction*. Cambridge, MA: Harvard University Press.

Gergen, K. J. (1995a). Postmodernism as a humanism. *The Humanistic Psychologist*, 23, 71–82.

Gergen, K. J. (1995b). Social construction and the educational process. In L. P. Steffe & J. Gale (Eds.), *Constructivism in education* (pp. 17–39). New Jersey: Lawrence Erlbaum.

Gergen, K. J. (1996). Theory under threat: Social construction and identity politics. In (pp. 13–23).

Gergen, K. J. (1997). The place of the psyche in a constructed world. *Theory & Psychology*, 7, 723–746.

Gergen, K. J. (1998a). From control to construction: New narratives for the social sciences. *Psychological Inquiry*, 9(2), 101–103.

Gergen, K. J. (1998b). Social construction and psychoanalytic promise: Commentary on paper by Michael J. Bader. *Psychoanalytic Dialogues*, 8(1), 45–53.

Gergen, K. J. (1999). *An invitation to social construction*. London: Sage.

Gergen, K. J. (2001a). Construction in contention: Toward consequential resolutions. *Theory & Psychology*, 11, 419–432.

Gergen, K. J. (2001b). Psychological science in a postmodern context. *American Psychologist*, 56, 803–813.

Gergen, K. J. (2001c). *Social construction in context*. London: Sage.

Gergen, K. J., & Gergen, M. M. (1991). From theory to reflexivity in research practice. In F. Steier (Ed.), *Research and reflexivity* (pp. 76–95). London: Sage.

Gergen, K. J., & Kaye, J. (1992). Beyond narrative in the negotiation of therapeutic meaning. In S. McNamee & K. J. Gergen (Eds.), *Therapy as social construction* (pp. 166–185). London: Sage.

Gergen, M., & Gergen, K. J. (2003). *Social construction. A reader*. London: Sage.

Gerrod Parrott, W. (1992). Rhetoric for realism in psychology. *Theory & Psychology, 2*, 159–165.

Giere, R. N. (1988). *Explaining science: A cognitive approach*. Chicago: University of Chicago Press.

Glock, H.-J. (1996). *A Wittgenstein dictionary*. Oxford: Blackwell Publishers Ltd.

Goodman, N. (1977). *The structure of appearance* (3rd ed.). Dordrecht: D. Reidel Publishing.

Grayling, A. C. (1992). Transcendental arguments. In J. Dancy & E. Sosa (Eds.), *A companion to epistemology*. Oxford: Basil Blackwell.

Greenwood, J. D. (1989). *Explanation and experiment in social psychological science: Realism and the social constitution of action*. New York: Springer-Verlag.

Greenwood, J. D. (1991). *Relations and representations: An introduction to the philosophy of social psychological science*. London: Routledge.

Greenwood, J. D. (1992a). On the kinds of things that are emotions: A reply to Scherer, and Fischer and Frijda. *New Ideas in Psychology, 10*, 29–33.

Greenwood, J. D. (1992b). Realism, empiricism and social constructionism. *Theory & Psychology, 2*, 131–151.

Greenwood, J. D. (1994). *Realism, identity and emotion*. London: Sage.

Grice, H. P. (1957/1967). Meaning. In P. F. Srawson (Ed.), *Philosophical logic* (pp. 39–48). Oxford: Oxford University Press.

Gross, P. R., & Levitt, N. (1996). *Higher superstition: The academic left and its quarrels with science*. Baltimore: John Hopkins University Press.

Guba, E. G., & Lincoln, Y. S. (1994). Competing paradigms in qualitative research. In N. K. Denzin & Y. S. Lincoln (Eds.), *Handbook of qualitative research* (pp. 105–117). London: Sage.

Guthrie, W. K. C. (1969). *A history of Greek philosophy* (Vol. III). Cambridge: Cambridge University Press.

Haack, S. (1993). *Evidence and inquiry: Towards reconstruction in epistemology*. Oxford: Blackwell.

Hacker, P. M. S. (1986). *Insight and illusion: Themes in the philosophy of Wittgenstein*. Oxford: Clarendon Press.

Hacker, P. M. S. (2003). Wittgenstein, Carnap and the new Americans. *The Philosophical Quarterly, 53*, 1–23.

Hacking, I. (1983). *Representing and intervening*. Cambridge: Cambridge University Press.

Hacking, I. (1999). *The social construction of what?* Cambridge, MA: Harvard University Press.

Hahn, H. (1959). Logic, mathematics and knowledge of nature. In A. J. Ayer (Ed.), *Logical positivism* (pp. 147–161). Glencoe: The Free Press.

Halling, S., & Lawrence, C. (1999). Social constructionism: homogenizing the world, negating embodied experience. *Journal of Theoretical and Philosophical Psychology, 19*, 78–89.

Hamlyn, D. W. (1967). Empiricism. In P. Edwards (Ed.), *The encyclopedia of philosophy* (Vol. 2, pp. 499–505). New York: Macmillan Publishing & The Free Press.

Hanson, N. (1958). *Patterns of discovery*. London: Cambridge University Press.

Harré, R. (1990). Exploring the human Umwelt. In R. Bhaskar (Ed.), *Harré and his critics: Essays in honour of Rom Harré with his commentary on them* (pp. 297–364). Oxford: Blackwell.

Harré, R. (1992). What is real in psychology: A plea for persons. *Theory & Psychology, 2*, 153–158.

Harré, R. (1993). *Social Being* (2nd ed.). Oxford: Blackwell.

Harré, R. (2002a). *Cognitive science: A philosophical introduction*. London: Sage.

Harré, R. (2002b). Public sources of the personal mind: Social constructionism in context. *Theory & Psychology, 12*(5), 611–623.

Harré, R., & Krausz, M. (1996). *Varieties of relativism*. Oxford: Blackwell.

Hastings, B. M. (2002). Social constructionism and the legacy of James' pragmatism. *Theory & Psychology, 12*(5), 714–720.

Heil, J. (2003). Levels of reality. *Ratio, 16*(3), 205–221.

Held, B. S. (1998). The many truths of postmodernist discourse. *Journal of Theoretical and Philosophical Psychology, 18,* 193–217.

Held, B. S. (2002). What follows? Mind dependence, fallibility and transcendence according to (strong) constructionism's realist and quasi-realist critics. *Theory & Psychology, 12*(5), 651–669.

Heshusius, L. (1986). Pedagogy, special education, and the lives of young children: A critical and futuristic perspective. *Journal of Education, 168,* 25–38.

Hibberd, F. J. (1995). Can a psychological statement be neither true nor false? In I. Lubek, R. van Hezewijk, G. Pheterson & C. Tolman (Eds.), *Trends and issues in theoretical psychology* (pp. 367–372). New York: Springer.

Hibberd, F. J. (2001). Relativism *versus* realism—a specious dichotomy. *History of the Human Sciences, 14,* 102–107.

Hibberd, F. J. (2002). Reply to Gergen. *Theory & Psychology, 12*(5), 685–694.

Hirst, R. J. (1959). *The problems of perception.* London: George Allen & Unwin Ltd.

Hollis, M., & Lukes, S. (Eds.). (1982). *Rationality and relativism.* Oxford: Basil Blackwell.

Holt, E. B., Marvin, W. T., Montague, W. P., Perry, R., B, Pitkin, W. B., & Spaulding, E. G. (1912). *The new realism: Coöperative studies in philosophy.* New York: The MacMillan Co.

Holzman, L., & Morss, J. (2000). A decade of postmodern psychology. In L. Holzman & J. Morss (Eds.), *Postmodern psychologies, societal practice, and political life* (pp. 3–12). New York: Routledge.

Husserl, E. (1900/1970). *Logical investigations* (J. N. Findlay, Trans. Vol. I). London: Routledge and Kegan Paul.

Irzik, G., & Grünberg, T. (1995). Carnap and Kuhn: Arch enemies or close allies? *The British Journal for the Philosophy of Science, 46,* 285–307.

John, I. D. (1994). Constructing knowledge of psychological knowledge: Towards an epistemology for psychological practice. *Australian Psychologist, 29,* 158–163.

Jones, R. A. (2002). The necessity of the unconscious. *Journal for the Theory of Social Behaviour, 32*(3), 344–365.

Katzko, M. W. (2002). The construction of 'social constructionism': A case study in the rhetoric of debate. *Theory & Psychology, 12*(5), 671–683.

Keeley, S. M., Shemberg, K. M., & Zaynor, L. (1988). Dissertation research in clinical psychology: Beyond positivism? *Professional Psychology: Research and Practice, 19,* 216–222.

Kerlinger, F. N. (1986). *Foundations of behavioral research* (3rd ed.). New York: Holt, Rinehart and Winston.

Kirk, R. (1999). *Relativism and reality: A contemporary introduction.* London: Routledge.

Kirkham, R. L. (1992). *Theories of truth: A critical introduction.* Cambridge, MA: The MIT Press.

Koslicki, K. (2004). Constitution and similarity. *Philosophical Studies, 117,* 327–364.

Kraft, V. (1953). *The Vienna Circle* (A. Pap, Trans.). New York: Philosophical Library.

Kuhn, T. S. (1970). *The structure of scientific revolutions* (2nd ed.). Chicago: Chicago University Press.

Kuhn, T. S. (1979). Metaphor in science. In A. Ortony (Ed.), *Metaphor and thought* (pp. 409–419). Cambridge: Cambridge University Press.

Kuhn, T. S. (1993). Afterwords. In P. Horwich (Ed.), *World changes: Thomas Kuhn and the nature of science* (pp. 311–341). Cambridge, MA: The MIT Press.

Kukla, A. (1986). On social constructionism. *American Psychologist, 41,* 480–481.

Kukla, A. (2000). *Social constructivism and the philosophy of science.* London: Routledge.

Kusch, M. (1989). *Language as calculus vs. language as universal medium: A study in Husserl, Heidegger and Gadamer.* Dordrecht: Kluwer.

Kusch, M. (2002). *Knowledge by agreement: The programme of communitarian epistemology.* Oxford: Clarendon Press.

Kvanvig, J. L. (2003). *The value of knowledge and the pursuit of understanding.* Cambridge: Cambridge University Press.

Leahey, T. H. (2004). *A history of psychology: Main currents in psychological thought* (6th ed.). Upper Saddle River, NJ: Pearson Prentice-Hall.

Liebrucks, A. (2001). The concept of social construction. *Theory & Psychology, 11*(3), 363–391.

Lincoln, Y. S., & Guba, E. G. (1985). *Naturalistic inquiry*. Beverly Hills: Sage.

Locke, J. (1706/1924). *An essay concerning human understanding* (5th ed.). Oxford: Oxford University Press.

Lovie, A. D. (1992). *Context and commitment: A psychology of science*. New York: Harvester Wheatsheaf.

Lyddon, W. J. (1991). Socially constituted knowledge: Philosophical, psychological, and feminist contributions. *The Journal of Mind and Behavior, 12*, 263–280.

Mackay, N. (2003). On 'just not getting it': A reply to McNamee and to Raskin and Neimeyer. *Theory & Psychology, 13*(3), 411–419.

Mackie, J. L. (1964/1985). Self-refutation—A formal analysis. In J. Mackie & P. Mackie (Eds.), *Logic and knowledge: Selected papers* (pp. 54–67). Oxford: Clarendon Press.

Mackie, J. L. (1967). Fallacies. In P. Edwards (Ed.), *The encyclopedia of philosophy* (Vol. 3, pp. 169–179). New York: Collier MacMillan Publishers.

Mackie, J. L. (1969). What's really wrong with phenomenalism? *Proceedings of the British Academy, 55*, 113–127.

Madsen, K. B. (1988). *A history of psychology in metascientific perspective*. Amsterdam: Elsevier Science.

Malcolm, N. (1958). *Ludwig Wittgenstein: A memoir*. London: Oxford University Press.

Mandelbaum, M. (1982). Subjective, objective, and conceptual relativisms. In J. W. Meiland & M. Krausz (Eds.), *Relativism: Cognitive and moral* (pp. 34–61). Notre Dame: University of Notre Dame Press.

Margenan, H. (1950). The nature of physical reality. New York: McGraw-Hill.

Margolis, J. (1991). *The truth about relativism*. Oxford: Blackwell.

Margree, V. (2002). Normal and abnormal: Georges Canguilhem and the question of mental pathology. *Philosophy, Psychiatry & Psychology, 9*(4), 299–312.

Marjanovic, A. (1990). Two paradigms in developmental studies of language: An old controversy in new clothes. In S. A. Wheelan, E. A. Pepitone & V. Abt (Eds.), *Advances in field theory* (pp. 135–148). Newbury Park: Sage.

Martin, J. (2003). Positivism, quantification and the phenomena of psychology. *Theory & Psychology, 13*(1), 33–38.

Mather, R. (2002). Gergen's social constructionism: Postmodern or post-Hegelian? *Theory & Psychology, 12*(5), 695–699.

Matthews, W. J. (1998). Let's get real: The fallacy of post-modernism. *Journal of Theoretical and Philosophical Psychology, 18*, 16–32.

Maze, J. R. (1991). Representation, realism and the redundancy of "Mentalese". *Theory & Psychology, 1*, 163–185.

Maze, J. R. (2001). Social constructionism, deconstructionism and some requirements of discourse. *Theory & Psychology, 11*, 393–417.

Maze, J. R. (2003). *Conversations in a vacuum: A comment on Shotter & Lannamann (2002)*. Unpublished manuscript.

McGeoch, J. A. (1935). Learning as an operationally defined concept. *Psychological Bulletin, 32*, 688.

McGeoch, J. A. (1937). A critique of operational definition. *Psychological Bulletin, 34*, 703–704.

McGrath, J. E., Kelly, J. R., & Rhodes, J. E. (1993). A feminist perspective on research methodology: Some metatheoretical issues, contrasts, and choices. In S. Oskamp & M. Costanzo (Eds.), *Gender issues in contemporary society. Claremont symposium on applied social psychology* (Vol. 6, pp. 19–37). Newbury Park: Sage.

McGregor, D. (1935). Scientific measurement and psychology. *Psychological Review, 42*, 246–266.

McLennan, G. (2001). 'Thus': reflections on Loughborough relativism. *History of the Human Sciences, 14*(3), 85–101.

McMullen, T. (1996). John Anderson on mind as feeling. *Theory & Psychology, 6,* 153–168.

Meiland, J. W., & Krausz, M. (Eds.). (1982). *Relativism: Cognitive and moral.* Notre Dame: University of Notre Dame Press.

Mente, D. (1995). Whose truth? Whose goodness? Whose beauty? *American Psychologist, 50,* 391.

Michell, J. (1988). Maze's direct realism and the character of cognition. *Australian Journal of Psychology, 40,* 227–249.

Mill, J. S. (1843). *A system of logic* (8th ed.). London: Longmans, Green & Co.

Misra, G. (1993). Psychology from a constructionist perspective: An interview with Kenneth J. Gergen. *New Ideas in Psychology, 11,* 399–414.

Mitchell, M., & Jolley, J. (1996). *Research design explained* (3rd ed.). Fort Worth: Harcourt Brace College.

Monk, R. (1990). *Ludwig Wittgenstein: The duty of genius.* London: Vintage.

Morss, J. (2000). Two cheers for postmodernism: Living the paradox. In L. Holzman & J. Morss (Eds.), *Postmodern psychologies, societal practice, and political life* (pp. 15–28). New York: Routledge.

Moyer, A. E. (1991). P. W. Bridgman's operational perspective on physics. Part 1: Origins and development. *Studies in History & Philosophy of Science, 22,* 237–258.

Neimeyer, R. A., Neimeyer, G. J., Lyddon, W. J., & Tsoi Hoshmand, L. (1994). The reality of social construction. *Contemporary Psychology, 39,* 458–463.

Nettler, G. (1986). Construing the world. *American Psychologist, 41,* 480.

Newton-Smith, W. H. (1982). Relativism and the possibility of interpretation. In M. Hollis & S. Lukes (Eds.), *Rationality and relativism* (pp. 106–122). Oxford: Basil Blackwell.

Nietzsche, F. W. (1971). *The portable Nietzsche* (W. Kaufmann, Trans.). London: Chatto & Windus.

Nightingale, D. J., & Cromby, J. (1999). Reconstructing social constructionism. In D. J. Nightingale & J. Cromby (Eds.), *Social constructionist psychology: A critical analysis of theory and practice* (pp. 207–224). Buckingham: OUP.

Nola, R. (1988a). Introduction: Some issues concerning relativism and realism in science. In R. Nola (Ed.), *Relativism and realism in science* (pp. 1–35). Dordrecht: Kluwer Academic Publishers.

Nola, R. (Ed.). (1988b). *Relativism and realism in science.* Dordrecht: Kluwer Academic.

O'Grady, P. (2002). *Relativism.* Chesham: Acumen.

O'Hear, A. (1995). Conventionalism. In T. Honderich (Ed.), *The Oxford companion to philosophy* (pp. 165). Oxford: Oxford University Press.

O'Neill, J. (1995). 'I gotta use words when I talk to you': a response to Death and Furniture. *History of the Human Sciences, 8,* 99–106.

Osbeck, L. M. (1993). Social constructionism and the pragmatic standard. *Theory & Psychology, 3,* 337–349.

Paranjpe, A. C. (1992). Problems and prospects for cognitive constructionism in postpositivist psychology. In C. W. Tolman (Ed.), *Positivism in psychology: Historical and contemporary problems* (pp. 145–154). New York: Springer-Verlag.

Parker, I. (1989). *The crisis in modern social psychology.* London: Routledge.

Parker, I. (1998). Realism, relativism and critique in psychology. In I. Parker (Ed.), *Social constructionism, discourse and realism* (pp. 1–9). London: Sage.

Parker, I. (1999). Against relativism in psychology, on balance. *History of the Human Sciences, 12,* 61–78.

Passmore, J. (1943). Logical positivism (I). *The Australasian Journal of Psychology and Philosophy, 21,* 65–92.

Passmore, J. (1944). Logical positivism (II). *The Australasian Journal of Psychology and Philosophy, 22,* 129–153.

Passmore, J. (1948). Logical positivism (III). *The Australasian Journal of Psychology and Philosophy, 26*, 1–19.

Passmore, J. (1966). *A hundred years of philosophy* (2nd ed.). London: Duckworth.

Passmore, J. (1967). Logical positivism. In P. Edwards (Ed.), *The encyclopedia of philosophy* (Vol. 5, pp. 52–57). New York: Macmillan Publishing & The Free Press.

Passmore, J. (1970). *Philosophical reasoning* (2nd ed.). London: G. Duckworth & Co.

Peeters, H. F. M. (1990). Limits of social constructionism: Beyond objectivism and relativism. In F. J. R. van de Vijver & G. J. M. Hutschemaekers (Eds.), *The investigation of culture: Current issues in cultural psychology* (pp. 77–90). Le Tilburg: Tilburg University Press.

Perry, R. B. (1925). *Present philosophical tendencies.* New York: Longmans, Green & Co.

Pittenger, D. J. (2002). *Behavioral research design and analysis.* Boston: McGraw-Hill.

Poincaré, H. (1902/1952). *Science and hypothesis* (W. J. Greenstreet, Trans.). New York: Dover Publications.

Poincaré, H. (1908). *Science and method.* New York: Dover Publications, Inc.

Popper, K. R. (1935/1968). *The logic of scientific discovery.* London: Hutchinson.

Popper, K. R. (1976). The myth of the framework. In E. Freeman (Ed.), *The abdication of philosophy: philosophy and the public good* (pp. 23–48). La Salle, Illinois: Open Court.

Potter, J. (1992). Constructing realism: Seven moves (plus or minus a couple). *Theory & Psychology, 2*, 167–173.

Potter, J. (1996a). Discourse analysis and constructionist approaches: theoretical background. In J. T. E. Richardson (Ed.), *Handbook of qualitative research methods for Psychology and the Social Sciences* (pp. 125–140). Leicester: British Psychological Society.

Potter, J. (1996b). *Representing reality: Discourse, rhetoric and social construction.* London: Sage.

Potter, J. (1998). Fragments in the realization of relativism. In I. Parker (Ed.), *Social constructionism, discourse and realism* (pp. 27–45). London: Sage.

Potter, J. (2000). Post-cognitive psychology. *Theory & Psychology, 2000*, 31–37.

Potter, J. (2003a). Discourse analysis and discursive psychology. In P. M. Camic, J. E. Rhodes & L. Yardley (Eds.), *Qualitative research in psychology* (pp. 73–94). Washington, DC: American Psychological Association.

Potter, J. (2003b). Discursive psychology: Between method and paradigm. *Discourse & Society, 14*(6), 783–794.

Potter, J., & Edwards, D. (1999). Social representations and discursive psychology: From cognition to action. *Culture & Psychology, 5*(4), 447–458.

Potter, J., & Edwards, D. (2001). Discursive social psychology. In W. P. Robinson & H. Giles (Eds.), *The new handbook of language and social psychology* (pp. 103–118). Chichester: John Wiley & Sons.

Potter, J., Edwards, D., & Ashmore, M. (1999). Regulating criticism: some comments on an argumentative complex. *History of the Human Sciences, 12*, 79–88.

Potter, J., & Wetherell, M. (1998). Social representations, discourse analysis, and racism. In U. Flick (Ed.), *The psychology of the social* (pp. 138–155). Cambridge: Cambridge University Press.

Price, H. (1988). *Facts and the function of truth.* Oxford: Basil Blackwell.

Putnam, H. (1981). *Reason, truth and history.* Cambridge: Cambridge University Press.

Quine, W. V. (1951/1990). Two dogmas of empiricism. In R. R. Ammerman (Ed.), *Classics of analytic philosophy* (pp. 196–213). Indianapolis: Hackett.

Quine, W. V. (1960). *Word and object.* Cambridge, MA: MIT Press.

Quine, W. V. (1970). On the reasons for the indeterminancy of translation. *Journal of Philosophy, 67*, 178–183.

Quine, W. V. (1994). Comment. In W. Salmon & G. Wolters (Eds.), *Logic, language, and the structure of scientific theories* (pp. 345–351). Pittsburgh: University of Pittsburgh Press.

Raskin, J. D., & Neimeyer, R. A. (2003). Coherent constructivism: A response to Mackay. *Theory & Psychology, 13*(3), 397–409.

Reichenbach, H. (1920/1965). *The theory of relativity and a priori knowledge* (M. Reichenbach, Trans.). Berkeley: University of California Press.

Reichenbach, H. (1938). *Experience and prediction.* Chicago: The University of Chicago.

Reichenbach, H. (1954). *The rise of scientific philosophy.* Berkeley: University of California Press.

Reichenbach, M. (1965). Introduction. In *The theory of relativity and a priori knowledge* (pp. xi–xliv). Berkeley: University of California Press.

Reisch, G. A. (1991). Did Kuhn kill logical empiricism? *Philosophy of Science, 58,* 264–277.

Richardson, A. W. (1998). *Carnap's construction of the world: The Aufbau and the emergence of logical empiricism.* Cambridge: Cambridge University Press.

Roche, B., & Barnes-Holmes, D. (2003). Behavior analysis and social constructionism: some points of contact and departure. *Behavior Analyst, 26*(2), 215–231.

Rorty, R. (1979). *Philosophy and the mirror of nature.* Princeton: Princeton University Press.

Rorty, R. (1991). *Objectivity, relativism, and truth: Philosophical papers* (Vol. 1). Cambridge: Cambridge University Press.

Rosenau, P. M. (1992). *Post-modernism and the social sciences: Insights, inroads, and intrusions.* Princeton: Princeton University Press.

Rouse, J. (2002). Vampires: Social constructivism, realism, and other philosophical undead. *History & Theory, 41,* 60–78.

Russell, B. (1912/1959). *The problems of philosophy.* Oxford: Oxford University Press.

Russell, B. (1918). The philosophy of logical atomism. *The Monist, 28,* 495–527.

Russell, B. (1946/1984). *A history of western philosophy.* London: Unwin Hyman Ltd.

Russell, L. J. (1928). Review of Bridgman's 'The logic of Modern Physics'. *Mind, 37,* 355–361.

Rychlak, J. F. (1992). Foreword. In R. B. Miller (Ed.), *The restoration of dialogue: Readings in the philosophy of clinical psychology* (pp. xv–xvi). Washington, DC: American Psychological Association.

Sankey, H. (1993). Five varieties of cognitive relativism. *Cogito, 7,* 106–111.

Sankey, H. (1994). *The incommensurability thesis.* Aldershot: Avebury.

Saugstad, P. (1989). Towards a methodology for the study of psychology. In I. A. Bjorgen (Ed.), *Basic issues in psychology: A Scandinavian contribution* (pp. 221–241). Soreidgrend: Sigma Forlag A/S.

Schermer, V. L. (2001). The group psychotherapist as temporary mystic: A Bionic object relations perspective. *International Journal of Group Psychotherapy, 51*(4), 505–523.

Schiffer, S. R. (1972). *Meaning.* Oxford: Oxford University Press.

Schlick, M. (1917/1979). Appearance and essence. In H. L. Mulder & B. F. B. van de Velde-Schlick (Eds.), *Moritz Schlick: Philosophical papers* (Vol. I, pp. 270–287). Dordrecht: D. Reidel Publishing.

Schlick, M. (1925/1974). *General theory of knowledge* (2nd ed.). Wien: Springer-Verlag.

Schlick, M. (1931/1979). The future of philosophy. In H. L. Mulder & B. F. B. van de Velde-Schlick (Eds.), *Moritz Schlick: Philosophical papers* (Vol. II, pp. 210–224). Dordrecht: D. Reidel Publishing.

Schlick, M. (1932/1979a). Causality in everyday life and in recent science. In H. L. Mulder & B. F. B. van de Velde-Schlick (Eds.), *Moritz Schlick: Philosophical papers* (Vol. II, pp. 238–258). Dordrecht: D. Reidel Publishing.

Schlick, M. (1932/1979b). Form and content: An introduction into philosophical thinking. In H. L. Mulder & B. F. B. van de Velde-Schlick (Eds.), *Moritz Schlick: Philosophical papers* (Vol. II (1925–1936), pp. 285–369). Dordrecht: D. Reidel Publishing Company.

Schlick, M. (1932/1979c). A new philosophy of experience. In H. L. Mulder & B. F. B. van de Velde-Schlick (Eds.), *Moritz Schlick: Philosophical papers* (Vol. II (1925–1936), pp. 225–237). Dordrecht: D. Reidel Publishing Company.

Schlick, M. (1932/1979d). Positivism and realism. In H. L. Mulder & B. F. B. van de Velde-Schlick (Eds.), *Moritz Schlick: Philosophical papers* (Vol. II, pp. 259–284). Dordrecht: D. Reidel Publishing.

Schlick, M. (1934/1979). On the foundation of knowledge. In H. L. Mulder & B. F. B. van de Velde-Schlick (Eds.), *Moritz Schlick: Philosophical papers* (Vol. II, pp. 370–387). Dordrecht: D. Reidel Publishing.

Schlick, M. (1935/1979). Introduction and on "affirmations" from Sur le fondement de la connaissance. In H. L. Mulder & B. F. B. van de Velde-Schlick (Eds.), *Moritz Schlick: Philosophical papers* (Vol. II, pp. 405–413). Dordrecht: D. Reidel Publishing.

Schlick, M. (1936/1979). Meaning and verification. In H. L. Mulder & B. F. B. van de Velde-Schlick (Eds.), *Moritz Schlick: Philosophical papers* (Vol. II, pp. 456–481). Dordrecht: D. Reidel Publishing.

Schlick, M. (1938). *Gesammelte Aufsätze*. Vienna: Gerold.

Schweigert, W. A. (1994). *Research methods and statistics for psychology*. Pacific Grove, CA: Books/Cole.

Scriven, M. (1969). Logical positivism and the behavioral sciences. In P. Achinstein & S. F. Barker (Eds.), *The legacy of logical positivism* (pp. 195–209). Baltimore: Johns Hopkins.

Searle, J. R. (2002). *Consciousness and language*. Cambridge: Cambridge University Press.

Seashore, R. H., & Katz, B. (1937). An operational definition and classification of mental mechanisms. *Psychological Records, 1,* 3–24.

Sennett, R. (1998). *The corrosion of character: The personal consequences of work in the new capitalism*. New York: W.W.Norton & Co.

Shotter, J. (1992a). 'Getting in touch': The meta-methodology of a postmodern science of mental life. In S. Kvale (Ed.), *Psychology and postmodernism* (pp. 58–73). London: Sage.

Shotter, J. (1992b). Social constructionism and realism: Adequacy or accuracy? *Theory & Psychology, 2,* 175–182.

Shotter, J. (1993a). *Conversational realities: Constructing life through language*. London: Sage.

Shotter, J. (1993b). *Cultural politics of everyday life: Social constructionism, rhetoric and knowing of the third kind*. Buckingham: Open University Press.

Shotter, J. (1993c). Harré, Vygotsky, Bakhtin, Vico, Wittgenstein: Academic discourses and conversational realities. *Journal for the Theory of Social Behaviour, 23,* 459–482.

Shotter, J. (1994). Is there a logic in common sense? The scope and limits of Jan Smedslund's "Geometric" Psychologic. In J. Siegfried (Ed.), *The status of common sense in psychology* (pp. 149–168). Norwood, N.J.: Ablex.

Shotter, J. (1995). In dialogue: Social constructionism and radical constructivism. In L. P. Steffe & J. E. Gale (Eds.), *Constructivism in education* (pp. 41–56). Hillsdale, N. J.: Lawrence Erlbaum.

Shotter, J. (1996). Living in a Wittgensteinian world: Beyond theory to a poetics of practices. *Journal for the Theory of Social Behaviour, 26*(3), 293–311.

Shotter, J. (1997). The social construction of our inner selves. *Journal of Constructivist Psychology, 10,* 7–24.

Shotter, J. (1998a). Resurrecting people in academic psychology: A celebration of the ordinary. In W. E. Smythe (Ed.), *Toward a psychology of persons* (pp. 245–271). Mahwah, NJ: Lawrence Erlbaum Associates.

Shotter, J. (1998b). Social construction as social poetics: Oliver Sacks and the case of Dr P. In B. M. Bayer & J. Shotter (Eds.), *Reconstructing the psychological subject* (pp. 33–51). London: Sage.

Shotter, J. (2003). 'Real presences': Meaning as living movement in a participatory world. *Theory & Psychology, 13*(4), 435–468.

Shotter, J., & Billig, M. (1998). A Bakhtinian psychology: From out of the heads of individuals and into the dialogues between them. In M. M. Bell & M. Gardiner (Eds.), *Bakhtin and the human sciences: No last words* (pp. 13–29). London: Academic Hebrew Language.

Shotter, J., & Lannamann, J. W. (2002). The situation of social constructionism. Its 'imprisonment' within the ritual of theory-criticism-and-debate. *Theory & Psychology, 12*, 577–609.

Siegel, H. (1984). Empirical psychology, naturalized epistemology, and first philosophy. *Philosophy of Science, 51*, 667–676.

Siegel, H. (1987). *Relativism refuted: A critique of contemporary epistemological relativism.* Dordrecht: D. Reidel Publishing.

Siegel, H. (1992). 'Relativism'. In J. Dancy & E. Sosa (Eds.), *A companion to epistemology* (pp. 428–430). Oxford: Blackwell.

Sismondo, S. (1993). Some social constructions. *Social Studies of Science, 23*, 515–553.

Slife, B. D., & Williams, R. N. (1995). *What's behind the research? Discovering hidden assumptions in the behavioral sciences.* Thousand Oaks: Sage.

Smith, B. H. (1997). *Belief and resistance.* Cambridge, MA: Harvard University Press.

Smith, C. (1967). Le Roy, Édouard. In P. Edwards (Ed.), *The encyclopedia of philosophy* (Vol. 4, pp. 439–440). New York: Macmillan Publishing & The Free Press.

Smith, H. (1988). The crisis in philosophy. *Behaviorism, 16*, 51–56.

Smith, L. D. (1986). *Behaviorism and logical positivism: A reassessment of the alliance.* Stanford: Stanford University Press.

Sokal, A., & Bricmont, J. (1998). *Intellectual impostures: Postmodern philosophers' abuse of science.* London: Profile Books.

Sosa, E. (1995). Phenomenalism. In T. Honderich (Ed.), *The Oxford Companion to Philosophy* (pp. 658). Oxford: Oxford University Press.

Spector, M., & Kitsuse, J. I. (1977). *Constructing social problems.* Hawthorne, NY: Aldine de Gruyter.

Stebbing, L. S. (1933). Logical positivism and analysis. *Proceedings of the British Academy, 19*, 53–87.

Stebbing, L. S. (1933–34). Constructions. *Proceedings of the Aristotelian Society, 34*, 1–30.

Steier, F. (1991). Introduction: Research as self-reflexivity, self-reflexivity as social process. In F. Steier (Ed.), *Research and reflexivity* (pp. 1–11). London: Sage.

Stevens, S. S. (1935a). The operational basis of psychology. *American Journal of Psychology, 47*, 323–330.

Stevens, S. S. (1935b). The operational definition of psychological concepts. *Psychological Review, 42*, 517–527.

Stevens, S. S. (1936). Psychology: The propaedeutic science. *Philosophy of Science, 3*, 90–103.

Stevens, S. S. (1939). Psychology and the science of science. *Psychological Bulletin, 36*, 221–263.

Stevenson, C. L. (1937/1952). The emotive meaning of ethical terms. In W. Sellars & J. Hospers (Eds.), *Readings in ethical theory* (pp. 415–429). New York: Appleton—Century—Crofts.

Stove, D. C. (1991). *The Plato cult and other philosophical follies.* Oxford: Basil Blackwell.

Stove, D. C. (1995). *Cricket versus republicanism.* Sydney: Quakers Hill Press.

Stove, D. C. (1998). *Anything goes: Origins of the cult of scientific irrationalism.* Paddington, NSW: Macleay Press.

Strawson, G. (2000). Esprit de core. A new way of viewing "the movie-in-the-brain". *Times Literary Supplement* (October 27), 12–13.

Suppe, F. (1974). Alternatives to the received view and their critics. In F. Suppe (Ed.), *The structure of scientific theories* (pp. 119–232). Urbana: University of Illinois Press.

Sutcliffe, J. P. (1993). Concept, class, and category in the tradition of Aristotle. In I. Van Mechelen, J. Hampton, R. S. Michalski & P. Theuns (Eds.), *Categories and concepts: Theoretical views and inductive data analysis* (pp. 35–65). London: Academic Press Ltd.

Sutcliffe, J. P. (1996). Ce que j'ai fait, et ce qui reste à faire. In C. R. Latimer & J. Michell (Eds.), *At once scientific and philosophic* (pp. 243–294). Brisbane: Boombana.

Tennant, N. (1994). Carnap and Quine. In W. Salmon & G. Wolters (Eds.), *Logic, language, and the structure of scientific theories* (pp. 305–344). Pittsburgh: University of Pittsburgh Press.

Terwee, S. J. S. (1995). Deconstructing social constructionism. In I. Lubek, R. van Hezewijk, G. Pheterson & C. Tolman (Eds.), *Trends and issues in theoretical psychology* (pp. 188–194). New York: Springer.

Tolman, C. W. (1992). Neopositivism and perception theory. In C. W. Tolman (Ed.), *Positivism in psychology: Historical and contemporary problems* (pp. 25–45). New York: Springer-Verlag.

Tolman, C. W. (Ed.). (1992). *Positivism in psychology: Historical and contemporary problems*. New York: Springer-Verlag.

Tolman, E. C. (1936). An operational analysis of 'demands'. *Erkenntnis, 6*, 383–390.

Uebel, T. E. (1996). Anti-foundationalism and the Vienna Circle's revolution in philosophy. *British Journal for the Philosophy of Science, 47*, 415–440.

Unger, R. K. (1989). *Representations: Social constructions of gender.* New York: Baywood Publishing Co.

Ussher, J. (2002). Premenstrual syndrome: Fact, fantasy, or fiction? In C. von Hofsten & L. Bäckman (Eds.), *Psychology at the turn of the millennium* (Vol. 2, pp. 497–527). New York: Psychology Press.

van Sant, G. M. (1959). A proposed property of relations. *The Journal of Philosophy, 56*, 25–31.

Verheggen, C. (2003). Wittgenstein's rule-following paradox and the objectivity of meaning. *Philosophical Investigations, 26*(4), 285–309.

Vulliamy, G., & Webb, R. (1993). Special educational needs: From disciplinary to pedagogic research. *Disability, Handicap and Society, 8*, 187–202.

Waters, R. H., & Pennington, L. A. (1938). Operationism in psychology. *Psychological Review, 45*, 414–423.

Weinberg, J. R. (1936). *An examination of logical positivism.* London: Kegan Paul, Trench, Trubner & Co.

Werkmeister, W. H. (1937). Seven theses of logical positivism critically examined (I). *The Philosophical Review, 46*, 276–297.

Wetherell, M., & Potter, J. (1998). Discourse and social psychology—silencing binaries. *Theory & Psychology, 8*(3), 377–388.

White, M. (1950/1952). The analytic and the synthetic: An untenable dualism. In L. Linsky (Ed.), *Semantics and the philosophy of language* (pp. 272–289). Urbana: University of Illinois.

Williams, M. (2001). *Problems of knowledge: A critical introduction to epistemology.* Oxford: Oxford University Press.

Williamson, T. (1996). Reference. In D. M. Borchert (Ed.), *The Encyclopedia of Philosophy. Supplement* (pp. 499–502). New York: Simon & Schuster Macmillan.

Wittgenstein, L. (1921/1974). *Tractatus logico-philosophicus.* London: Routledge & Kegan Paul.

Wittgenstein, L. (1953/1967). *Philosophical investigations* (G. E. N. Anscombe, Trans. 3rd ed.). Oxford: Basil Blackwell.

Wittgenstein, L. (1975). *Philosophical remarks.* Oxford: Basil Blackwell.

Wittgenstein, L. (1982). *Last writings on the philosophy of psychology* (Vol. I). Oxford: Basil Blackwell.

Zeddies, T. J. (2001). Out of the consulting room and into the world: Hermeneutic dialogue, phronesis, and psychoanalytic theory as practice. *American Journal of Psychoanalysis, 61*(3), 217–238.

INDEX

Printed in the United States
56455LVS00002B/7-12